BECOMING A SEXUALLY INTIMATE PERSON

by
James R. Barbour

The University of Vermont

R & E Publishers

This book is sold with the understanding that the subject matter
covered herein is of a general nature and does not constitute legal,
accounting or other professional advice for any specific individual or
situation. Anyone planning to take action in any of the areas that this
book describes should, of course, seek professional advice from ac-
countants, lawyers, tax and other advisers, as would be prudent and
advisable under their given circumstances.

R&E Publishers
P.O. Box 2008, Saratoga, CA 95070
Tel: (408) 866-6303   Fax: (408) 866-0825

Book Design and Typesetting by **elletro** Productions

Book Cover by Kaye Quinn

ISBN 1-56875-042-0

Library of Congress Cataloging-in-Publication Data
Barbour, James R.
Becoming a sexually intimate person / James R. Barbour.
    p. cm.
    ISBN 1-56875-042-0 : $12.95
    1. Sex instruction for youth--United States. 2. College students--
United States--Sexual behavior. 3. Intimacy (Psychology)
I. Title
HQ35.2.B37   1993
306.7'0835--dc20
                                                        93-24214
                                                        CIP

Designed, typeset and totally manufactured in the
United States of America.

For Marilyn

CONTENTS

CHAPTER 1

Bill and Meredith: Not Your Average Couple

Bill and Meredith are not your average couple. Oh, they look pretty much like other young adults, and if you met them you wouldn't notice anything unusual or remarkable about either one. But after getting to know them, I realized that they were quite extraordinary in terms of their sexuality. Let's go back to my initial encounter with them when they were juniors in college, and see what it was that I found so intriguing about this couple.

Meredith and Bill were both twenty-one at the time, and were enrolled in my Human Relationships and Sexuality course at the University of Vermont. I invite my students to come see me if there is something they would like to talk about, and the two of them were following up on this invitation. They started by giving me a history of their relationship, and described the kinds of issues they had been dealing with recently.

"Meredith and I met second semester of our sophomore year, in a History course we were taking," Bill began. "I noticed Meredith the first day of class, and decided to keep my eye on her and find out more about what she was like. Meredith told me later that she saw me that day, too, and had similar thoughts about me. During the second week of classes the professor had us work in small groups, and I managed to get into Meredith's group. After seeing her operate in the group I knew this was someone special, someone I was definitely interested in getting to know better." Bill paused a moment, and smiled at Meredith. She smiled back, and taking his hand in hers moved her chair so they could be closer together.

"A couple of weeks after this," Bill continued, "some of my friends and I were sitting around one night when the phone rang and my roommate said it was for me. I almost fell off the chair when I discovered it was Meredith, calling to see if I wanted to come over to her place later for a pizza. I was so excited that after I told her yes, I hung up the phone before I asked her where she lived. Fortunately, Meredith realized this, too, and called me right back."

"Well, I guess you could say that from that point on, one thing kind of led to another," Meredith said, as she joined in recounting their story. "We started doing things together like going to the movies and meeting for dinner, and we spent an awfully lot of time just talking. Over the next few months as we got to know one another, we realized that we were feeling very different about this developing relationship than we had about any others we had before. There was a kind of warmth and closeness which really felt different for me, and I think Bill felt the same way."

"Oh, I definitely did, Meredith," Bill chimed in as he shifted his position so he could prop his arm on Meredith's chair. As he lightly caressed her hair, Bill picked up where Meredith left off. "It was also clear to both of us that there were some very strong sexual feelings there, and although we hadn't done anything more than hold hands and kiss a little bit we knew these feelings were becoming progressively more intense. I fantasized about Meredith, and I realized that I wanted to act on my fantasies. I secretly hoped that Meredith was having the same kind of fantasies about me, and as it turned out she was."

"No question about it, Bill, my feelings were just as strong as yours," Meredith said, as she looked intently into his eyes. "But I'm not as slow a learner as you are, so it was easier for me to conceptualize a way to achieve our mutual goal before we graduated from college," Meredith teased. "So one night after a movie I decided I would talk with Bill."

"Let me tell you something," Bill interjected, beaming with pride. "This is one beautiful woman I have as a partner. It really amazed me how forthright she was in talking about her sexual feelings. I'll never forget it."

"Basically, all I said was 'Bill, I'm coming to feel very close to you, and I would like that closeness to become more sexual. I don't have a lot of sexual experience, but I feel ready to expand on this part of our relationship. I'd like to sleep with you and have sexual intercourse, and I'm wondering whether you're feeling the same way about me.'"

"Well this sounded almost too good to be true," Bill said, "because of course I felt the same way, and I was just about bursting inside I was so happy with the idea. But I knew there was something more than simple lust involved here, because it felt very different from the kind of pure sexual feelings I had about women in the past. I guess you could say it was a kind of burning passion, a sense of wanting to experience Meredith in a very total way."

"So I said, 'Meredith, nothing would make me happier than to make our relationship more sexual. Suppose we talk about some of the things we'll need to do in order to mole toward this goal.' Actually, I think I said something like 'Wow!' or 'Holy Crow!' first, I was so excited."

"What you said was, 'Hot shit!' Bill, but I knew by the way you said it that you were as excited about this as I was," Meredith said, as she picked up with the next part of their story. "I'm an engineering student," she continued, "and tend to take a logical approach in dealing with personal as well as professional issues. So I got out a piece of paper and we began to brainstorm a list of things we felt we needed to do or think about if we were going to have a sexual relationship. I knew that I was concerned about not wanting to get pregnant, so I put contraception first on the visit. Bill said that if we were to expand our relationship it would require more time from both of us, so his first item was relationship time. Well, we went back and forth with this idea for about two straight hours, and came up with a list that seemed pretty impressive. One of the things we decided to do at that very moment was to hold on to the list, so we could refer back to it in the future. We brought it along to share with you," Meredith said, as she pulled a carefully folded sheet of paper out of her jacket pocket and handed it to me.

Although I had worked with young adults for many years and thought I had seen just about everything, I must admit that Meredith and Bill's list was a first for me. Printed in Meredith's crisp engineer hand were the following "Things to Consider."

Things to Consider		
Contraception	Relationship Time	Study Time
Sex Talk	Roommate Issues	Parents' Feelings
Sexual Health	Friends	Trust & Fidelity
Sexual Values	Living Together	Commitment Issues

I was astonished when I realized how deliberate these two had been in planning their sexual relationship, and found it difficult to imagine how young adults could harness their sexual attraction for one another in such a rational way. I wondered what kinds of experiences they had while they were growing up that might have prepared them for such a positive and assertive entry into genital sexual expression.

"You look stunned," Bill said, as both he and Meredith grinned at me in self-delight. "You must think we're pretty weird, being so rational about this, but believe me we really aren't. Meredith and I both grew up in families where our parents talked with us a lot about our sexual development, so our approach to initiating a sexual relationship just seemed to be an extension of what we had been learning all our lives. Most of our friends don't believe us when we talk with them about this, and I think it's because they feel that sex should be spontaneous or it won't be any fun. What they don't seem to understand is that our sexual relationship is a lot more fun **because** we approached it like we did."

Bill's explanation certainly gave me some insight into why he and Meredith seemed to have such a solid relationship. Everything I knew about family development told me that children whose parents were open in their discussions about their developing sexuality were more likely than others both to delay first intercourse as well as to use contraception in their initial sexual encounters. But I was eager to know more about what Meredith and Bill had done with their list, and whether they had reconciled all their issues before they began any sexual activity. Meredith was ready with a response.

"One of the things we realized when we began to talk about our concerns was that we wouldn't really be able to understand some of these issues fully until we began interacting sexually. It's like you can't make an informed judgment about something until you get some data, and we felt we needed some sexual data before we could honestly reconcile some of our concerns. That might sound like a copout or like we were just trying to rationalize becoming sexually active, but we didn't feel that way at all. We had already accepted the idea that we wanted to expand our sexual interactions, so in that sense we really had nothing to rationalize. Bill, I remember that when we were talking about this you brought out some points that I hadn't thought much about before. Do you know what I'm referring to?"

"Sure I do, Meredith, I remember it very clearly," Bill replied, as he stood up and walked over to one of my bookshelves. As he pulled one of the paperbacks off the shelf, he continued. "As we've been talking I've been looking at your books, and I noticed Nathaniel Branden's **The Psychology of Romantic Love**. I read Branden's book in one of my psychology courses last year, and I was really struck by some of the things he said about the power and potential of sex in people's lives. One thing in particular had to do with the way sexual expression has the potential of giving people a reflection of their own sexuality in a way that other experiences simply don't provide. Branden talked about how we use other people like mirrors to get a reflection of our psychological sense of self. He said that when we interact with a person sexually in a way that produces a high level of joy and pleasure, that an essential part of the joy we experience comes from getting a pleasing reflection of our own sexuality from our partner. In that sense, then, only certain people reflect back to us a picture that appears fully congruent with our own perception of our sexual self. But this also means that we don't get that information unless we are involved in a sexual relationship of some kind. I think this is what you were thinking about, isn't it Meredith?"

"You're right," Meredith said, as Bill handed her Branden's book. "Bill suggested I read this book, too, and I'm glad I did, because it helped me get a clearer understanding of how important it is to learn about intimate relationships by actually **being in them,** and not just talking about them. It's amazing how many of our friends are avoiding intimate relationships, saying they don't feel ready for them or don't have the time. One of my friends said she's too busy trying to get into medical school to have a serious relationship, but it's hard for me to imagine a time later on when she will be less busy than she is now. I think people who talk this way are probably deluding themselves. I mean what does she think, that after she graduates from medical school she will take a sabbatical leave and develop an intimate relationship? Everything I've heard about the so-called "real world" out there tells me that things get **more busy**, not **less busy** when you finish your education. And if you have kids, not only must life be busier, it must be an awfully lot more complicated than it is for us in college."

As I reflected for a moment on what Meredith and Bill had been talking about I realized that they had internalized one of the most compelling principles of human development, which is that we grow in our real knowledge of close relationships only to the extent that we are directly involved in such close relationships. This concept seems pretty fundamental and self evident to me, but it's one that I find young adults in general are quite skeptical about. I was eager to find out which items on their visit they had dealt with right away, and which they decided to put on the back burner; I wasn't surprised by their response.

"We had very little trouble in rank-ordering our list of concerns, with maybe one or two exceptions," Bill said, as he replaced Branden's book and sat down along side of Meredith. "I guess you could say that our most immediate concerns were health related," Bill said, "in the sense that we wanted to be sure we wouldn't start a pregnancy, or if we had a sexual disease of some kind we wouldn't give it to the other person. I think we also had the feeling that since we knew we would be having sexual intercourse pretty soon, we'd better face those practical issues before passion got the better of us. Just the thought of having intercourse with Meredith was enough to put my hormones into a state of near rage," Bill chuckled.

"So we decided to go to the health center," Meredith continued, "and have an STD checkup and choose a contraceptive method. The people at the center were great, and helped us make a decision about a birth control method that would be best for us. Bill waited outside while I had a pelvic exam, and I guess that since he had never seen me nude before this was a good idea. Since that first time, though, he's been with me during all my pelvic exams—I like having him there and I think it helps him understand problems women have that men just don't have to worry about."

"I think you're right about that first exam, Meredith," Bill added. "But I'm glad I've been able to be with you since then. I had no idea what was involved with female reproductive health care, and I really appreciate your desire to have me present during your exams, Meredith. Most of the guys I know don't have a clue about what's involved in a pelvic exam."

"The doctor said that everything was fine with me," Meredith continued, "and then checked Bill out. Bill told me later he was a little surprised when the doctor examined his penis and testes---I guess you weren't used to having a doctor poking around in that part of your body, were you?"

"I think that what I wasn't used to was a **female** doctor checking out my sexual equipment," Bill laughed, "but I must say I learned a lot from that examination. I never knew that men in my age category are at greater risk for testicular cancer than either older or younger males, so I was relieved when she didn't find any lumps or anything. The doctor showed me how to feel my testes for lumps and also how to locate each epididymis, which feel kind of like little knots in your scrotum. When I was done with my exam the doctor talked with the two of us together, answered some questions we had about the contraceptive method we had chosen, and then we were all set."

"On the way home from the health center we made plans for a special picnic in two weeks on a hill that overlooks the lake," Meredith continued. It was a very private place, and it seemed like a perfect setting to make love for the first time. It was a beautiful day, and the experience was one I'll never forget. It's not like it was the most exciting or creative sexual encounter we've ever had, but it was really intense and fulfilling, and felt especially good because we had planned for it together."

"For me, Meredith, it was pure ecstasy," Bill said. "I agree with you, too, that from a technical point of view our first intercourse wasn't so dazzling that you'd want to write home about it. As a matter of fact I was so excited that I came in about thirty seconds, which certainly wasn't enough time to stimulate Meredith to orgasm. But I was just so happy that it really didn't matter, because I knew we had our whole relationship in front of us and that we would have many more opportunities to fine-tune our sexual technique. Of course, the sexual part of our relationship **has** improved tremendously since that first time, but I wouldn't trade anything for the memory of our hilltop picnic!"

With the background of their sexual history laid out, Bill and Meredith settled back in their chairs. I thought to myself that their story sounded almost too good to be true; but of course they weren't joking. My problem was that I wasn't used to working with young adults who planned their sexual lives like Meredith and Bill, and it was a bit of a shock to contemplate what the world would be like if everyone went about life the way they did. What I wondered, though, was why they had come to see me in the first place. Delighted as I was to hear their story, it wasn't at all clear why they had chosen to disclose it to me. I was about to find out.

"But we didn't come to see you just to tell you how our relationship began," Meredith continued, resuming the serious mood of our earlier discussion. "The longer Bill and I have been together the more we've come to realize how difficult it is for people on this campus to develop and maintain sexually inti-mate relationships, and we thought you might be in a position to improve this situation around here. We really would like to live together, and have been thinking how great it would be to have some resident halls designated for couples. Everybody knows that people have sex in their rooms and sleep over at their lover's room, but the university really doesn't actively foster this kind of living arrangement. If anything, they do just about everything they can to discourage it."

"Meredith's right," Bill chimed in. "I mean they have dorms that are co-ed by floor, co-ed by wing, co-ed every other room, but no dorms that are just plain co-ed. And it doesn't seem to occur to anyone around here that gay men and lesbians have even more difficulty maintaining sexually intimate relationships within the university system. It just seems hypocritical for the university to put so much emphasis on the importance of diversity, and not speak to the real needs of students who would like to live together in the resident halls instead of in an apartment downtown. And we're not just looking for a place to sleep in the same bed—we want a full program of seminars, workshops, and social activities that would help all the hall residents learn more about sexuality and intimate relationships. Maybe even a course with credit."

"It seems to me," Meredith pressed on, "that the real issue here is the way the university views its role as educator of the whole student. It feels to us like what they're saying is that it's not really the responsibility of the university to help students learn about intimacy, that their job is to prepare us for the world of work and we should learn how relationships function on our own time, probably in the future. That's where Bill and I disagree strongly with the university, but I guess this place is no different from most other colleges in this respect. It just seems like the college years would be a great time to help young people practice being intimate, and help them learn how they can be both good students and good lovers. And this is important for all of us, whether we're heterosexual or whether we're gay or bisexual."

"I couldn't agree with you more, Meredith," Bill said. "There are so many things to learn about sex and intimacy, things I never really thought much about before I met Meredith. Since we've been in your Human Relationships and Sexuality course it seems we've learned something new about each other almost every day, because you encourage your students to explore things that can be a little scary, they're so personal. And like we said before, we were pretty fortunate to have parents who were open with us about sex while we were growing up, so it's not hard to imagine how difficult it is for most young people to deal with sexual issues. Meredith and I thought that since you work with so many people who are interested in intimacy, that maybe you could convince the university to get involved with the kind of resident hall programs we're talking about. That's really why we came to see you. What do you think—is it worth trying to convince the administration to see our point of view?"

Meredith and Bill had introduced the $64 question, one that I have spent a lot of time thinking about during the last ten years. I was in full agreement with their suggestion, and in fact have discussed this idea with the residential staff of the university. Most everyone I talk with thinks the concept is an interesting one, but that the practical problems in implementing such a program are insurmountable. The two responses I usually get to this suggestion are, "Can you imagine what would happen if the state legislature ever got wind of this idea?" and "Parents would have a fit. An absolute fit!" Most colleges and universities acknowledge the fact that many of their students have sexual relationships, but few of them do much, if anything, to actually foster such relationships. As Meredith and Bill pointed out, universities are very cautious about doing anything that might suggest that they **advocate** sexually intimate relationships between their students, although many of them provide programs to help students understand and accept responsibility for their sexuality. Many campuses offer reproductive health care in their student health services, and conduct workshops about contraception and sexually transmitted diseases in their resident halls. Yet all but a few stop short of providing accommodations for couples who want to live together unmarried on campus.

Meredith and Bill's request reminded me of how little progress has been made on this issue. Over twenty years ago, Robert Rimmer wrote **The Harrad Experiment**, a best-selling novel about a college with just such a program. Harrad College was designed around the ideas that love and close relationships were essential for maintaining a high quality of human life, and that colleges and universities could play a major role in teaching young adults how to be good intimate partners. Students at Harrad had to agree to room with a member of the opposite sex, and although they were under no obligation to develop a sexual relationship with their roommate, most of them did. They did this in part because they had been carefully matched for compatibility, but also because of a basic premise of human relationships: people who live in close quarters for a sustained period of time often develop sexual feelings for one another. Despite the popularity of Rimmer's book, no one took up the gauntlet he tossed down and turned his fictional utopia into a living experiment. As a culture, we have such an enormous amount of ambivalence over the role that sex should play in human life that we just aren't ready for this bold step.

So I had to tell Meredith and Bill that I didn't think the university would come around to seeing things their way in the near future, certainly not before they graduated. But I encouraged them to keep up the good fight.

"Well if you can't do that," Meredith said, "why don't you consider writing a book for young adults that would help them get a handle on sex and intimacy. I think most young adults would really be eager to read a book that was pitched directly at them, especially if it dealt with these issues in the same way you do in your human sexuality course."

"I think that's a great idea, Meredith," Bill continued, as he gathered up his knapsack and jacket. But it's got to be the kind of book a young adult like us would pick up and read, not a heavy duty technical thing. In terms of learning about sex, there are lots of textbooks for students and there's Playboy and Penthouse, but there is very little in between that holds much interest for people in their late teens and twenties. I don't think it should be so much a fact book, like 'This is a penis, and here's how it works,' but rather its focus should be more on how it feels to have a penis, and what issues having a penis present to males. It's not that having the facts isn't important; it really is, but it's that other piece of it that you never get from a text, good as it might be. I think that what young adults could really use is a book that speaks directly to them about their own sexual attitudes and behaviors, and challenges them to examine how these things have been influenced by their family and their culture."

"Maybe, too, you could use the data you gather from students in your classes to illustrate your ideas," Meredith said, as she stood up and prepared to leave. "I would think that the thousands of projects your students have written would be a gold mine of anecdotes and examples of what really happens to young adults, and how we really feel about our sexuality."

Bill and Meredith's idea was intriguing. After this conversation I became convinced that indeed there was something missing from most books for young adults about sex and intimacy, and what was missing had to do with how young people really **feel** about these topics, and what meaning they attach to their sexual behaviors. In addition, none of the books I've seen talk to young adults directly about the antecedents to or consequences of their sexual attitudes and behaviors.

Here's an example to illustrate what I mean. It's no secret that many men enjoy having a partner go down on them

(I'll have a lot more to say about oral-genital sex in a later chapter). You may also be aware that men more often than not enjoy **receiving** oral sex more than they do **giving** it. But have you ever talked with your parents or your friends or your lover about **why** this is so? Probably not. In fact, even though most young men and many young women enjoy receiving oral sex, few of them have developed sexual scripts that allow them comfortably to ask a partner to pleasure them this way. How comfortable would you be saying to a partner something like this?

"Wow, I'm really enjoying all this kissing and petting we're doing, and I'd love it if you went down on me. I'd love to go down on you, too, and we could hop in the shower together and clean up our collective acts, and if you're worried that I'll ejaculate in your mouth just let me know, and I'll tell you when I'm about to come."

My guess is that this kind of script for oral sex is not one you presently feel comfortable with, although you may enjoy giving and getting oral sex a great deal. The reasons you probably don't feel at ease with this kind of sexual language are directly related to what you have learned about sex in general while you were growing up. But chances are that few people, including your parents, have been willing to talk with you openly about sex and sexual development, so you have been left to wiggle your body and hope that your partner will understand just what your wiggling is trying to say to them.

I think it is both possible and desirable for young adults to be able to communicate their sexual needs without having to gyrate their hips and pray. It's possible and desirable for you to talk directly with a partner about what you want, and to do things that will maximize the likelihood that you will indeed get what you **do** want, and not get or do what you **don't** want. But being able to get and give what you want sexually requires that you know quite a bit about sex and sexuality, and also means that you are in touch with your sexuality.

This book is intended to help you understand yourself as a sexual being, and help you become the kind of sexual person you would like to be. It's not really a "How To" book, in the sense that I won't be giving you **SEVEN WAYS TO INSERT TAB A INTO SLOT B.** But it is very much designed to help you create and maintain sexually intimate relationships that are satisfying and fulfilling for you and your partner. The context of sexual experience I most favor is that which occurs within committed intimate relationships, so what I discuss in this book about sex is almost always done with this in mind.

Whether you are a student or are out in the work world inhabited by other young adults like you, there is plenty here for you to think about.

Most of what I have learned about the sexual issues that concern young adults has come directly from college students, a result of teaching a course in Human Relationships and Sexuality for fifteen years at the University of Vermont. This course attracts some eight hundred students a year, and although I get to know personally only a small fraction of that number, I am able to form relationships with a good number of them. Students often come to see me to discuss a sexual or relationship concern, and they also just drop by my office to chat about what's going on in the course. These direct conversations keep me abreast of what's happening sexually on our campus, and also give me clues into how young adult sexual and relationship concerns change over time.

A second important way I learn about young adults' sexual behaviors and attitudes is through a survey administered each semester in our sexuality course. The survey covers a wide range of areas related to sexual learning, attitudes, and behavior, and serves to give my students a chance to compare the data derived from their class with similar surveys described in their text. I'll be using the data in these surveys throughout this book, primarily to illuminate a particular topic being discussed. The data from my students at the University of Vermont will not be identical to what you might find at another college or university, but the **trends** in the data very much conform with national trends related to sexual attitudes and behaviors of young adults in general.

Let me give you a simple example to explain what I mean. Surveys from my students over the years have consistently shown that about 85 percent of the males and 40 percent of the females in my course masturbate with some frequency, say once a week. If we administered the same survey at another college or university or to a population of young adults in the work world, the figures might be 90 percent males, and 45 percent females, or 80 percent males and 30 percent females, or 40 percent males and 10 percent females. The important point to make is that the difference in masturbation rates **between** males and females is quite consistent: males in their late teens and twenties are likely to be masturbating at roughly twice the frequency of females.

So the percentages themselves, while important, will usually be less significant than what the numbers **mean**. The largest differences in behavior and attitudes occur not as a function of where you live, but rather are linked to your gender. A central theme of this book is that these gender differences create a lot of problems for us as men and women as we seek to create and maintain satisfying sexual relationships. And this is true whether we're straight or whether we're gay or bisexual.

The third, and probably most important way I learn about young adult sexuality is by reading projects my students write which trace the development of their sexual identity. These projects, which are evaluated anonymously, give students a chance to think about the important influences on their sexual development, including their sexual experiences. Over the years, hundreds of students have given me copies of their papers after they have removed any information that might identify them, and have granted me permission to quote this material in my writing. The sexual "stories" told by students run a wide range, from euphoric to tragic. Many students, especially women, describe situations in which they were sexually abused, often by someone they trusted not to exploit them. Some students are petrified to act on their sexual feelings, worried that they will be rejected by someone they care for. Others worry that their bodies aren't attractive, or their sexual organs aren't big enough, or that they won't be able to please their sexual partner, or that they can't have orgasms when they want to. Virtually **all** students feel that **other** students are much more sexually active than they are!

An underlying question that emerges over and over again, whether in a student's project or in a classroom session discussing survey data or in a counseling session in my office is, "Am I normal?" This question isn't always stated explicitly—sometimes it is hidden, and the student isn't sure just how to ask it. Here are a few examples of how this question gets stated.

- ✿ "Sometimes I think my breasts are too small, but my boyfriend says he likes them the way they are. I guess that's what matters."
- ✿ "Whenever I have intercourse for the first time with someone I always ejaculate real quick, sometimes in just a few strokes. I always worry about this."
- ✿ "It's like I lead two different lives: one with my straight friends, many of whom are on the field hockey team with me, and another with my gay friends and my lover. A lot of my lesbian friends say I should come out, and make it clear that I'm a lesbian, but I don't feel like rocking the boat any more than I have to."

✿ "I can never reach orgasm when I have intercourse with my partner, and he says I should try masturbating when I'm with him. But this whole idea sounds pretty scary—I mean, do people really do this kind of thing?"

✿ "When my sister was seventeen and I was eighteen, she said she wanted to lose her virginity to me. Because we loved each other and knew we always would, we didn't see how this could hurt either one of us. We made love a number of times, and it was a really beautiful thing. But when I told some of my friends about this they said I'm sick, like some kind of a pervert. Now I'm beginning to wonder about it, although it still seems OK to me."

Each of these individuals was concerned that maybe there was something about their sexuality that wasn't quite right, that wasn't normal for people like them. A few years ago a nineteen year old man came to see me because he was convinced he would never be able to maintain an erection long enough to have sexual intercourse. This fear arose from the fact that when he was seventeen he and his girlfriend did some heavy petting in the back seat of his car, attempted to have intercourse, but were unable to because he could not maintain an erection. His girlfriend later told some of their mutual friends that they **did** have intercourse, and when his friends asked him about it, he went along with the lie and said they had. On two subsequent occasions with different women he again tried to maintain an erection, both times without success.

Faced with three episodes of an uncooperative penis, he was sure his sex life was over and was ready to give up on the whole idea of ever becoming "sexually mature." He was absolutely convinced that he was the only male in New England who had ever experienced this kind of sexual difficulty. When I told him that many young men, as well as older ones, have difficulty in maintaining an erection with a new partner, it was as if I had lifted a huge weight off his shoulders. He said that I was the first person he had ever talked to about this problem, a secret that he had been carrying around for two years.

This young man is a typical example of someone concerned about being normal, and it is a shame that because of societal attitudes about sex he felt he had to keep this secret for so long. It would not surprise me at all if you are concerned with issues similar to those described by my students, so a major goal of this book is to have you come away feeling that you are not alone with your worries, that with knowledge and insight you will discover that you are indeed the "normal" kind of person you wish to be.

People often have difficulty distinguishing the difference between behavior that is truly abnormal and inappropriate from behavior that is atypical, or different from the norm. When someone asks a question like whether it's normal for lovers to masturbate together, they are usually not thinking of the word normal in sociological terms (the opposite of which would be deviant or abnormal), but rather are wondering whether this kind of sexual behavior indicates that something is significantly different about the concerned individuals or their relationship. As this example shows, the **shoulds** and **oughts** regarding how lovers reach orgasm are so firmly imbedded in the socio-sexual scripts of people that it's often hard to break away from them, even when other scripts might produce far more desirable outcomes. Gaining a better understanding of where these dysfunctional scripts come from will in itself help to free you from many of the fears and worries that may be blocking you from enjoying yourself as a sexual person.

This book may represent the first instance in your life in which an adult has suggested to you that it is normal and desirable to enjoy yourself as a sexual person. Although advertising and media messages tell young people today that sex is an important part of the adult world, most parents don't do much to teach their children how to become sexually healthy, and in fact often do a lot to inhibit this kind of growth. Many of the topics discussed in this book will take you into areas where you haven't been invited before, because the adults around you didn't think you were old enough to hear about them or didn't think they were proper topics for **anyone** to discuss.

And I will ask you to think about aspects of your sexual attitudes and behaviors that may make you feel uncomfortable at times, because it may be difficult for you to admit to yourself that you feel the way you do. For example, you may drink alcohol in social situations, but probably haven't thought much about what influence alcohol and other drugs you might use occasionally have on your sexuality. While I'll be giving you permission to think about elements of your sexuality that you may not have explored before, I will also be raising questions that you may find troubling.

But my hope is that when confronted with some of the more compelling features of human relationships and sexuality, you will feel encouraged to talk with your friends, your parents, and your lovers about these issues, and will become engaged in a process of thought, dialogue and behavior that will lead to real growth. I have enormous trust in your ability to make good decisions on your own behalf once given the full opportunity to understand what informs these decisions. I have a tremendous concern about the decisions many young adults are making in regard to their sexuality, but I also believe that the major responsibility for their making poor decisions rests with the adults who have nurtured them up until this time in their lives. This book represents my personal contribution as an adult to change this condition.

In developing an approach to each topic discussed in the book I've tried to keep foremost in my mind that readers represent a broad range of social, economic, and educational backgrounds, and also are representative of a range of sexual orientations. The central themes of the book will apply to you whether you are straight or gay or bisexual, because our dominant socializing forces have more influence on our gender than on our sexual orientation. In other words, heterosexual and homosexual females have more in common in terms of their sexuality than do heterosexual females and heterosexual males. Likewise, heterosexual males have more in common with homosexual males in terms of their sexuality than they do with heterosexual females. There will be many instances when I will discuss issues that pertain only to heterosexual interactions, and sometimes I will focus exclusively on homosexual interactions. But I have worked hard to make this a book in which all readers feel welcome, regardless of their gender or their sexual orientation, and there are some specific ways I've gone about doing this.

One way I've done this is to use the phrase **whether you're straight or gay** in discussing the broad influences that society has on our sexual development and behaviors. It may be hard for you to accept this fact, but straight people and gay and bisexual people share similar goals in life in terms of work, love, sex and money—the so-called big ticket items. This isn't to say that the experience of growing up gay or lesbian or bisexual is identical to that of growing up straight. Growing up gay presents many more problems, and is much more difficult than being straight in a predominantly straight world. There is a great deal to be gained from becoming more tolerant of other people's sexual orientations, and an important way to increase this tolerance is to become familiar with what it's like to have a certain orientation.

I have also chosen words which are gender neutral and non-sexist, which at first may appear a bit awkward to you. Young men and women often refer to females as **girls**, and to males as **guys**. Straight young adults usually refer to their dating partner as their boyfriend or girlfriend, terms used less frequently by gay men and lesbians to describe their sexual partners. Gay men and lesbians are more likely to use the terms lover or partner in this instance.

In this book and in my day-to-day conversations, I use only the terms woman and man to refer to people who are young adults, whether they are in high school, college, or out in the work world. Although many of my colleagues refer to young adults as kids, in my opinion this term has no place in a vocabulary describing young adults. You may be a **young** adult, but you're not a kid any more, and I don't intend to talk to you like a kid. I prefer the terms **partner** or **lover** to girlfriend and boyfriend, again because they are gender-neutral, and also speak of a more mature relational condition. Using a term like partner takes some getting used to, but once you acquire this habit I think you'll like it.

I think we're ready to move on now into the real substance of the book, but before we do I want to tell you about two very difficult editorial problems I faced as I worked on this manuscript. From the very beginning, I wanted to write in a style that would keep you engaged with what you were reading, yet at the same time I did not want to trivialize the subjects I was discussing by using language or examples that might offend you. So I often felt I was walking a very fine line between pushing you too hard or not pushing hard enough. Many of the examples I use are totally absurd in the sense that such conversations or situations just don't happen in real life. But my point in creating these examples was to illustrate how absurd so much of what we are taught about human sexuality really is. I am relying on your ability to sort out reality from my deliberate exaggerations, and to realize that there is a playful spirit at work in most of the dialogues and examples throughout the book.

The second issue I faced had to do with creating a writing voice that would speak directly to my intended audience, which consists of individuals roughly ages eighteen to mid-twenties. On one hand, I realized as I wrote that there are many sixteen and seventeen year old young adults for whom this book is just what they have been looking for to help them explore their sexuality and intimate relationships. On the other, I knew there are some individuals in their mid-twenties who are already familiar with many of the book's ideas. But from the comments that I received from the many young adults who read the manuscript while I was working on it, the voice issue seems to have worked out quite well.

Our journey begins in childhood, where so many of our ideas about sex and sexuality are established. If reading this book is half as much fun as writing it has been I'll feel like my goal was accomplished. I'd like very much to hear from you with questions you have about sex or relationships, or with your reactions to the book as a whole or to some aspect of it that especially interested you. You may write to me at the address listed at the end of the book---I'll do my best to send you a reply.

CHAPTER 2

Growing Up Sexual

I want you to form a mental picture of your mother and father making out. Let's put them on the living room couch, since they feel comfortable there now that you and your brothers and sisters are out of the house. Some cool jazz is playing softly on the stereo in the background, and they seem the picture of contentment as they sit there kissing and petting, murmuring sweet pet words and nibbling a bit on one another's ears. After a while they work themselves into a frenzy of passion, a kind of fiery desire they know can only be quenched by more direct and explicit action. They begin to tear at one another's clothes, both now eager to touch and explore the other's naked body. Before you can say "sixty-nine," your parents are a tangled mass of heaving bodies engaged in an episode of oral sex that could pop every circuit breaker in the house.

After ten minutes of this high-pitched pleasuring, your parents seem to sense a turning point in their lovemaking, and as if by practiced cue, they simultaneously pivot their bodies into the missionary position. After fifteen minutes and as many different positions, both of them sense an impending conclusion to their efforts, and check with the other to be sure they are ready. Through a series of nonverbal but distinctly understood signals, they approach the crest of their now unrestrainable buildup, and in a marvelous show of solidarity crash together through the final barriers of orgasm.

After dozing together for a while on the clothes-strewn floor in front of the couch they rise slowly, kiss and embrace lovingly and head out to the kitchen to fix a snack. While your mom is slicing up some fruit and cheese, your dad takes a pencil and adds a hash mark to a row of tallies that are written on the back of a cabinet door over the refrigerator. You have seen these marks before, have noticed that they increase over time, and have even been skeptical of your mom's explanation that they keep track of the number of Ketchup bottles your father has used since the family moved into the house. But nothing has quite prepared you for what happens next, for as your dad closes the cabinet door, he glances toward your mom, and with a sly grin remarks that "There seems to be plenty of room left on this door for at least seventy more." To which your mom replies, "Not to worry. There are twelve more cabinet doors in this kitchen, and when we run out, we can always move to another house and start all over again."

I'll bet you had a little trouble conjuring up this picture of your parents getting it on, didn't you? It's easy enough to think of a young stud and his beautiful partner going through this kind of script, but when you try to put your parents into the starring roles the whole scenario goes bust. It wouldn't surprise me if, while you were reading this, you were experiencing a wrenching kind of internal conflict. On the one hand, you were a little titillated by the sensual imagery of a passionate sexual encounter, while on the other you were no doubt thoroughly disgusted by the thought of your parents having sex on the living room couch where everyone sits around at night and watches TV together! You may also have felt embarrassed by the thought of being a voyeur to your own parents while they engaged in such a private act.

But the biggest difficulty you probably had with this little vignette is that of imagining your parents as sexual beings, and for this problem you are not entirely to blame. Many factors contribute to a perception held by children that their parents have little if any sexual interaction except for an occasional and perfunctory session of intercourse after a Saturday night party. There are at least three important reasons why children tend to view their parents as being asexual. First, our culture tends to associate sex with youth, and with being young. Media images typically consist of young and beautiful men and women, and erotica and pornography utilize young models with sleek bodies. In part, this equating of youth with sex is in keeping with the societal attitude that values new things over old things, but it goes well beyond this idea and includes a more prevalent assumption that older people simply don't have sexual needs of the same intensity as do younger ones. Many older people, of course, buy into this idea too, and allow cultural stereotypes about sex and age to inhibit their own sexual activities. If sex declines with a person's age, it is probably not because their sexual needs have diminished, but rather that other factors interfere with their ability or desire to experience the sexual part of themselves.

A second reason why young people often underestimate the extent of their parents' sexual behaviors is that most parents give little direct evidence to their children that they indeed **are** sexual. Most young adults report that they rarely see their parents being physically affectionate with one another, nor do their parents talk with them about the physically pleasurable aspects of their relationship. So an important part of your perception of your parents as asexual is accurate, in that the extent of their physical intimacy is much less than it was when they were younger, and is more than likely **much** less than what you might prefer in your own intimate relationships.

But perhaps most important in this discussion about your parents' sexuality is the idea that it is very difficult for you to see your own present sexual behaviors as being similar to those of adults your parents' age. Although many young people do things that they think make them appear to be older than they are (such as drink and smoke), few young adults want to identify with most of the behaviors and attitudes of adults their parents' age. When your parents say they're too old to try something that you like to do, such as wind surfing or disco dancing, you are likely to feel a bit smug about the fact that you can do a lot of things your parents have given up on. Young adulthood is really your first full opportunity to excel in many areas that your parents cannot, and perhaps never could, and sex is just another item on this list. I frequently hear young people say that they do sexual things their parents would never dream of doing, and although there may be some truth to this statement, the purpose in making it seems to be based on a desire to set their own sexual identity apart from that of their parents'. I fully understand your desire not to identify with your parents' sexuality. I'm sure that you hope your own sexual life will be more fulfilling than your parents', and since you are apprehensive over what life might be like if you follow in their sexual footsteps, you are putting plenty of distance between your own sexual identity and theirs.

Something else is at work here as well, and that is a kind of conspiracy of silence that exists between you and your parents. As their children get older, many parents form a tacit agreement with their children that says, "We won't ask questions about your sex life if you won't ask about ours." This kind of agreement helps these parents rationalize not talking with their children about sex, and is also a way for them to avoid dealing with the many sexual and relational issues that they themselves are frequently faced with. On their part, your parents are as likely to **overestimate** the extent and variety of your sexual behaviors as you are to **underestimate** theirs. Your parents may assume that you are more sexually experienced than they were at your age, in part because statistically you are, but also because it helps them support the myth that sexual activity naturally declines with age. It's only natural, they can say, that you would be enjoying sex more than they are, since "everyone knows" that as people get older they lose interest in sex. If you and your parents keep quiet about what's really happening, you can both preserve your own cherished illusions.

The Link Between Our Childhood and Adult Intimate Relationships

When I indicate to young people that there is a good chance they will choose a marriage partner whose qualities are similar to their own other-sex parent, they usually react with disbelief. When I go on to suggest that their own adult intimate relationships will in some ways mirror that of their parents, they just about give up on me. These reactions are predictable; however much we may love and respect our parents, most of us are unwilling to accept the notion that we might follow in their relational footsteps. But since our parents' relationship is usually a central image for us in terms of learning about the nature of intimacy, it is not surprising that as we enter adulthood most of our relationship skills and insights reflect what we have learned from the model presented by our parents.

The power of a parental model to influence the course of our own adult relationships is enormous. And there is a paradox at work here as well which many of us don't fully appreciate until we have children of our own. Although most young people say they received little if any instruction from their parents about human sexuality, their parents nevertheless taught them a great deal about sexuality. For many people, the words sex and sexuality immediately evoke only images of arousal, eroticism, and genital stimulation. But the concept of human sexuality is much broader than this, embracing a range of attitudes and behaviors related to self and others. One's sexuality can be seen as a developmental process, beginning at birth and continuing throughout all of life. To refer to our sexuality means to speak not only of the physical characteristics and capacities we have for specific kinds of sexual behaviors, but also of the psychological learnings we have acquired, our values, norms, and attitudes about these behaviors. Included also are the attitudes we have about ourselves and others regarding masculinity and femininity, and those aspects of identity related to our sexual orientation. When we gain a fuller appreciation of the broader meanings of human sexuality, it is easy to see how parents do indeed have a tremendous influence on their children's developing sexuality.

The most potent instruction comes in the form of direct or indirect messages about body image, gender, family roles, and affection and intimacy. Unfortunately for many of us, the instruction our parents gave us about these aspects of our sexuality was heavily laden with "shoulds, oughts, don'ts, and be carefuls." Much of what parents teach their children about human sexuality can be considered "sex negative," in the sense that the instruction emphasizes the downside risks of human sexual behaviors, while virtually ignoring their life enhancing potentials. This is why it is so important for you to think about the messages you received as a child as you think about your self as a young adult. Let's examine the four areas of our sexuality I just mentioned in order to see just what your parents may have taught you about them.

Body Image

There is no question that the way we feel about our bodies affects the way we express our sexuality. We typically compare our bodies with the ideals presented in advertising and the media, and quite frequently our bodies don't measure up to these ideals. It's usually a matter of not having enough, or having too much. Young people often express the problem this way: the women would like to lose ten pounds; the men would like to gain two inches! But equal to these media influences are the messages our parents give us about our bodies that pertain to their function as well as their appearance.

Many parents emphasize to their children that boys should **do**, and girls should **be**, which helps to explain why such parents are not overly concerned when their sons' clothing becomes soiled in play. Parents are more likely to encourage their daughters to be attractive, and to dress and groom them in ways that enhance their appearance. Just consider the amount of time and effort the "typical" adolescent girl puts into learning how to use makeup, style her hair, shop for and select clothing and accessories, and talk on the phone with friends, and you'll get a sense of how a girl's socialization trains her for "being" rather than "doing." Saying this does not diminish the many girls who are in fact "doers," active in sports and other physically demanding enterprises. These active girls are able to overcome their gender constraints, and many of course become quite competent as both "do-ers" and "be-ers."

An important consequence of this difference in socialization among boys and girls is that most boys grow up feeling they own their bodies, whereas many girls learn they should prepare their bodies for others to use. We don't use the term "puts out" to refer to anyone but a female, do we? We don't ever say, "Bob puts out for any woman with two legs," because we expect Bob to have control over his body, and to use it only if he fully desires to use it. Males learn at an early age to use a female's body for their own sexual enjoyment, and it is only an incidental matter if the female herself derives any pleasure from the sexual interchange. **Males learn to be the initiators, females the limit setters.** These two ideas are firmly embedded in the different messages boys and girls get about their bodies.

Children learn another important lesson about their bodies from their parents' attitudes and practices related to nudity. Parental styles and rules about nudity around the house vary quite a bit from family to family, but the vast majority of young people report that, at least implicitly, nudity is forbidden in their homes. Seeing a member of the other sex nude is the most problematic for families, especially when one of the individuals is a parent. Most difficult among the various combinations is that of a parent being seen nude by an other-sex child, a situation that intensifies as the child grows older. Parents tend to tolerate their very young children seeing them nude, but they become increasingly uncomfortable with this practice as their youngsters near adolescence. There seem to be several reasons for parental concern related to nudity.

The first issue relates to the possibility that either the child or the parent might become sexually aroused if they see the other person nude. Some parents worry that if their child sees them nude the child might develop sexual feelings that would be confusing or potentially harmful. These same parents may be concerned that they themselves will develop inappropriate sexual feelings for a child if they see them nude. Both these possibilities exist, of course, but neither is very likely to happen if the nudity occurs in the context of dressing and bathing, in which being nude is always appropriate. It's not unusual for parents and children to have occasional sexual thoughts about one another, but these thoughts don't mean that either desires to act on them. Parents and children have these thoughts whether or not they ever see the other nude; most of us occasionally have sexual feelings for people we know, without ever desiring to act on these feelings.

The second issue for parents about nudity is more personal than interpersonal, and has to do with the level of comfort they themselves have with their own bodies. If you don't feel good about the way your body looks, it is not likely you'll want **anyone** to see it, including yourself. Since so many adults have such a low opinion of the way their body looks, it's no wonder they are reluctant to expose it to family members or anyone else. Ann Landers has occasionally written about husbands or wives who undress in the bathroom or a closet before coming to bed, and for whom sleeping in the nude would be unthinkable. And finally, many parents avoid appearing nude in front of their children because to do so raises the possibility that their children will ask them questions about the sexual parts of their bodies, questions they would rather not have to deal with. Parents who feel comfortable with their nude bodies are less likely to evade such situations, and instead welcome the chance to use their own bodies as "live models" for teaching their children about their sexuality.

Gender Learning

In a later chapter I will discuss the ways our sex role learning directly affects our sexual attitudes and behaviors as young adults. But since our sex role socialization begins at birth, it will be useful here to introduce some ideas about this process that will be helpful to keep in mind throughout the book. What you learned about being male or female as a child has had a tremendous effect on your sexual attitudes, values and behaviors. Not only does American society have different expectations for male and female sexuality, but more important, it places a different value on the relative worth of males and females. Parents play a very important part in teaching their children about what they consider to be appropriate gender behaviors and attitudes, although they don't usually transmit their ideas directly. Rather, they tend to express their views about gender in the way they live their lives--by the ways in which they themselves conform to gender role norms, and the things they imply about the importance of making clear-cut boundaries for sex role development.

Research studies have now documented well that parents respond differently to their children according to their gender. These differences in response begin when a child is born, and include such things as assigning different attributes to the sleeping, eating, and crying behaviors of infant males and females. From their baby's earliest days, parents handle their male and female babies differently, they talk to them differently, and they assume that they have distinctly different characteristics because of their gender.

Perhaps because we live in a democracy, parents are apt to say that they treat their children the same, regardless of their gender; but everything we have been able to learn about parent-child interactions suggests just the opposite. Although parents would like to believe that their son or daughter can grow up to be President, their day-to-day behaviors toward their children don't support this belief.

It probably has not escaped your notice that boys and girls continue to be separated from one another, both physically and psychologically. If you have ever purchased a gift for a young child you know that although there are toys which are androgynous, most are clearly either "boy toys" or "girl toys." Even today you can see single-sex lines of boys and girls waiting to go into an elementary school after recess, and in their youngest years, boys and girls are discouraged from competing against each other in sports and many games. Subjects in school such as home economics and industrial arts are elected primarily by only girls or boys, and the separation of the sexes is especially apparent in sports and extra-curricular activities. Cheerleaders are still primarily girls. Class presidents are more likely to be boys, class secretaries girls. More boys take math and science, especially at the advanced levels, and girls are more likely than boys to take typing and secretarial courses. More girls than boys baby sit, more boys than girls deliver newspapers. Of course there are many exceptions to these choices that boys and girls make, but they continue to constitute the dominant trends in American life.

Not only do boys and girls engage in different and separate activities, but perhaps more important, what they do is valued differently by their peers and the adults around them. One of the clearest indicators of the different value placed on the activities of girls and boys can be seen in the amount of money a community spends in support of their endeavors, and the numbers of each gender that participate in any given activity. Although girls have made rapid and extensive gains in the extent of their athletic programs, primarily as a result of Title IX, [a federal law requiring equal access] attendance and revenue from ticket sales for boys games still far exceeds that from girls. Female athletes are still considered by many to be less committed to their sport than males, and only in the area of tennis have women made a dent in the high paying professional sports market.

Children learn very early that boys and girls should exercise different responses in controlling their emotions and feelings. This psychological separation of children occurs most directly through the different messages they receive about whether to express or contain their feelings. Boys learn not to cry when they hurt, and to be brave in the face of pain. Girls learn to preserve relationships even if it means suspending or ignoring the rules of a game. Boys learn to "put up or shut up," girls learn to win through charming. Much of this learning comes directly from parents, whose beliefs about the ways males and females should think and act profoundly influence what they say and how they behave toward their children.

Reaction among parents over whether males and females **should** have distinctly different roles in life is quite mixed. A great many parents feel that children should have an opportunity to take up any occupation, regardless of their gender, even though a close observation of their daily statements would likely show that their belief is continually being mediated by messages that contradict this idea. Many parents maintain a nagging suspicion that both their sons and daughters might benefit from a softening of attitudes toward gender role behaviors and opportunities. But it is very difficult for parents to know how to go about this task, especially when it comes to their sons. In their daily exchanges, fathers more than mothers are likely to caution their sons about not acting like girls; no male who has grown up believing that females are weak wants his son to take on this attribute. For parents who themselves live rather rigidly structured role-bound lives, the difference between what they say and do is readily apparent to a child, and the message is surely received as an ambiguous one.

It is much easier for most parents to see their daughter become an astronaut than it is to see their son become a cosmetologist. Some of this difference can be explained by the fear many parents have in fostering homosexuality in their sons, a fact that is more true for fathers than mothers. This fear of homosexuality that many fathers have is clearly reflected in the difficulty that so many of them have in being open with their sons about bodily learning. The other part of such a concern by parents grows from their awareness that an astronaut has a higher social status than a cosmetologist, so from this perspective, parents might well want their son **or** daughter to aspire to a career with more social value. Gender differences continue to be seen at the college and university level and have a significant impact, not only on the way men and women feel about themselves but also the way they feel about and treat the other sex.

Family Roles

Young men and women today often say that their generation is completely different from that of their parents' in terms of family roles, but it's very difficult to find much evidence to support this contention. Look at these responses students made in our most recent survey.

Who Should Be The Provider?

Should the husband be the major provider
for his family, even if his wife works?

	FEMALES	MALES
YES	27%	47%
NO	58%	39%
AREN'T SURE	15%	14%

It's pretty clear that most of these young men see them-selves as taking up the breadwinner role when they become adults, despite their protests that they see themselves becoming partners in egalitarian marriages. It is very difficult to shake off twenty years of socialization about what responsibilities we should assume as adults, especially when we are unsure what impact a new ap-proach might have on our relative power in a relationship.

Another survey question illustrated in the next chart asks to what extent the individual expects to perform child care activities if they marry. The kind of child care activities we're talking about include feeding, bathing, doctor visits, transporta-tion, and basic day and night time care.

How Much Child Care Will You Provide?

	FEMALE	MALES
The same as my spouse.	56%	83%
More than my spouse.	43%	5%
Less than my spouse.	1%	12%

The men who said they expect to spend as much time in caring for their children as their spouse are certainly well intentioned, and perhaps they really have this genuine desire. But it's unlikely that their own role as parents will be much different from that of their fathers. And this means that the estimations made by the women are also unrealistic, although they are much closer to the mark than the men's in the sense that they expect to do quite a bit more child care than their spouse.

An important piece of your sexuality was shaped as you watched and participated in the various roles within your family. Many of the things you learned about relationships came by observing the way your father and mother related to one another, and this is especially true about roles. A great deal of this learning may have taught you that your father enjoyed a special kind of status when it came to household tasks and child care. This fact may not have meant much to you while you were growing up, but chances are you have internalized the underlying message here, which is that males are valued more than females. As much as you would like to believe that you are of similar worth and value as anyone, irrespective of their gender, if you are a male your behavior is likely to reflect a deeply held belief that indeed you are superior to females.

Why is this issue of household tasks and child care so important to your sexuality? Mainly because it's very hard to have an equal relationship with someone unless you are pulling half the load. Wait a minute, you're thinking. What if the husband is the breadwinner, and his wife is staying home with the kids? Isn't he doing his share in the equality equation if he works all day to provide a living for his family? Well, he's doing his share during the day while he's at work. But most men in this situation feel entitled to stop working when they arrive home, although they expect their wife to continue working until the last child is in bed. They expect their wife to do this despite the fact that she, too, has been working all day.

The problem is much more basic than this when we think about families in which both husband and wife work full time, a condition which exists in well over half of all American families. Even in these families, the amount of household tasks and child care that husbands provide is a small fraction of that done by wives. Husbands don't even correctly report the amount of time they spend in these chores, typically overestimating their contribution by as much as half. Are professional couples, who have more control over the demands of their job, different in this respect? Not really. Professional husbands do only a small amount more of these tasks than do non-professionals; and in probably only ten to fifteen percent of marriages do husband and wife share these responsibilities equally.

Here's a third piece of survey data, which speaks to the question of whether spouses will change their full-time work status when a child arrives.

Child Care in the Younger Years

If you were to have children some day, during their younger years, would you expect that...

	FEMALE	MALES
You would work part time for at least a while and your spouse would remain fully employed?	62%	3%
Your spouse would work part time for at least a while and you would remain fully employed?	1%	57%
Both you and your spouse would work part time for at least a while?	17%	21%
Both you and your spouse would remain fully employed, except for a short leave of absence?	15%	19%

Why aren't men pulling their weight around the house? One reason is that many of them continue to think of cooking and cleaning as "women's work," and therefore beneath their dignity. It doesn't matter whether they are high powered executives or assembly line workers, many men consider household tasks as menial work, and avoid them like the plague. An important message we get by watching our fathers rationalize their lack of involvement in the home and in child care is that women are less powerful than men, since they are the ones who get stuck with the dirty work. The message for a girl is, "I'm not as important as boys, because I have to do things from which boys are exempt."

Another consequence of a father's avoidance of housework is that he misses many opportunities to interact with his children and to talk with them about things that concern them, including those that pertain to their sexuality. In most families, when a child does have a question about sex they go to their mother for an answer. When fathers perform housework and child care their children invariably see them as being more accessible than if they don't, and this accessibility encourages children and fathers to communicate more openly with one another. Some young people have told me that a major reason why their father doesn't contribute more to housework is that their **mother** is opposed to the idea. This may sound a bit crazy at first but if you think about it, it's easy to see why some women might do this. After all, many women feel they have bought into a system which provides them with certain benefits they wouldn't enjoy if they weren't in it, and they are reluctant to rock the boat. Even if they work, such wives are likely to be earning less than their husbands, and it's not easy to challenge a husband who contends that his higher wages entitle him to more power in family decision making.

Affection and Intimacy

I've already indicated that many parents never show much affection for one another, either physically or verbally. We learn other things about affection and intimacy from our parents by seeing how they interact with their friends, with other family members, and with us. Isn't there a great contrast between the touching "styles" of your mother and father? If she is like many women, your mother probably touches and hugs many different people, from friends and family members to other children to whom she has no family ties. Perhaps as many as sixty percent of mothers report they touch and hug in this manner. By contrast, over seventy percent of fathers report they **almost never** touch or hug their friends this way. Most of our fathers stopped touching and hugging us when we reached junior high school age, and this is even more likely to be true if we are male. Our mothers, on the other hand, tend to touch us throughout our lifetime.

As children, we see our mothers cry and be visibly upset far more often than we see our fathers express their feelings in this way. And we see our mother's tears brought on by a whole host of circumstances and events that range from sadness and loss to anger and outrage. We also see our mothers cry when we accomplish major goals or receive special awards or recognition, and we sometimes evoke their tears just by doing something loving for them. By contrast, we rarely see our fathers cry, largely because they **don't** cry very often. Most men can cite the specific circumstances in which they cried during the past five years, if indeed this has happened at all.

It's easy to see the effects of this kind of parental modeling on children. Girls are much more likely than boys to express their affection through hugging, caressing, nurturing and caretaking behaviors. Girls are encouraged to behave in these ways, and through baby sitting responsibilities they typically have more opportunities to do so. On the other hand, boys are systematically discouraged from kissing, hugging, being gentle, and asking for help. One of the most severe lessons a young boy must learn is that he must not be physically affectionate with his male friends. About the only opportunity a male has to express such affection is in a team situation where, after scoring a goal it is safe for the boys to hug one another. It appears safe to males under these circumstances because everyone can **see** that these boys are not sexually involved in any way. And it is the fear of homosexuality and the desire to avoid being perceived as being "like girls" that acts so strongly to suppress the expression of affection among males.

For most boys, there don't appear to be many options for expanding the range of their affectionate behaviors. They see their mother being open and affectionate, their father being guarded and inexpressive. If boys are rarely hugged or kissed by their fathers, rarely see their fathers touch or hug others, how can they possibly conclude that they should behave any differently? The need to touch and be touched is so strong a human need, however, that there are many negative consequences for a society that deprives its children of this form of nurturing. It's no wonder, then, that adolescent and young adult males are frequently labeled as "wanting only one thing—sex." What these young males probably want more than anything is what all human beings want and need: to be touched, held, and nurtured. For many males, though, the only way they know how to be touched is through a sexual encounter.

So instead of growing up seeing the many opportunities that affection and intimacy offer to all human beings, boys and girls learn very different things about these major features of life. For adults to change drastically the way they respond to their friends physically and emotionally requires something of a major overhaul of their interpersonal value system. You already know a lot about your own needs for affection and intimacy, but being able to meet your needs will likely require that you change some of your ideas and behaviors.

It's unfortunate that most parents don't talk with their children very much about sex. But since **they** didn't have sexuality education courses when they were in school, and their parents probably didn't talk with **them** about sex, it's at least understandable why today's parents don't do more with this kind of instruction. Will you be any different in this respect if and when you have children? You won't be unless you take some deliberate steps to prepare yourself to be a good sexuality educator, and it's not too early to begin. Whether or not you ever have children, you can count on being in situations where children will ask you questions about sex.

Even as a young adult you can do many things to prepare yourself to become a good sexuality educator. First, you can learn more about your own sexuality and work to feel more comfortable with yourself as a sexual person. You can increase your knowledge about sex and intimacy by reading, taking courses, and talking openly and sharing information with your friends. You and your friends or partner can practice responding to questions that children are likely to ask, and can critique one another's responses. And you also can just talk with children about anything, in order to gain some experience with the world of childhood and how children think and express their ideas. If you can talk comfortably with children about sex, there's a good chance that you will also be able to talk with your lover about sex, although there are elements in adult sex talk that require new learning and practice. So learning to talk with children may produce some very real benefits to you in terms of improved communication with your sexual partner.

There are several other ideas about your childhood that we should consider before we move on. The first is that you need not be limited by the constraints your parents may have imposed on your developing sexuality. I often hear young adults say things like, "I grew up in a strict Catholic home..." or "My parents never told me **anything** about sex..." or "What I got from my parents about sex was totally negative." I have no reason to doubt that these statements are true, and also acknowledge how powerful the influence of parents is on our sexuality. But you also have the opportunity to develop your own value system about sex and intimacy, and you need not let your parents' views color your world forever. This doesn't mean you have to reject everything your parents ever taught you. Most of us can point to many things we learned from our parents that we truly value and cherish. Most of us love our parents, even though we may disagree with some of their ideas.

I don't want to underestimate how difficult a task this may be for you, because I know that a key issue for you as you struggle with your developing sexuality is that you may be concerned that your parents would not approve of you if they knew the extent of your sexual activities. I ask my students two questions about this on their survey, and their responses help explain why you, too, might find it difficult to break away from your parents' sexual value system.

How aware are your parents of the extent and variety of your sexual experience?		
	FEMALE	MALES
They are fully aware	10%	10%
They know little about them	48%	56%
They know almost nothing	42%	34%

Assumimg your parents were fully aware of the extent and variety of your sexual experiences, how approving would they be of you as a sexual person?		
	FEMALE	MALES
Fully approving	7%	19%
Approving for the most part	44%	33%
Disapproving	49%	48%

Feeling that their parents do not approve of their sexual behaviors doesn't seem to prevent most young adults from being sexually active, but it often does interfere with the process of self-acceptance. A topic I'll discuss in greater detail in another chapter is what you can do as a young adult to help your parents feel more accepting of the sexual part of you.

Another point to bring up here is that although most of us were very fortunate to have had safe and secure sexual lives while we were growing up, a sizable portion of young people were victims of sexual abuse at the hands of family, friends, or strangers. If you yourself were such a victim, I hope that you have obtained help from counselors and friends in understanding and dealing with the impact of this kind of abuse. If you have not obtained help with this issue and would like to, you should contact local mental health or rape crisis centers, or call one of the following agencies for assistance in finding help near where you live:

✿ Incest Survivors Anonymous (ISA). P.O. Box 1653, Long Beach, CA 90805.
310-428-5599.
✿ SARAH, Inc. (Sexual Assault Recovery through Awareness and Hope).
P.O. Box 20353, Bradenton, FL 34203.
813-746-9114.
✿ Survivors of Incest Anonymous.
P.O. Box 21817, Baltimore, MD 21222.
301-282-3400.

CHAPTER 3

Different Strokes for Different Folks

Children discover the pleasure of touching their genitals at a very early age. While on the changing table, infants will often touch their genitals, the results of which in a male can be plainly seen in a tiny erection. As they get to be toddlers and preschoolers, most children develop a finer appreciation for the pleasures of their own touch. While they don't display the same task-oriented approach of adolescents or adults, young children certainly can be said to masturbate, because they engage in self-pleasuring.

While waiting in line at the check-out counter of the Grand Union a few years ago, for example, I observed a girl of about four standing behind her mother as the clerk rang up a cart full of groceries. This little tyke had both her hands stuffed into the front pockets of her Osh Kosh B'Gosh overalls, and was slowly rubbing her crotch. It would have been clear to even the casual observer that as she rolled her half-closed eyes around, rocked back and forth on her heels while slowly gyrating her hips, this child had found an enjoyable way to pass the time. Although she didn't seem to be bothering a soul, I would certainly not suggest that children masturbate in the Grand Union. If her mom had seen her, a little distraction would have been in order, with perhaps a suggestion after they got into the car that when she wanted to masturbate it was a good idea to do so in private, perhaps in her room. Her mom could say that some people get a bit uncomfortable when they see another person masturbate, and by masturbating in private she would be respecting such a person's feelings.

I can well understand why you might be wondering at this moment whether this entire chapter is devoted to the topic of masturbation. It is, and for good reasons. Although masturbation is not something that most people feel comfortable talking about, it is a sexual behavior that represents a doorway into one's erotic sexual self. Masturbation provides us with insights into what we enjoy about the pleasures of our own sexual arousal, and this information serves as a key in our helping a partner understand what feels good to us. While masturbation may be an area of your sexuality you feel uncomfortable about, it is none-the-less true that if you are able to love and pleasure yourself it will be much easier for you to be loved and pleasured by a partner.

In this chapter you will encounter a number of accounts of masturbation written by young adults like yourself. If you already feel comfortable about masturbating, these accounts will validate your experience. If you have negative feelings, you will no doubt be challenged to think about where these thoughts came from, and how your feelings about masturbation affect other aspects of your sexuality.

How We Learn about Masturbation

Males are socialized to masturbate by other males, and often utilize magazines like Penthouse and Playboy to stimulate their fantasy imagery. This form of erotica is a readily available part of their culture, perhaps as handy as the living room coffee table. Since orgasm and ejaculation are two different physiological events, it's not uncommon for boys to have their first orgasmic experiences well before puberty. But there does seem to be a link between the amount of the male sex hormone testosterone the testes make and the urgency to experience sexual arousal, so the extent of masturbation usually picks up as a boy nears puberty. By the time they reach their mid- to late teens, most males have masturbated to orgasm at least once, and many have done so quite regularly. Contrary to what many people think, boys are less likely than girls to discover masturbation on their own. Having a penis hanging around all the time doesn't mean that a young boy will realize by first grade that it is in need of constant attention.

Females, on the other hand, are more likely to discover masturbation on their own, but do so at an older age than males. There are a number of reasons why females not only discover masturbation later than males, but also masturbate less frequently, especially in their younger years. The most important is that females are socialized to believe they should not be sexual, and thus should have minimal sexual needs. Second, females learn that their bodies exist for the pleasure of males, and not for their own pleasure. Female modesty includes modesty about one's own body, and certainly stimulating one's own body constitutes a serious violation of this modesty injunction. Third, learning to masturbate can be difficult for some females, since they may lack a clear understanding of the association between clitoral stimulation and orgasm. And unlike a penis, the clitoris is located in a less obvious place. But from the many descriptions of masturbation we have from women, it is clear that social pressure and sexual learning, not anatomy, are the factors that most inhibit masturbation among females.

The taboo about masturbation arises in part because so many people have mixed feelings about its benefits. A rather strange situation exists, in which a very common behavior is treated with great disdain, something that is obvious when we think about the slang words that describe it. There are a tremendous number of slang terms used to describe masturbation, and it is no coincidence that most of them apply to male masturbation. Can you think of a single slang term for female masturbation? Probably not.

Slang terms for male masturbation include the following: jerk off, beat off, whack off, beat your meat, pound your pud, flog your log, choke the chicken, cuff the puppy, and spank the monkey. By the time he is eighteen, the average male's penis has been jerked, beaten, whacked, pounded, flogged, choked, cuffed and spanked, and this has happened repeatedly. This hardly sounds like a pleasurable experience to me!

What we have is a situation in which a sexual behavior is labeled as being unacceptable, and yet is practiced by a large percentage of the population. Young people especially often make fun of masturbation, and deny that it plays a positive role in their lives. To take a vocal stand on the importance of masturbation will probably put you in a distinct minority among your peers. Because of this negative attitude, it can even be difficult to find a private place to masturbate. If you are in college or have a roommate like Charlie does, it may call for some careful planning to find the opportunities for self pleasure.

Can you imagine this scene, in which Frank returns to his room in the middle of the evening to find his roommate Charlie masturbating:

"Charlie, what the hell's going on here, anyway?"
"Oh, Hi Frank. I'm just masturbating. Give me, oh, ten or fifteen minutes, and I'll be through. I'll be heading over to the library soon, if you'd like to take a whack at it yourself in a while."

This isn't too likely to happen, is it? If Frank were to "catch" Charlie masturbating like this, he'd probably head straight to his floor advisor's room, and demand another room or a new roommate. He'd burst into the RA's room and blurt out something like,

"Hey, Jack, you'll never believe what happened. I just walked into my room, and found Charlie on the bed jerking off! I mean, he was just lying there, with the lights out, going at it."

It's just as unlikely that if this scenario did take place, Jack would reply by saying something like this:

"Now Frank, calm your hormones! You know darn well that it's normal and healthy for people to masturbate, and that you do it as much as Charlie does. I'm sure that with a little planning you two guys can work something out so your masturbation won't interfere with one another's plans. What do you say the three of us sit down and talk about this together and come up with a schedule or something?"

Some Interesting History about Masturbation

If you spend any time at all talking with young men and women about the topic of masturbation, you will see how ambivalent they are about this sexual practice. Those who don't masturbate, or do so only occasionally, often express both distaste for the behavior as well as indicate that it reveals a kind of depravity or perversion. Those who do masturbate, while usually enjoying it and considering it to be an important aspect of their sexuality, frequently describe feeling guilty or concerned over what the behavior might mean about them as persons. Why are there so many negative attitudes about masturbation?

Many factors contribute to the generally negative attitudes we have about masturbation. All of them grow out of some piece of our cultural heritage, and are closely interwoven with our present notions of appropriate sex roles and sexual ideologies. Religion and medicine account for much of the unpleasant imagery that surrounds masturbation today, just as these two institutions have influenced all other kinds of sexual behavior. Although it may sound unfair to say that the basis for the church's concern for limiting sexual expression lies in its desire to perpetuate a patriarchal view of the world, it's hard to find a better explanation. Likewise, many physicians continue to look with contempt on women and men whose education and training is inferior to their own. Since people in all cultures have looked to their priests and medicine men for guidance in so many spheres of life, it's no wonder that these two groups have had such a profound effect on the behavior of their followers.

Of the major western religions, Catholicism seems to be the most consistent in its condemnation of any sexual behavior other than that of sexual intercourse without contraception, between husband and wife. The Church has maintained a clear position that the purpose of sex is procreation, and that to engage in other forms of sexual activities is to defeat God's plan and desire. Although some individual priests may take a more tolerant approach toward the sexual practices of their parishioners, they do so without the support of Rome. In 1975, the Vatican stated that masturbation represented a seriously disordered act, all the while acknowledging that there was no psychological or sociological evidence to support this contention. This position of the Church has not changed.

Closely aligned with Catholicism on this topic are fundamentalist Protestant churches whose doctrines espouse "traditional family values," code words for patriarchy. These same churches oppose legal abortion, sexuality education in the schools, and an active role for women in the leadership of the church. Their belief that the husband should be the bread winner and family supporter helps explain why they oppose women in the work world.

Although traditional Judaism forbid the kind of touching of the genitals involved in masturbation, contemporary Jewish thinking is much more tolerant about this, resembling that of mainstream Protestantism. Many of the more liberal Jewish congregations and Protestant denominations accept masturbation as being a healthy and normal part of a person's sexuality.

At least during the past two centuries, physicians have exercised as much negative influence over human sexuality as have priests and other churchmen. It's embarrassing to think of how people have looked to physicians for common guidance for so long, never realizing that most physicians were no better equipped to talk openly about sexual issues than was anyone else.

Incidence and Techniques of Masturbating

Males begin masturbating at an earlier age than females, and do so with greater frequency throughout their lives. But this difference in frequency does not mean that masturbation is any less important for females than for males. Rather, the difference reflects the socialized idea that women should not really be sexual, and that if they must be, there should be a man's arm attached to any hand that touches their clitoris. As men and women reach their mid-thirties, their frequency of masturbation tends to become more alike. On the other hand, compared to men, single women experience a considerably higher percentage of their orgasms through masturbation than they do from other means of stimulation, a trend that appears to begin in the late teen years. My surveys have produced data about masturbation that has remained remarkably stable over time. The following chart summarizes responses to a question about whether the person has masturbated to orgasm.

Masturbation to Orgasm: In Percentages		
FREQUENCY	FEMALE	MALES
Never	55%	9%
Once	3%	7%
Several Times	22%	17%
Frequently	20%	67%

It is clear that the percentage of masturbating females is significantly less than that of males. By the time they are in their thirties, however, the percentages will look much more like those of the males, with as many as 70-90 percent reporting they masturbate with some frequency. Since for many women masturbation is the only way to reach orgasm, it's easy to see why this behavior increases with age.

Although women and men employ many different methods to masturbate, most of them involve the basic principle of applying some form of direct or indirect pressure to the glans (the most sensitive end part) of the clitoris or penis. Many women stroke the area of the labia and vaginal opening while massaging the clitoris in a side-to-side rocking motion. Instead of rubbing the glans of the clitoris directly, a woman is more likely to manipulate it through the folds of the clitoral hood, a technique similar to that of a man pulling his foreskin over the glans as he strokes his penis up and down. Some women lie on their back to masturbate, while others prefer to lie on their stomach. And there are some males who like to lie on their stomach and rub their penis against a pillow or blanket without touching their penis with their hands. Some women use vibrators to intensify the pressure on their clitoris, something which has no negative effects on their interpersonal sexual practices. Men, too, occasionally use a vibrator while masturbating, using it to stimulate the base of their penis and the area around the anus. Some men insert a lubricated finger into their anus while masturbating, and are able to reach orgasm by gently stimulating their prostate gland. Water from a shower massager is a perfect trigger for a number of women, and with a soapy body a bath is a wonderfully sensual atmosphere for this kind of sexual pleasuring. Both women and men sometimes use a lubricant such as massage oil or soap while in the shower to heighten the pleasurable sensation while masturbating.

Women appear to employ a wider range of techniques in masturbation than do men, but all strategies have the net effect of producing a high state of arousal and orgasm. In addition to the methods just mentioned, women sometimes masturbate by simply squeezing their thighs together, rubbing their vulva against an object such as a sofa arm, or inserting objects into their vaginas. A small percentage of women can achieve orgasm simply by caressing their breasts, or through fantasy alone.

Contrary to popular belief, men are no faster than women in their ability to achieve orgasm through masturbation. The notion that women require more time than men to reach orgasm grows out of the images surrounding orgasm in intercourse, an idea I'll discuss more fully in another chapter. Suffice it to say here, if you put Jack and Jill on the masturbators' starting line, said, "Ready, Set, Go!", they'd cross the finish line in a dead heat. But of course nothing could be sillier than seeing how fast you can reach orgasm, unless you're late for a meeting or your friends are waiting downstairs for you to go shopping! Most people like to pace their masturbation in a way that takes into account how much time they have, how tired they are, and their general psychological mood. If anything, masturbation seems to be a nice way for men and women to take their time, to enjoy things at a casual pace, and soak in the sensualness of their own bodies.

There is amazing variety to the way young people describe their masturbation techniques. Although there are some differences between the ways women and men describe their masturbation, I have noticed a number of common threads among the descriptions. Men and women agree that masturbation calms and relaxes them, often assisting them in falling asleep after a busy day. They also agree that it helps them learn about their own bodies and what makes them feel good, and allows them to do something special, just for themselves. Many people feel glad that they can relieve their sexual tensions on their own when they don't have a partner, or when their partner is not available. And some women and men feel strongly that masturbating with their partner gives them an added sense of closeness, allows them to meet their own individual orgasmic needs, helps their partner understand their own sexual feelings better, and opens the door to increased communication about sex.

Different Strokes for Different Folks

As I've worked with young people over the years I have developed a real appreciation for their inventiveness and ability not to take themselves too seriously. I have found these two qualities to be especially true in descriptions of their developing sexuality. Consider, for example, the following account written by one of my students who risked a lifetime of potential pleasure in order to try out a tip he'd picked up in his shop class.

Taken to the Cleaners

"I can remember precisely when I started to masturbate to orgasm. It was in ninth grade shop class, when some of the guys started locker room talk. We were getting pretty crude when one of the guys said how his friend's brother put his penis in a vacuum cleaner and got an erection. Well curiosity got the better of me, and before I knew it, I was experiencing my first orgasm at the age of fifteen, with vacuum cleaner in hand.

"Since my first orgasm was four years ago, at seven orgasms a week on average, that gives a rough estimate of 1,456 orgasms in my life. This is no bull. I really don't know if this will present problems later in life or not, but right now I'm willing to take that chance. I'm a little worried that the hand will take precedent over a sexual partner, though. I've found that the ideal conditions for me to masturbate is with the lights on, looking at a centerfold, and masturbating my penis with a wool sweater. Real wool feels very soft, and stimulates my penis quite easily. After reading this, you might think that I'm very weird, perverted, or totally into my body, but this isn't true. I'm as normal as the next guy."

Do you suppose this young man is trying to pull the wool over our eyes? I don't think so, but I do think he is very lucky that he didn't try this stunt with a commercial vacuum cleaner. He really doesn't have to worry though about developing a preference for masturbation instead of doing something sexual with another person. Most people feel that masturbation is just one part of their sexuality, a part that some of them call on more frequently when they are younger. As people get older they often realize that they can have it both ways: a partner and their own hand, without doing a disservice to either one of them.

In contrast to the young man we just discussed, the following woman discovered masturbation on her own, something much more likely to happen to females than males. I admire her perseverance.

Rubber Duckie, You're My Friend!

"I can't remember how old I was when I first became sexually aroused, but the circumstances were very strange. I vividly recall taking a shower, and using our brand new shower massager. At first this appeared to be just a more forceful and directed jet of water, which didn't phase me in the least until I brought it close to my genitals. WOW!! What a sensation. This was the first time I had ever experienced an orgasm, and I enjoyed it so much it was almost scary.

"I repeated this act a number of times because it felt so good. I never knew it was a form of masturbation, nor did I know that my clitoris was what was being stimulated by the water jet, or that I could stimulate it with my own hand as well. All I felt was that I was doing something wrong, and that no one else did anything this crazy.

"For a long time I denied myself the pleasure of masturbation, and until recently I wasn't really sure exactly what masturbation actually was. When I gained more information from a book about it I dared to try it myself. Being the closet case that I am, I waited until no one was home, and then locked myself in the bedroom. Very skeptical about the whole exercise, I went about massaging my clitoris just as instructed. It felt good, but in order to reach orgasm I had to rub quite vigorously, and this created soreness afterwards. But the euphoric sensation stemming from my genitals created an unbelievable high throughout my body. It felt very similar to the orgasm I had experienced when the water forcefully propelled itself against my clitoris.

"My feelings about masturbation really changed after this experience. I think all women owe it to themselves to try masturbating, especially those who get such little stimulation from sexual intercourse. But there's no need for anyone to look at this as second best, with sexual intercourse as being first best, or believing that masturbation is only for individuals who can't get 'the real thing.' Masturbation has added greatly to my sexual development, as well as increased my knowledge of my own body rhythms."

Like so many other people, this young woman had learned somewhere along the way that there was something wrong with experiencing the kind of pleasure she achieved from the shower massager. The idea of denying herself this pleasure is symptomatic of two more general cultural attitudes about sex. The first is that sexual pleasure should be taken in small doses, since this kind of pleasure should only be the occasional reward for good behavior in unspecified areas of life. The second is that only a partner should provide pleasure to one's body, and the partner must be of the other sex. Fortunately, many of us are able to overcome these strong cultural sanctions and judge for ourselves how much pleasure we are entitled to, and under what circumstances we obtain it.

But many individuals persist in believing that masturbation is a perverse and damaging practice. For the two women whose descriptions follow, masturbation is unacceptable, but it is interesting to see that "Pro Choice" raises an issue that transcends the usual kind of concerns about masturbation.

No Thanks

"I've masturbated two or three times. I think it's a little kinky and I would really back away from someone I knew masturbated a lot. It seems to me to be a sign of desperation or sexual frustration. I don't think I could ever respect a guy that beat off a lot, or a woman who played with herself. I think I'll always consider them odd and strange, and I wouldn't want anything to do with them if I knew they masturbated regularly."

Pro Choice

"I have never masturbated, and don't have the desire to masturbate. My feelings on masturbation were basically pro-choice until I found out that my partner masturbated. It wasn't the idea of masturbation that disturbed me. I just felt that I wasn't satisfying him enough, and it bothered me that naked women in dirty books turned him on."

It is unlikely that we will convince the first woman that she need not fear her masturbating friends; she seems quite set on the idea that masturbation is disgusting. But chances are she already has many male friends who "beat off a lot," and knows and respects women who "play with themselves." This argument sounds very much like the one cited by individuals who say they don't know anyone who is gay. These people indeed **do** know gays, they just don't **know** that they're gay. And since masturbation is such a taboo subject to discuss, it is unlikely that this woman would ever be exposed to the facts of her friends' masturbation patterns.

"Pro Choice," on the other hand, raises what appears to be a very valid point about her partner masturbating while looking at "dirty books." It is probably not true that she isn't satisfying him enough, since most adults who masturbate do so because it represents a special form of sexual pleasuring, not because their partner is not satisfying their sexual needs. But what "Pro Choice" may be most concerned about is that fact that her partner uses pornography to stimulate his sexual fantasies. There are a couple of things she and her partner could discuss together related to this practice, and it would help immensely if they could begin their discussion by acknowledging that each of them has been sexually socialized in very different ways.

On the one hand, the individual fantasies each may have while masturbating or day-dreaming cannot possibly be harmful to them. No sexual thought, no matter how strange or perverted it appears, will ever harm someone. On the other hand, "Choice's" partner needs to know that his pornography offends her and does so for a variety of reasons, not the least of which is that it objectifies human beings. So what is the difference between having private sexual thoughts you conjure up yourself, and those stimulated by pornography?

On the surface, maybe not a lot. But at a deeper level our relationships are heavily influenced by the messages we get from things like pornography, so when we choose not to read it or look at it we're making a strong statement about our beliefs in the value of rejecting cultural stereotypes as a means of attaining mutual relationships. And as we'll see in a later chapter, rejecting this kind of image is fundamental to making changes and improvements in our intimate relationships. If "Choice" confronts her partner about this matter in a loving and supportive way she may find that not only is he willing to change this part of his behavior, but also that her negative feelings about masturbation in general may be modified as well.

When I talk with young people about masturbation, a question that frequently comes up is, "Can a person masturbate too much?" The big problem in answering this question is in knowing how much is too much. Whenever I hear this question I'm reminded of the scene in the movie **Annie Hall,** in which a psychiatrist asks Diane Keaton and Woody Allen how often they have sex. Diane Keaton replies, "All the time, like three times a week!" while Woody Allen says, "Hardly ever, only three times a week!" When it comes to frequency, one's individual perspective becomes very important.

To illustrate this idea, let's consider the case of "Addicted," who, among other things masturbates when he's suffering from DSB (Deadly Sperm Buildup).

I'm Addicted

"I masturbate a great deal. At least once every three days, in the evening, morning, afternoon, any time I feel that build-up of semen. I have done it in a lot of funny places, like a bus, train, and plane bathroom.

"There are two reasons why I would like to stop masturbating, or at least cut down on the amount. First, I think that I am addicted to it, and it is often hard to go a week without doing it. And second, I would like to be less dependent on masturbation as the only relief from the pressures and tensions of the day.

"Whenever I masturbate during a particular morning or afternoon, I will stay away from intimate situations with women. What if they wanted it, and I would have to say to them, 'Sorry, I just masturbated earlier today, and will not be able to work tonight!'"

Masturbating once every three days doesn't seem like too much to me. Even three times a day isn't unusual, at least during certain periods in a person's life. One good way to deal with this whole masturbation frequency issue is to ask yourself questions like these:

- ✿ Am I masturbating so much that I don't have time to do the things I'm supposed to, like study, bathe, socialize with friends, walk the dog, lace my shoes up all the way?
- ✿ Am I so obsessed with masturbating that it occupies most of my waking thoughts?
- ✿ Have I torn ligaments in my arms or wrists as a result of continually rubbing my genitals? Do my genitals have serious abrasions or contusions resulting from such abuse?

If the answers to these questions are no, you need not worry. If any of the answers are yes, you may indeed be masturbating too much. But your problem probably isn't masturbation; rather, masturbation may be serving as the only way you are coping with the pressing issues currently in your life. If you played racquetball all day, or felt a compulsion to ride your bike ninety miles before breakfast, or spent the better part of every afternoon combing your hair, you'd be doing things that suggested you **were** having difficulty keeping your priorities in order. In this kind of a situation it would be a good idea to discuss the matter with a counselor or therapist. These folks are experts at helping people with this kind of issue.

Let's suppose for a minute that "Addicted" is indeed addicted to masturbating. When he goes for more than a few days without masturbating he develops incredibly painful withdrawal symptoms that range from a general tightening of the skin on his scrotum to an uncontrollable shaking in his right arm. Can this be harmful? Apparently not. I have searched the medical literature high and low and have been unable to find even a single study that adequately documents the so-called "Masturbator's Syndrome." Have you ever heard of someone being hospitalized because they were masturbation addicts, or had to take methadone, or attend Masturbators Anonymous meetings? Of course you haven't, and the reason is that masturbation tends to be a self-limiting activity: you just can't do it all the time, because after you do it a while you get tired, and fall asleep.

It looks like "Addicted" might benefit from some additional activities in his life like sports or volunteer work. These kinds of things will help him take his mind off the tensions and pressures he describes, which may result in less masturbation. And when he develops an intimate relationship with someone he will not need to fret about saving his semen. Although his worry about not being able to "service" a partner is a common one among his peers, most young men can ejaculate a couple of times a day if the circumstances are appropriate. In an intimate relationship, "Addicted" and his partner can work out a schedule for their lovemaking that will permit regular, mutually desired emissions.

If "Pro Choice" and "Need Not Apply" had general concerns about their masturbating friends, they would surely be stunned by the thought of masturbating with a partner. What I'm referring to here are individuals who masturbate in the presence of their partner, either simultaneously or one at a time. The woman who wrote the excerpt that follows had described in a previous paragraph that prior to her current relationship she had felt considerable guilt whenever she touched her genitals. It is clear to see that the trust she felt for her partner was encouraging her to experiment in ways that were expanding her sexual development in a favorable way.

We Do It Together

"I always thought it was wrong to touch down there, so I was always hesitant to do so. In my present relationship, however, I have experienced a new feeling. My boyfriend encourages me to masturbate, and assures me that it is OK. We began to masturbate together and find it a very stimulating act of foreplay before lovemaking. I feel at ease and very comfortable in his presence. I like to masturbate with him, but gradually I have begun to do it on my own. Due to the distance between my partner and me we only see each other on weekends, and it can get very lonely without him. Masturbating helps to ease the longing I have for him. I feel masturbation is important in that it lets you feel more open with your body and feelings."

It's no wonder that masturbating with a partner seems like such a scary activity. If most people are unwilling even to talk about masturbation it stands to reason that they are even less likely to actually do it in another's presence, even that of their partner. But those couples who do enjoy masturbating together report that this practice is an especially beneficial one. It is often very exciting just to watch your partner masturbate, perhaps in part because you're doing something that is thought by many to be taboo. Watching a partner masturbate allows you to see them experiencing something that may have happened to you many times before, and this kind of information provides you with a level of appreciation that cannot be found easily in other sexual behaviors. When you hold your partner while they masturbate you're letting them know they can trust you with one of their most private and personal behaviors. And when couples masturbate simultaneously, they can pace themselves so as to achieve orgasm together, probably one of the few ways in which this phenomenon can occur. And there are times when only one partner wants to reach orgasm and the other is tired or not feeling well, but not too sick and tired to hold and nurture the other while they masturbate.

What's The Bottom Line on Masturbation?

So what's the bottom line on masturbation? If you're not a Certified Masturbator, should you run to the library to find a book that will teach you how? If you feel guilty when you masturbate, should you stop? If you feel good about masturbating, should you write a book explaining why you feel this way? These deep and penetrating questions don't deserve to be dealt with by citing a simple formula, but here is some advice that I think will hold up quite well.

First, masturbation won't hurt you. If certain people or your church tell you that you shouldn't masturbate because it is against God's will or some other similar reason, you are certainly free to take their advice. But it is important to know that their advice is based on their belief system, and not on the fact that masturbation can hurt you in any way. Masturbation is probably one of the safest sexual activities known to modern civilization, much safer than sexual intercourse, pregnancy, or even kissing someone who wears braces. And no states require that seat belts be worn while masturbating.

Second, it won't hurt you if you don't masturbate. One of the great things about both personal and interpersonal sex is that you have total freedom to participate or not. Because many people masturbate doesn't mean you have to. You may not masturbate now but find that as you get older you would like to do so. Or vice versa. Not masturbating is not a sign of sexual immaturity any more than wearing pajamas is a sign you sleep in a cold bed.

Third, masturbation has many benefits, in spite of the fact that it is sometimes accompanied by feelings of guilt. These guilt feelings seem to diminish as people get older, and as they learn to feel more comfortable with the many other discontinuities in their lives. Things that are unacceptable at twenty often become fully integrated practices just a few years later. Masturbation is a way to gain personal sexual knowledge, and to enjoy oneself as well, and there are few other pleasures in life that are so inexpensive.

And finally, masturbation isn't second best to anything. You may prefer other forms of sexual expression, especially ones that are interpersonal, but to think of masturbation as a substitution for "real sex" rather than as a sexual act with its own set of meanings and values is to reflect a limited view of the nature of human sexuality. As Woody Allen once said, "Masturbation for me is like having sex with a very special person---me."

CHAPTER 4

◀❙❉❙▶

Just the Two of Us

Most of us can easily recall when we first realized we were a boy or a girl. These early childhood memories often include incidents like bathing with other-sex siblings or cousins, seeing an other-sex parent nude, being dressed in clothing that was stereotypically male or female, or being chastised for not acting like a boy or a girl should act. These earliest recollections about our gender can be traced to our pre-school years, frequently to about ages three or four. It's also not too difficult for most people to identify their first romantic or sexual interest in another person, which might have occurred as early as the second or third grade. Our childhood interests in a person of the other sex typically are at the romantic level, and although we may hold hands or play kissing games, we aren't usually concerned with sexual arousal. In the middle school and junior high, teachers, coaches, and older high school students may become the objects of our romantic interests, which we describe by saying we have a crush on the person.

Many young people report that their first real awareness of becoming sexually aroused occurred in the junior high or early high school years, and these initial experiences were triggered by a variety of stimuli. Sometimes it was a matter of discovering their father's **Playboy** or **Penthouse** magazines and becoming very excited at the sight of nude bodies and the erotic language of the letters and fantasy articles. Both males and females indicate that looking at their father's "sex magazines" was risky, and this risk factor certainly seems to heighten the general level of sexual excitement. Sex and risk often go hand-in-hand, something that people often mention when they describe having sexual intercourse in dangerous places like elevators, airplanes, or restaurant bathrooms.

Young adults often say that it was their first "real" kiss that fully awakened their sexual arousal system, and quite frequently this sexual response was not really anticipated. Young men are likely to report that they had erections during this kind of kissing experience, which was embarrassing because they thought their partner would notice it. Young women more often report a generalized warm and glowing feeling in their groin accompanied by a sensation of wetness, which they too were certain others would somehow be able to detect. Thus while they were dancing, for example, such young couples would become sexually aroused but try very hard to look cool and contained so as not to give any clues to chaperons or others that might tip off what was really going on.

Middle school and junior high school boys and girls whose initial feelings of sexual attraction are for a member of the same sex are faced with a considerable problem, since for them to act on these feelings is likely to subject them to taunts, harassment, and rejection by their peers. Epithets like queer, faggot and dyke are the stuff of junior and senior high hallway and locker room discourse, so young people who are becoming aware of their homosexual orientation learn quickly how to disguise their attractions in order to fit into their predominantly heterosexual world. At the same time their heterosexual friends are beginning to actualize their needs for sexual connection to others, homosexual boys and girls often are struggling with just the opposite problem, that of suppressing and denying their desires. There are few secrets in life more terrifying for a young person than that of being homosexual, since this is a secret they feel they may never be able to share with anyone.

No matter what their sexual orientation, early adolescence is not an easy time for many young people, so being gay or lesbian often compounds an already problematic period in one's life. This is not to say that adolescence is a tough time for all youth: many young adults, including gays, recall this period of their life as a very positive and affirming one. But the pressure on all youngsters to begin dating and to carry out a heterosexual script is formidable, and therefore many gay and lesbian youth do go out with other-sex friends and try to act as if they were straight. The need for acceptance is so great during this time in a person's life that they will go to great lengths to appear to be "normal," which in this instance means appearing to be heterosexual.

So kissing is the first kind of arousing experience that most of us have with another person, and kissing usually proceeds to "making out," which is a form of extended kissing. While you might think that by the time they reach their late teens all young people would have some kissing experience, our surveys have consistently shown that between one and three percent of our respondents report they have never kissed anyone. Reasons for this vary, but most of these folks indicate that they simply have never had the opportunity to try kissing, though they feel quite open to the possibility that it will happen in the future. For heterosexual couples, making out sets in motion a sexual script which can be applied to other more advanced forms of arousal, a script heavily flavored by gender role learning.

Petting

The basic script of sexual interaction between hetero-sexual couples casts each actor into a designated role, with the male being the **initiator**, his female partner the **limit setter**. Petting is a good example to demonstrate the stylized way in which sexual interactions advance from kissing. Petting involves touching the body below the neck, although it also frequently includes touching the body above the shoulders, such as caressing the face and head. In a scripting sense, the male's role is to pet, the female's is to be petted, and also to determine how far the petting is to proceed. She is the pettee, but also the enforcer. He is the petter, but must be guided by her permission granting.

If you have been paying attention, you know that the male's first step in the petting routine is to touch his partner's breasts through her blouse or sweater. If she gives even the slightest indication that she likes this he will proceed to insinuate his hand under her shirt, and touch her breasts directly. If again this action is met with a favorable response, he will continue to advance his touching to caress his partner's thighs and vulva, first through her dress or jeans, and then directly after removing some of her clothes, perhaps with her assistance.

Now an interesting thing about this petting script is that the male doesn't know what his limits are until they are set by his partner, since most people don't discuss these limits explicitly before they begin petting. Wouldn't it be unusual to hear the following kind of conversation from a couple who were making out passionately for the first time?

Jill   "Oh, Jack, this is really nice, all this kissing and so on. I'm really getting hot, and I'd like it ever so much if you would touch my breasts. But since it's our first date, I'd like our petting to be limited to this. How's that sound to you?"

Jack   "That sounds just fine to me, Jill. If we find that we'd like to advance our petting to include our genitals, we can talk about it, and decide then what to do."

Almost by definition in this script, the male must touch beyond his partner's permissible zones, since he doesn't know what his limits are until he has exceeded them, if only briefly. It is not coincidental that the term "going all the way" fits into this script, since it means that the couple has acted in concert to test and conquer each border of the sexual terrain leading them toward sexual intercourse. And it is a truism that once a boundary has been established it is permissible for the couple to return at least to that point in any subsequent sexual encounter. Although the female is free to ease her border defenses voluntarily and can actually invite such an advance, it is more likely that her partner will make his own attempts to breach the next obstacle on his way to getting what he wants. This all sounds a bit like warfare, doesn't it?

Petting the genitals is likely to be the first means by which partners evoke orgasm in one another, although this might have occurred during an episode of "dry humping," in which partners rub their crotches together while both are fully clothed. It's quite an eye opener to discover the discrepancies in the ways in which young adults perceive and report their orgasmic experiences achieved through petting. The following chart presents two sets of data: first, the percentage reporting they have been petted to orgasm by a partner, and second, those reporting they have petted a partner to orgasm.

Have you ever been petted to orgasm by a partner?		
PERCENT RESPONDING	FEMALE	MALES
No, this has never happened	34	18
This happened one time	11	8
This has happened several times	29	33
This has happened many times	26	41
Have you ever petted a partner to orgasm?		
PERCENT RESPONDING		
No, this has never happened	13%	9%
This happened one time	9%	12%
This has happened several times	33%	34%
This has happened many times	45%	45%

You don't have to be a mathematical genius to see that there is something puzzling about the data in these charts. Simple arithmetic demonstrates the following inconsistencies:

- ✿ 45 percent of the males report they have petted a partner to orgasm many times, whereas,
- ✿ Only 26 percent of the females reported they have been petted to orgasm many times. On the other hand,
- ✿ 45 percent of the females reported they have petted a partner to orgasm many times. And you're not going to believe it, but
- ✿ 45 percent of the males say they have been petted to orgasm many times.

What's going on here, anyway? How come the women are pretty much right on the money in reporting their partners' orgasms, but the men are way off target in accounting for **their** partners' orgasms? When I discuss this data with my students, they have two predictable responses: women **KNOW** when their partners come (the evidence has been squirted here, there and everywhere), and thus report accurately this half of the equation; the men, on the other hand, lacking similar objective evidence of their partners' orgasms and not having a clue as to what female orgasm is all about, report their petting results with less than perfect accuracy. My students explain this discrepancy by saying that the women are faking and/or the men are exaggerating. I think they are absolutely right in these explanations, so let's examine why women might fake orgasm when they are petted, and why men might exaggerate or "over report" the incidence of their partners' orgasms.

Why would any woman in her right mind fake an orgasm while being petted, or for that matter at any time? There are several really good reasons. Perhaps the most important one is that she has learned well the lesson that when a man pets her, she **should** reach orgasm. You might say it's her job to orgasm when petted. This little rule exists even though the woman may never have reached orgasm in her life before, from masturbation or any other form of stimulation. Her sexual history really doesn't matter much here, if she is going to be a good little girl she'd better play by the rules. So whether she comes or not, or whether she has even the remotest idea of what it feels like to orgasm, her job is to put on a show that will convince her partner that he has been a good boy and done his job well. She needs to boost his ego—certainly not deflate it! She can do this by gyrating her torso, moaning and groaning with increasing emphasis, and finally collapsing in feigned ecstasy. Or she can give few objective clues to her partner regarding whether or not she comes, but say reassuring things to him like, "Oh, Baby, that was great—you really know how to put a girl into orbit!" If her partner is the kind of man who likes to be sure he's been successful, and asks her directly, "Did'ja come?" or "Was it good for you?" she can say something clever like, "Do cows moo? Is the moon up there in the sky? Would your Mamma lie to you, Baby?" Men love to believe lines like these.

Another good and very practical reason why a woman would fake orgasm is to put an end to the torture being inflicted upon her clitoris and surrounding tissues. Unless a partner has given them some detailed instructions in how to manually pleasure her clitoris, many men simply fumble and rub, and assume that if they rub long and hard enough their partner will reach orgasm. This approach rarely proves to be effective, but this fact doesn't deter most petters. Since a woman is supposed to assume that her partner is skilled in all matters sexual, including petting, it could seem forward or downright insensitive of her to give him specific instructions in how to pleasure her. If a woman leaves her partner to his own devices, she runs a considerable risk of acquiring a good set of rope burns on her labia and clitoris if she doesn't give him some clear indication that his work is over, that his goal has been accomplished.

A woman could avoid this fake-or-not-to-fake bind by responding with one of the following kinds of scripts:

♣ "Sweetie, I love it when you stroke my breasts and vulva, and massage my clitoris with your fingers. But I want you to relax about trying to make me come. At this point in my life, the only way I can come is by masturbating, and it just makes my clitoris really sore if you rub it too much. At some point you can hold me while I masturbate, and that way we'll both be able to enjoy the beneficial effects brought about by orgasmic release."

—OR—

♣ "I don't want to fake an orgasm with you, Honey, 'cause I know you wouldn't want me to make you think something happened when it really didn't. The truth of the matter is that I haven't really discovered quite how to reach orgasm yet, but I'm not at all bothered by that. I'm learning that my orgasm is **my** responsibility, and when I figure out how I can bring you into this little act you'll be the first one to know. I'm learning how to masturbate, which will probably help me a lot in getting a handle on this, so to speak. In the meantime, I really enjoy having you pet my vulva and clitoris—just don't worry about needing to go anywhere with it."

I know these scripts sound contrived and too polished to have been said by real people, but these rather simple and straightforward approaches would help a couple enjoy a petting experience with the maximum pleasure for each partner. Of course any scripts like these require that the actors feel reasonably secure with their sexuality, something that is easier said than done.

Let's now consider the men whose reporting of their partners' orgasms was exaggerated. Why would a man report that his partner comes when in fact she doesn't? He has some good reasons, too, the most significant of which is that he is simply reporting what he **should** report. Have you ever read a **Penthouse** or **Playboy** letter or fantasy piece in which a male writes that he was unable to please his partner—something like the following?

> "My partner was writhing around the couch as I stroked her clitoris, but nothing I was able to do seemed to be sufficient for her to reach orgasm. At one point, she said 'I just can't figure out what's going on here—none of my other boyfriends ever had any problem bringing me off.' I mean, man that kind of talk can really hurt a guy, if you know what I mean."

Yes, we know what he means. Although he may not have the vaguest idea what he's doing, a man will proceed to pet his partner anyway, and it's not too likely that he'll ask her what she would like, nor show her how to pet **him** for that matter. Sadly for many men, the only way to be a real man means to be in control, even if you don't know what you're doing. So some men report what they **think** they should; but there are others whose exaggerated figures reflect a true desire of what they would like for their partners. Most men enjoy orgasmic release, and they would like their partners to experience the same.

If women have some kind of objective evidence that their male partner comes, men have only their partners' direct statements or body language to go on. That men can be fooled by a partner into believing that they came reveals just how little men understand female orgasm. It's worth pointing out that men usually lack this knowledge because their partners have not helped them conceptualize what female orgasm is like. If we take this puzzle apart it is easy to see how each partner gains some sense of what orgasm for an other sex partner is like.

A woman knows when her male partner comes when she pets him because when he ejaculates she sees or feels his semen, and correctly deduces that if he has ejaculated he has also reached orgasm. But let's say that the petting is going on in the dark (which is often the case), but the woman is unable to see or touch her partner's semen. In this situation, she has only the subjective evidence of his moans and groans to go on, and is no better off than he would be in assessing her orgasm under similar circumstances. If she's holding onto the shaft of her partner's penis while he is ejaculating, she can't **feel** his penis pulsating with each orgasmic contraction. His penis doesn't reverberate in her hand with a BOOM! BOOM! BOOM! effect. When a male reaches orgasm during sexual intercourse, his partner usually doesn't **feel** his orgasm. If he's not wearing a condom, she feels his ejaculate trickle out of her vagina, and has this evidence of his orgasm, but her vagina doesn't typically pulsate and throb as a result of her partner's orgasm. If she wanted to **feel** her partner's orgasm she could place a finger in his anus, or at the base of his penis, where she could detect small contractions.

Since men lack the evidence of ejaculation from their partners, developing a concept of female orgasm can be more difficult or even totally elusive. As I already mentioned, a fairly high proportion of young women hasn't yet experienced orgasm, so if a man is to get a sense of what female orgasm is like he will need to have a partner for whom orgasm is readily attainable. The key to gaining a clear understanding of female orgasm results from having a finger or thumb in your partner's vagina while she's coming. The contraction action during female orgasm is at the introitus, or opening into the vagina, and a finger or thumb so placed in the vagina can experience the firm, rhythmic contractions that accompany orgasm. The easiest way for a male to experience his partner's orgasm in this manner is probably while she is masturbating, although it would also be possible during petting or oral-genital sex. During sexual intercourse, the glans of the penis, the super-sensitive smart part, is nowhere near the orgasmic contractions. And because the shaft of the penis is less sensitive in these respects, it is not likely to detect the contractions at the introitus.

It should be obvious that if sexual partners talked with one another about what was going on between them, we wouldn't have the mixed-up data about petting and orgasm that I've been describing. Partners may not be talking to one another because they don't know what to say, because they don't want to admit they might not know everything there is to know about orgasm, or, as in the case with some women, because they don't **want** their partner to discover that they know how to orgasm. A woman might worry that her partner would label her a slut if he felt she knew too much about her own sexuality.

Developing scripts for petting may stretch your creative imagination, but the results will be more than worth whatever energy you put into the endeavor. It is always a good idea to ask for what you want, as well as to ask your partner what he or she wants. Be as graphic and precise as you can in specifying what you desire. If you are not sure what you really like because you don't have enough experience to know, ask your partner to experiment with different ways of pleasuring you, and guide them verbally and with your hands toward those activities you most enjoy. Part of the enjoyment of petting for both partners results from the knowledge that what they each do is efficacious—that is, it works. When touching a partner's genitals produces an erection or vaginal lubrication, the pettee feels good because the condition of sexual arousal feels good, and the petter feels good and becomes more sexually excited because their touching has been effective. Using the suggestions in the little chart that follows may help you enjoy an activity that most people feel is something of a foundation to sexual interaction, that is touching their partner and being touched in ways that are mutually pleasing and stimulating.

PRINCIPLES OF PETTING 101

1. You are entitled to be touched where you like to be, and in a manner that you enjoy and most benefit from.

2. You are most likely to be touched effectively if you give your partner explicit verbal instruction. It may be hard to put into words what you would like, but the rewards outweigh the risks.

3. Combine words with guiding assistance, and provide feedback which asseses how well your partner is meeting your needs. Such a sequence might look like this:

a. "I really like to have you stroke my penis firmly, pulling the foreskin over the glans."

b. Place your partner's hand on your penis where you want it, clasp it as tight as you desire.

c. "Yes, that's it. Now stroke it about like that."

d. "That;s perfect. Just keep going, only a little faster, Right, that's it."

4. Be frank with your partner about whether or not orgasm is important to you. Don't fake orgasm--satisfying sexual experiences depend on honesty and candor, even if it means acknowledging that you haven't yet developed some aspect of your sexual repertory.

Oral-Genital Sex: A Dialogue

Remember Frank, the young man I described earlier who walked in on his roommate Charlie while Charlie was masturbating? Not too long ago Frank came to see me about another issue that doesn't get talked about very often, but is one which concerns quite a few people, young and old alike. Our conversation went something like this.

Frank: "Hi, Jim. Got a minute?"

Jim: "Sure, Frank. How are things going with you and Charlie?"

Frank: "Just fine--we worked out a swell arrangement, and since I've been taking your Human Relationships and Sexuality course I've come to appreciate just how important it is to be able to talk about this kind of thing. Which is why I came to see you. I was wondering if I could talk with you about something else?"

Jim: "Sure, Frank. What's on your mind?"

Frank: "You know how in class the other day you were talking about oral sex? Well, the guys in my dorm are **always** talking about oral sex and how incredibly great it is and everything. But then some of the things they say about it are really pretty gross."

Jim: "Oh, really? What kinds of things do they say?"

Frank: "Well, for one thing, they're always saying how great it feels when their girlfriends do it to them, but when it's the other way around, it's a completely different story. I mean they make it sound like a woman's crotch is just about the last place on earth you'd want to be, certainly not the kind of place you'd want to take a friend."

Jim: "That's very interesting. Just what is it about the female crotch that your friends find so objectionable?"

Frank: "Oh, they say things like it's a mean and nasty place, that it smells disgusting."

Jim: "Unlike men's crotches.

Frank: "Right. But all the guys I read about in **Playboy** say they really like to go down on their partners, and their partners go wild when they do it."

Jim: "Sounds like you're confused, Frank. On one hand, oral sex sounds pretty exciting, but on the other, there are some things about it that seem unappealing. I'm not surprised your friends talk about oral sex this way."

Frank: "Yeah--what I want to know is whether it's really as bad as they say it is. And also whether it's as **great** as they say it is."

Jim: "I can understand why you're concerned about all this, Frank. Suppose we take a look at some of the data I just tabulated from our course--I think it's a good place to start talking about this issue. These two charts show how the students in your class feel about giving and getting oral sex."

Which Statement Best Describes Your Feelings About Performing Oral-Genital Sex for a Partner?		
RESPONSE	FEMALE	MALES
HAVE NEVER DONE IT	13	9
DON'T ENJOY IT	36	11
ENJOY IT; SATISFIED WITH AMOUNT	46	54
ENJOY IT; WOULD LIKE MORE	5	26

Which Statement Best Describes Your Feelings About Performing Oral-Genital Sex for a Partner?		
RESPONSE	FEMALE	MALES
HAVE NEVER DONE IT	12	4
DON'T ENJOY IT	12	3
ENJOY IT; SATISFIED WITH AMOUNT	52	29
ENJOY IT; WOULD LIKE MORE	24	64

Frank: "Wow! Look at how much more both the guys and the girls want to **get** oral sex than they want to **give** it! And the girls don't really seem to like it all that much either way. What's going on here, anyway?"

Jim: "Got any ideas yourself about what might explain all this, Frank?"

Frank: "Well, if girls' crotches really are smelly, that would explain why the guys aren't that excited about increasing the amount they go down on girls. And the guys say it's great when someone goes down on them, so that explains why so many of them want more of it. But is it true what they say about the way girls smell."

Jim: "Well, first of all, any crotch has a lot of sweat glands, whether it belongs to a female or a male, so it's natural for there to be a certain amount of body odor there. And in women, the normal secretions produced by the vagina and cervix combine with perspiration, and can intensify the smell a bit."

Frank: "But wouldn't taking a shower cure that problem for both partners in a situation like this?"

Jim: "Sure it would, especially if they showered just before they began making love. But lovers aren't always near a shower when they want to engage in oral sex, which is probably what accounts for some of the stories your buddies in the dorm talk about. If they are going to put down women's crotches for being smelly, though, they should be willing to own up to the fact that their own crotches can smell just as bad as a woman's."

Frank: "I'll buy that."

Jim: "Have your friends ever talked about the fact that the smell of a woman's vulva can be a real turn on for them?"

Frank: "Yeah, as a matter of fact this guy Marty who lives in my suite was making that very point the other night, but the other guys said he was crazy, and just making it all up. They all said that nobody in their right mind would ever say that a girl's crotch smelled **good**."

Jim: "Your friend Marty sounds like he's wired up pretty good, certainly a lot better than the other men in your suite. The natural secretions from a woman's cervix and vagina, especially near the time she ovulates, typically have a powerfully pleasant aroma which most lovers find quite arousing. So you could find plenty of people who would take strong exception to the idea that a woman's vulva is either unfriendly or unpleasant to smell."

Frank: "I'm really glad we could talk about this, because I'm feeling better already about this whole business of oral sex."

Jim: "For women, though, there is another issue, and that is menstruation. You're probably aware that historically, menstruation has been seen as unhealthy and unclean, and this image persists despite the fact that we live in a more enlightened time. There are still companies that make deodorant products they advertise will help women feel better on those 'special days of the month,' an approach which capitalizes on these negative images of menstruation. And this kind of thing makes some women feel that there really **is** something wrong with this part of their body."

Frank: "Yeah, I've seen a lot of ads like that in magazines. I guess if I were a woman I might believe them too, and be pretty uncomfortable with the whole idea of oral sex. And when guys read these ads, they probably get the same message."

Jim: "They sure do. Have you ever thought about the words that men use to describe giving oral sex to women?"

Frank: "You mean like muff diving? Or biting the beaver? How about eating out at the 'Y'?

Jim: "Exactly. Not the kind of words to make your mouth water, are they?"

Frank: "Well, I wouldn't put it quite that way, but I am beginning to see how this gross language really can interfere with people's sexual enjoyment."

Jim: "It certainly does, and in lots of ways. Many women grow up feeling that there is something wrong with their vulva, and are ashamed of them. So it's easy to understand why they might be reluctant to have someone go down on them."

Frank: "But what about the fact that girls don't like to go down on guys as much as the guys would like?"

Jim: "Well, I can think of a couple of concerns that women would have about going down on a partner. One of them has to do with learning how to avoid gagging, which can take some practice. Another is the whole business of swallowing semen."

Frank: "Swallowing semen?"

Jim: "Right. Part of the anxiety of oral sex for some women is the fear that their partner will come in their mouth, and at least initially the idea of swallowing semen can be pretty disgusting. Gay men learn how to deal with fellatio, and with their feelings about swallowing semen, but non-gay men don't think about it very much. They may like it from a conceptual standpoint, but not many of them have swallowed a sample of their own semen in order to develop an empathic understanding of what it might be like for a partner."

Frank: "You can say that again. I can just imagine how the guys I know would react if you suggested they swallow a semen sample so they'd know what it would be like for a partner. They'd think you were nuts."

Jim: "I'm sure they would. And they would probably also dislike the idea that oral sex is often portrayed as a power issue. But if you watch almost any heterosexual porno film you'll find that one of the first images to appear is that of a woman on her knees, performing fellatio on a man who is either standing or sitting above her. It's no secret that this kind of pose involving oral sex makes a very clear statement about who is in control of the situation."

Frank: "From everything you've said it sounds like oral sex really can be pretty terrific, but a lot of stuff gets in the way of having it turn out that way. If it's so great, you'd think there would be things people could do that would help them cut through all the bad stuff, and enjoy it without giving it a bad name."

Jim: "I couldn't agree with you more, Frank. And of course there are a number of things partners can do to increase the likelihood that both of them will enjoy oral-genital sex. First of all, they can talk with each other about how they feel about it, and if they have some apprehensions make them known. Partners can include a shower as part of their routine lovemaking, which will take care of the possible issue of body odors and will also give them an opportunity to enjoy the pleasures of mutual showering. Soaping up one another in the shower is a pretty sensual experience in itself, and can be a nice love making feature in its own right. A male can let his partner know that swallowing semen is not an issue for him, and can reassure her that he will let her know when he is about to come. She can then decide whether or not she wants to swallow his semen."

Frank: "You make all this sound pretty easy, and I guess if people did the kinds of things you suggested they really **would** feel a lot better about asking for and getting what they want. Of course they have to be able to get the words out in the first place, which must be pretty hard to do sometimes. I mean what are you supposed to say, 'I'd really like it if you went down on me?' Wouldn't a girl freak out if you just came right out and said something like this?"

Jim: "Maybe some women would see this request as too direct, but I think most would prefer to respond to a specific request than try to figure out what you want on the basis of the way you wiggled your torso in front of their face. Perhaps because it's still considered somewhat taboo, some people consider oral-genital sex to be a more intimate act than sexual intercourse, so women especially are likely to feel more comfortable with the whole idea if they are experiencing this kind of sexual interaction within the context of an intimate relationship. If you can learn to talk openly with a partner about this kind of sexual activity you'll discover that you can talk with them about a whole lot of other sexual topics."

Frank: "You've really given me a lot to think about, Jim, and the next time the guys start ragging on oral sex I think I'll be prepared to challenge them."

Jim: "Frank, I'm glad you stopped by— keep me posted on how things progress.

CHAPTER 5

◄◄◊◊►►

The Big S. I.

My students sometimes refer to sexual intercourse as **THE BIG S.I.**, which conveys a pretty powerful picture in just eight letters. Penis-in-vagina intercourse is probably the single most dominant image in the landscape of human sexuality, and there are very good reasons why this is so. Human beings ascribe great meaning to sexual intercourse because of its enormous potentials, not the least of which is the creation of new life. For most of us, however, the reasons for having sexual intercourse far transcend that of reproduction; we have progressed well beyond the need to produce a child every year or so in order that one or two of them might make it to adulthood. While our reproductive capacity spans anywhere from thirty-five to seventy years, producing 2.1 children takes but a moment of our lifetime's fertility quotient. It remains to be seen whether the period of fertility of human beings will be reduced as we gain greater control over the diseases that have threatened life since its inception.

Broadly speaking, most people have sexual intercourse for two reasons: first, for the pleasure it brings them, and second as a means of expressing the feelings they have toward their partner. This means that people sometimes have sex just for the pleasure they will derive, and attach little or no significance to feelings they have toward a partner. Sex with casual acquaintances and with prostitutes, as well as one night stands are good examples of this kind of intercourse, but it is also important to point out that many loving couples sometimes have intercourse more for the raw pleasure of the experience than as a means of expressing their loving feelings. Their strong feelings are often expressed under these conditions, but this may not be the primary motivation for such intercourse. Conversely, couples also enjoy sexual intercourse because it affords them a way to express the close and loving feelings they share for one another, and the level of their sexual arousal and pleasure may be of less significance to them at the moment than is their desire to be close to their partner. A primary goal in such instances may be to provide pleasure to a partner rather than to experience it oneself. And of course such couples often engage in intercourse to fulfill the promises of both pleasure and love.

These two significant potentials of sexual intercourse, pregnancy and pleasure, are what explain the power it holds for us as human beings. Until very recently the potential pleasure that a couple could obtain through sexual intercourse was almost always tempered by the risk or threat of an unintended pregnancy, and this fact is so deeply imbedded in the human consciousness that it continues to influence sexual behaviors in an age of effective contraception. Sexually transmitted diseases have always been a risk associated with sexual intercourse, but sexual monogamy has and will continue to permit couples to minimize this potentially negative consequence. But sexual fidelity does not prevent conception any more than it guarantees sexual pleasure.

No matter how sexually experienced or sexually sophisticated you feel you are, virtually all your attitudes about sex, as well as your sexual behaviors, have been shaped and defined by your culture's beliefs about the meanings of sexual intercourse. Sexual intercourse isn't something that just exists out there, it's not just a penis in a vagina. Sexual intercourse **means something.** If it didn't, I wouldn't be writing this book, pro-lifers wouldn't be "rescuing unborn babies," and priests and nuns could be married and have children if they wanted to. Perhaps most of the meanings developed about sexual intercourse have been informed by the potentials it affords to people: pregnancy and pleasure. Unfortunately, the meanings of sexual intercourse have been defined throughout history almost exclusively by men, whose concept of human sexuality has often operated on the premise that they are superior to females, and therefore should be in charge of all matters related to sex and human sexuality.

You may feel that you have escaped the most negative forms of sexual socialization. Maybe. But if you breathe the air around you, you have been exposed to so many sexual messages in so many different ways that many of them have seeped into you in spite of yourself. What I'd like you to do in this chapter is to look closely at what you have learned about the meanings of sexual intercourse, and begin to identify creative ways to move your sexual understandings and behaviors toward the goal of mutuality and equality in sexual relationships.

The Languages of Sexual Intercourse

Let's begin by considering the varieties of language people use when talking about sexual intercourse, either in casual conversation or while actually engaged in intercourse. Intercourse itself is usually only one of a number of arousing activities a couple engages in, but terms like "having sex" tend to place the central emphasis on there being a penis in a vagina at some point during the action. If you say, "Bill and Meredith had sex," most people will understand this to mean that they had sexual intercourse. If Bill and Meredith merely took off all their clothes, kissed passionately, petted one another's body, went down on one another and both reached orgasm, then spent the night sleeping soundly cuddled up together in Meredith's bed, you'd probably say they didn't have sex, but rather might agree that they did "everything but actually have sex." But if you happened to stumble into Meredith's room while all this was going on, you probably wouldn't be impressed if they said they weren't having sex. "Oh, sure" you'd say, "I suppose you're doing a history assignment together." If your parents "caught" you and your lover in similar circumstances, **they** probably wouldn't be impressed with such an explanation, either. The important idea about all this is that people place a very special significance on whether a penis has been in a vagina, even if it only **appears** to have been.

Words and phrases that describe sexual intercourse and the various behaviors that surround the act can be divided into several categories of language. Words like coitus and intromission are considered **scientific** language, and are often used by physicians and other kinds of clinicians. As recently as the 1960's, the only people who could get away with writing popular books about sex were physicians, and books like **A Doctor Speaks on Sexual Expression in Marriage,** by Dr. Donald W. Hastings (Little, Brown & Company, 1966), are filled with this kind of clinical and supposedly objective language. Terms like making love, going all the way, and having sex represent examples of **common discourse,** and although they often serve as euphemisms for the term sexual intercourse, they are used so commonly today that people even invent euphemisms for euphemisms! Terms used in common discourse usually communicate the intended message pretty clearly, although a term like "fool around" is quite subject to interpretation unless the partners have previously agreed that this expression includes certain specific acts.

Terms like fuck, ball, screw, poke a pussy, get laid, score, hump, and bang are usually thought of as **street language,** and are notable because they typically convey a sense of power, and often are used in a demeaning way. But just because words like these are usually spoken in a pejorative (demeaning, downgrading) way doesn't mean that they are **always** used in this manner.

Sexual partners tend to personalize their sexual activities, by giving names to their sexual organs, for example, or by claiming the use of certain sexual words to convey a more precise meaning of a particular sexual act. When lovers are so hot for one another that everything they touch gets scorched, the term "making love" may just not do. So one might say to the other, "I'm so hot I want to fuck until your eyeballs pop right out of their sockets!," and have this statement interpreted as a wonderful, loving invitation. **You** might never use the word fuck in this way, but many people do, and feel quite comfortable doing so. Language is what we make it to be, and words in themselves don't hurt us. Intelligent people are able to distinguish between an epithet like, "Fuck you, Charlie!" and the word fuck as used by the lovers in the example I just gave.

All this not withstanding, it's important to realize that pejorative terms continue to dominate the sexual talk of many young men. Many men talk about "getting laid," discuss which of the women they know "put out," describe "scoring with a chick the first time out," and refer to women in general as "cunts" or "pussies." Most young women don't talk about getting men drunk so they can "get laid." But for many young men, this kind of talk is quite routine, and even if you are a male who abhors this language and way of thinking about women, chances are you are frequently exposed to it. As long as some men continue to talk about women in this way, all males will be influenced to some degree. And as long as "enlightened" males accept or tolerate this kind of talk from other males, it will continue.

How Your Parents Learned about Sexual Intercourse

If your parents got married in the sixties or early seventies they might have read a book like the one I just mentioned written by Dr. Donald Hastings. There were a number of other books written by physicians available at the time, but all of them took a similar approach in their instruction, which was to teach the groom how to sexualize his new bride. This is how Hastings described the ideal approach for a groom to take with his bride on the first night of their honeymoon.

First Intercourse

The virginal female, or one with very little experience, can be expected to have anxiety about what is to come. It may take her considerable time to develop a receptive frame of mind. Hence the male should go slowly, spend a long time (several hours if need be) in hugging, kissing, stroking, lightly touching her legs and the inner aspects of her thighs, brushing the mons veneris and pubic hair in passing....As the man's penis comes to erection, he gently slips it between the girl's legs just below the vaginal entrance and lets it rest against the lips of the vagina, but making no attempt to enter. As the girl becomes increasingly aroused, she will lift her upper leg and thigh, letting it come to rest over the man's upper leg. This exposes her vaginal entrance and separates the vaginal lips. Still no attempt is made to push the penis into the vagina. Gentle probing movements are made with it by lightly pushing its head in and out of the vaginal entrance, perhaps half an inch or so....As sexual excitement mounts and the man senses that his partner is ready, he gently rolls her on her back and comes to lie on top of her, resting his weight on his elbows and knees. She will instinctively spread her legs and bend her knees, thus raising her thighs....On this first occasion, the penis can be introduced gradually full length into the vagina. When that has been accomplished, the purpose of the initial sexual experience has, in a sense, been achieved. The penis has entered full length, the hymen if present has been broken, and the girl has begun her sexual life....It is probably best for the man, after he has penetrated full length, to concentrate on reaching orgasm and ejaculation as rapidly as he can...there is probably little point in attempting to produce orgasm in the virgin by prolonged coitus at the time of her first intercourse....She will probably have some vaginal soreness, and it is the unusual girl who will be brought to orgasm the first time she experiences sexual relations.....During the early days of the marriage it is also best that the husband make no demands which, at this stage of her sexual development, the wife might regard as unusual or even abnormal. Thus, mouth-genital relations, to pick one example, should not be insisted upon. If erotic play of this type is to be practiced, it can come later, after the wife begins to feel sure of herself sexually, is experiencing orgasms regularly, and is ready to increase her sexual sophistication.

A Doctor Speaks on Sexual Expression in
Marriage
Donald W. Hastings, M.D.
Boston: Little Brown and Company, 1966

Twenty-five years after it was written this advice sounds pretty absurd, doesn't it? One wonders how anyone in their right mind presumed to write such nonsense, let alone a distinguished professor, chairman of the Department of Psychiatry and Neurology at the University of Minnesota School of Medicine. But I don't think Dr. Hastings was mean-spirited. I think he was well-meaning, and had the best interests of his readers at heart when he wrote this book. His problem was that he was a male physician, and had inherited a system of male privilege that he simply took for granted. Hasting's book says a lot about the way human sexuality continues to be regarded in the last decade of the twentieth century, so it's worth spending a few minutes discussing this passage.

It is clear from the outset that the "man" is to be in charge of this scene. The husband is the man, his wife the "girl." Implicit in all the instructions to the husband is the tacit understanding that he is not wholly inexperienced in sexual matters, since it is hard to imagine how an inexperienced lover could possibly remain as cool and collected as Hastings presumes the groom to be. It is the groom's job to treat his bride like a princess, to be gentle, reassuring, and in control of himself. Consider just a few of the things the groom must deal with as he conducts the first real sexual symphony of his life.

- ✿ He is to spend "adequate" time in the preliminaries to intercourse, **hours** if necessary! In other words, it is his job to warm up his wife. She is like a diesel engine—you have to warm them up a long time before they're ready to go. The bride supposedly just lies there waiting for her loving husband's work to take effect.
- ✿ Having completed the first part of his task, the husband reaches a checkpoint in the operation: he "senses that his partner is ready." Dr. Hastings implies that this ability to sense a partner's sexual readiness is built into males, like radar. One assumes it would be impolite of the groom to **ask** his bride if she is "ready," since this would put her in the embarrassing position of having to **talk** about sex.
- ✿ The groom is to insert his penis gently into his bride's vaginal entrance, pushing its head in and out, "perhaps half an inch or so." In all your life have you ever heard of

a penis that had even the remotest awareness of the concept half an inch? Here we have a young man about to have sexual intercourse with his beloved wife for the first time, and he is instructed to operate his penis as if it had a built-in micrometer. Most men in similar circumstances would already have ejaculated by this point, having become completely overwhelmed by their excitement.

✿ Guidelines for the groom make his goal clear: to launch his bride into her sexual life. This goal is accomplished when his penis has been "introduced full length into the vagina." The previously hermetically sealed vaginal vault of his bride has been entered, and the purpose of the initial sexual experience has, "in a sense," been achieved. Work, work, work!

✿ Having followed his instructions faithfully, the groom is now reminded that being penetrated by a blunt instrument can be painful. Therefore, he must **concentrate** on reaching orgasm and ejaculate "as rapidly as he can." Oh, great. Now he tells us! Would anyone who knew even a little bit about male sexuality presume that the groom would be able to loll around inside his wife's unbelievably tight vagina and take his merry time at reaching orgasm?

✿ Besides, there is little point in trying to "produce orgasm in the virgin." Right. She wouldn't want her husband to think she was an "unusual girl" who could be brought to orgasm the first time she had intercourse.

✿ And finally, the groom must be the guardian of his bride's sexual sensibilities, and not "insist" on sexual behaviors which she might think are disgusting. **He** wouldn't consider something like oral-genital sex disgusting, of course, but given that the bride lacks her husband's sense of "sexual sophistication," this admonition should make perfect sense.

How Attitudes about Sexual Intercourse Have Changed

As silly as Hastings' advice sounds to us today, his underlying ideas about male and female sexuality continue to influence heterosexual relationships. Let's look at some contemporary data related to young adults' sexual attitudes and behaviors as a means of illustrating how closely they are tied to their historical sexual apron strings. We will begin by considering some of the assumptions young people have about the capacities males and females have to respond to sexual stimulation.

Men by Nature Are More Easily and Quickly Aroused to Readiness for Sexual Intercourse than are Women		
RESPONSE	FEMALE	MALES
AGREE	54	54
UNCERTAIN	22	21
DISAGREE	24	25

In the 1990's, these well educated young adults feel that men **by nature** get hotter more easily and more quickly than females. Only one-fourth of these young men and women disagreed with this statement, which suggests to me a tremendous residual of that 1960's warm-up drivel Dr. Hastings was talking about. This kind of thinking puts a real damper on quickies. Can't you just imagine a phone conversation like this one?

Jack: Hi, Jill. Guess what? I just found out that my boss is going to be out of the office for the **whole** afternoon. How about I pick you up and we sneak over to my place for a quick romp in the hay instead of eating lunch today?

Jill: Oh, Jack, that sounds like a wonderful idea, conceptually speaking. But you know how long it takes for me to get hot, and well, I'm afraid there's just not enough time during our lunch hour. Sorry, Jack. But it really was a good idea, at least conceptually speaking.

The idea that many contemporary young adults believe that males by nature are more sexual and require more frequent sexual release is further demonstrated in the next two charts.

By Nature, Males Have Recurring Needs for Orgasmic Release to a Greater Degree than do Females		
RESPONSE	FEMALE	MALES
AGREE	37	36
UNCERTAIN	32	28
DISAGREE	31	36

Almost two-thirds of these respondents believe or are uncertain as to whether or not males have some kind of biological predisposition requiring orgasmic release. I'm not aware of any controlled research studies that have demonstrated this fact, but it's obvious that many people believe it to be true. So many of our of sexual needs have been conditioned by what we have learned they **should** be that it's impossible to separate out the biological from the social influences on this question.

But it follows that if males by nature require more frequent orgasmic release than females, they might seek this release through sexual intercourse. A sizable number of my students concur with this idea, as illustrated in the next chart.

By Nature, Men Want to Have Sexual Intercourse More Often than do Women		
RESPONSE	FEMALE	MALES
AGREE	19	29
UNCERTAIN	24	28
DISAGREE	57	43

Although only a minority of both males and females agreed with this statement, a majority of the males either agreed or were uncertain about this. As with all the data I've been presenting, the "uncertain" category of response is a very important one, because it reveals those individuals who don't know what a correct or factual response might be. Being uncertain about whether males **by nature** want to have intercourse more than females, or have greater needs for orgasmic release than females, or become aroused for readiness for sexual intercourse more easily than females must surely affect how you proceed in any sexual interaction. Being uncertain about these kinds of things is as likely to influence your sexual behaviors as is agreeing or disagreeing with them, so it is not as if being uncertain permits you to behave in ways free from attitudinal influence.

Each of these beliefs—about arousal, orgasmic release, and the desire for intercourse—are formed by our culture, they are not biologically programmed into you. But you have been taught through your socialization that males by nature are more sexual than females, and this idea is constantly reinforced through advertising, print and video media, pop songs, the business community, and our families. Despite the fact that there is not a shred of empirical evidence to support this contention, the belief persists. Have you ever wondered why? I have. I think it persists to a large degree because it perpetuates the power males have to control females. If males are thought to be more sexual by nature than females they will then be assumed to deserve both to participate in more sexual activities than females, and also be granted special privileges because of their increased needs. It is precisely this kind of logic that underlies the double standard of sexual intimacy with which we are all so familiar. Are today's young adults making any progress in overcoming the double standard? Yes, I believe they are, largely because of the effects of the women's movement. But I'd be hard pressed to say that the goal of equality between the sexes is even close to being accomplished; the data that follows speaks clearly in this regard.

First Intercourse Experiences

About eighty percent of the women and a little over ninety percent of the men in my sample have had sexual intercourse at least once. Except for the difference between the percentage of virgins, the intercourse experience of males and females appears to be quite comparable. The same can be said for the age at

Have You Ever Had Hetersexual Intercourse?		
RESPONSE	FEMALE	MALES
NEVER	19	7
ONCE	5	6
SEVERAL TIMES	25	31
MANY TIMES	51	56

which these respondents had sexual intercourse for the first time. During the last ten years, the percentage of my students reporting they have had intercourse at least once has gradually increased, by seven or eight points for the women, and about five for the men.

How Old Were You When You First Had Intercourse?		
RESPONSE	FEMALE	MALES
AGE 15 0R UNDER	18	21
AGES 16-18	66	69
AGES19-21	16	10

Most of these students had their first intercourse experience before they got to college, or during their freshman year. People tend to remember their first intercourse, although the sexual aspect of it is more likely to be described as "just O.K.," than terrific. Sometimes first intercourse occurs as a result of careful mutual decisions, while at others it seems to be done to get it over with. Both males and females are usually at least somewhat apprehensive as they contemplate their first intercourse experience, the women perhaps anxious about the potential pain involved and the risk of pregnancy, the men worried about whether they will be able to maintain an erection and not ejaculate too soon.

The amazing thing about having had sexual intercourse at least once is that it forever more conveys on you a certain status, that of non-virgin. The status non-virgin may appear to give you a kind of credibility not possessed by virgins, but this credibility is totally independent of the **quality** of any of your sexual experiences. Non-virgins assume they possess this credibility, and they make similar assumptions about their friends and acquaintances. If you were sitting around with a group of friends and the conversation turned to sexual experience, it could be quite reassuring for you to say that you have had intercourse, knowing that it would be easy to fudge on the details if necessary. You might have had intercourse only one time two years ago, in a frantic thirty second episode of sex that occurred in the back seat of a Volkswagen. But if someone asks, you could honestly say, "Shit, yeah, I've had sex. It's no big deal, really." Small wonder, then, that some people have intercourse just to "get it over with." Among those respondents who had **not** had intercourse when they completed my questionnaire, it's interesting to see that the males were least pleased with their virginal status, which makes good sense when you realize how much more peer pressure there is on males to be sexual.

If You Have Not Had Sexual Intercourse, Which Statement Best Describes Why You Have Not?		
RESPONSE	FEMALE	MALES
DON'T FEEL I'M READY	19	10
RELEGIOUS BELIEFS	12	20
NOT INTERESTED JUST NOW	42	10
WOULD LIKE TO, BUT HAVEN'T HAD THE OPPORTUNITY	27	60

Intercourse Frequency and Satisfaction

The double standard for contemporary young adults is no more dramatically illustrated than in the number of lifetime sexual partners they report. Given that both males and females indicate they began their intercourse experiences at about the same age, the males have been active with considerably more partners than the females, as demonstrated in the following chart. Compared with students in 1978, however, the increase in the proportion of women reporting four or more partners has almost doubled, up from 22 percent, whereas the increase in males has been only about a third, up from 42 percent. Knowing the total number of sexual partners you may have had provides us with one kind of information, but this number alone tells us nothing about the quality or enjoyment the you experienced with any given partner. Nor does having had intercourse with many different partners promise that you will really know a lot more about sex and human sexuality than someone with fewer partners.

In Your Entire Lifetime, With How Many People Have You Had Sexual Intercourse?		
RESPONSE	FEMALE	MALES
ONE	22	19
TWO	19	10
THREE	20	8
FOUR OR MORE	39	63

If your sexual intercourse experience has occurred primarily in one night stands, you may know a great deal about how to have sex in a one night stand. But the carry-over of this knowledge to relationships of long duration is quite minimal, and in fact may actually be detrimental. **Almost universally, people describe their best sexual intercourse experiences as those that took place in long term, stable intimate relationships.**

Some people have suggested that the data in the following chart supports the notion that males by nature want to have intercourse more than do females, but there is more to this data than meets the eye. To me, the statement being made by the young men is that they are not having intercourse as often as they would like to, not that they have a greater desire than females to have intercourse. The questions to ask are, "Why aren't most of the males having intercourse as often as they want to?"

Would You Like to Have Sexual Intercourse More Often, Less Often, or With About the Same Frequency You Have it Now?		
RESPONSE	FEMALE	MALES
MORE OFTEN	35	65
LESS OFTEN	2	0
ABOUT THE SAME AMOUNT	63	35

and, "Why are a third of the women not having intercourse as frequently as **they** would like to?" There are probably several answers to these questions.

In general these young people are having sexual intercourse either as part of a stable, sexually intimate relationship, or are doing so through what they would call casual sexual experiences. These casual sexual experiences might be one night stands, but are as likely to be occurring in the early part of what might otherwise have developed into a long term relationship. In this scenario, partners may go out with one another a few times, have intercourse a couple of times, and then move on. Or sexual intercourse might spill over into the relationship of long term friends whose friendship is a more central feature of the relationship than is sex. What this all means is that from this data alone it is not possible to tell whether those respondents in stable relationships are desirous of more intercourse with their present partners, or whether people who are not in sexual relationships would in general like to be having intercourse more frequently. As a result of reading hundreds of projects over the years, however, it is my observation that a great many partners in stable relationships, as well as individuals in general would like to have intercourse more frequently. Several factors help explain why both these groups are not getting what they want, and the reasons tend to be similar for both.

Men who are not in durable sexual relationships may not be having as much intercourse as they want because women in general are more eager to have intercourse as part of an intimate relationship than through casual sexual experiences. The risks of pregnancy and sexually transmitted diseases coupled with the potential damage to their reputation place women in a position of being more discriminating about who they have intercourse with than men are. Another way to say this is that men would increase the likelihood of having as much sex as they desired if they entered and maintained sexually exclusive intimate relationships, and to the extent that they are uninterested or unwilling to do so there will always be large numbers of sexually unfulfilled males.

Either partner in a stable relationship might desire a higher frequency of intercourse, but here too males are the ones more likely to be making such a request. A common reason why such males are not having intercourse as often as they would like hinges on their partner's overall satisfaction with the couple's sexual relationship. Since women are more likely to view **relationship** as the key word in the term sexual relationship, their needs are more likely to center on loving and caring rather than on genital behaviors. But many women are not having their loving and caring needs adequately met in an episode of love making that includes sexual intercourse, as can be seen in the next chart.

In an Episode of Sexual Interaction that Includes Intercourse, Which Set of Behaviors Would You like to Increase in Terms of the Amount of Time Spent?		
RESPONSE	FEMALE	MALES
KISSING AND PETTING	37	16
INTERCOURSE ITSELF	18	45
POST-INTERCOURSE TIME	20	12
AM SATISFIED WITH TIME IN EACH	25	27

The fact that twice as many women as men want to increase the amount of time spent in kissing, petting, and post-intercourse loving is probably because these are the behaviors that most satisfy women's needs for being loved and cared for. In addition, since most women do not reach orgasm during intercourse, they are likely to place less emphasis on this aspect of love making. It is highly likely that women's desire for intercourse would increase if their partners met more of their affectional needs, since they would then be more likely to see their sexual relationships as being mutual and therefore be more willing to meet their partner's intercourse needs. And it is also likely that if orgasm was a routine part of women's intercourse experiences, they might well desire to increase their intercourse frequency.

Orgasm in Intercourse

Of all the aspects of sexual intercourse that get discussed on talk shows and written about in the popular press, surely the one that tops the list is orgasm. Something that is nothing more than a basic reflex generates enormous interest among Americans, and is as likely to be the topic of idle cocktail conversation as it is to be the subject of scholarly articles in scientific journals. Many people experience orgasm in a variety of ways, such as through masturbation, petting, oral genital stimulation or sexual intercourse, but it is orgasm achieved through intercourse that seems to represent our greatest fascination. Remember Dr. Hastings' statement about the groom "bringing his partner to orgasm" at the time of their first intercourse? Apparently there is something thought to be very special about orgasms that take place when penis and clitoris are mutually stimulated during the act of sexual intercourse. Perhaps the reason so much emphasis is placed on this kind of orgasm is that it occurs so infrequently, and therefore is considered to be something people should work to achieve!

So powerful is the image of orgasm during intercourse that myths have been constructed around the idea. One of the more insidious of these myths is that women who don't orgasm don't enjoy intercourse as much as those who do, an idea embraced by many young adults. I think there are several ways to explain the data in this chart.

A Woman Who Does Not Experience Orgasm Regularly During Sexual Intercourse Probably Does Not Enjoy Intercourse as Much as One Who Does		
RESPONSE	FEMALE	MALES
AGREE	29	43
UNCERTAIN	18	27
DISAGREE	53	30

Since orgasmic release is such a common element of sexual intercourse for most males, it's easy to understand why almost half of them would link orgasm to enjoyment. In responding to this question, these men may have thought about how **they** would feel if they did not experience orgasm regularly during intercourse, and concluded that women would feel the same way. From the women's point of view, we might assume that the 53 percent who disagreed with this statement did so on the basis of their own personal experience, a speculation that is reasonably consistent with the conclusions of more comprehensive research studies. The 20 percent of the women in my sample who had not had intercourse could account for the uncertain responses, leaving about 30 percent whose own personal experiences may again have confirmed their affirmative responses. In any event it is clear that these men and women are not communicating with one another about the relative importance of female orgasm to the overall enjoyment of sexual intercourse. Orgasm is such a subjective experience that it is impossible to assume with any confidence that a partner will or will not consider it crucial to their enjoyment of intercourse. I do know, however, that most of my students **would like to orgasm during an episode of lovemaking that includes sexual intercourse,** as can be seen in the chart that follows.

In Thinking About the Role of Orgasm in a Sexual Experience Which Includes Intercourse, Which Statement Best Describes Your Feelings?		
RESPONSE	FEMALE	MALES
PREFER TO ORGASM, USUALLY DO	42	96
PREFER TO ORGASM, USUALLY DON'T	54	4
DON'T USUALLY ORGASM; THAT'S O.K.	4	0

Desiring to reach orgasm and your enjoyment of sexual intercourse are mutually exclusive ideas, however, which means that most people consider these events as separate experiences. In other words, both men and women can enjoy intercourse for the special pleasures this activity affords them, and can do so without reaching orgasm. And conversely, most people can enjoy the special pleasures brought about by orgasm whether or not it is evoked while they are having sexual intercourse. All of this does not mean that individuals don't have a **preferred** way in which they most like to experience orgasm. They often do. For example, although both men and women frequently report that orgasm evoked by masturbation is more intense than by any other means, both sexes often prefer to orgasm while having sexual intercourse with a loved partner.

The above chart and the one that follows, however, clearly indicate that my female students are not having their desires for orgasmic release satisfied by means of sexual intercourse. The data in the chart below reflects a condition very similar to

The Last Time You Had Sexual Intercourse, Did You Experience Orgasm?		
RESPONSE	FEMALE	MALES
YES--FROM THE STIMULATION OF INTERCOURSE ALONE	15	43
YES--WITH A COMBINATION OF STIMULATION PROVIDED BY INTERCOURSE AND MANUAL OR ORAL STIMULATION	38	51
NO	47	6

that reported by Shere Hite in her study of a large sample of American women (**The Hite Report: A Nationwide Study of Female Sexuality.** New York: Dell Books, 1976), which is that a relatively small proportion of women, about one-third, report that they regularly reach orgasm from the stimulation of intercourse alone. Given that my students are considerably younger than those in Hite's sample, the fact that only fifteen percent orgasm in this way is not surprising.

We can probably divide the women who are not reaching orgasm during an episode of lovemaking that includes intercourse into three categories. First are those who are not yet experiencing orgasm through any form of stimulation. These women may reach a very high point of arousal, sense that the arousal can be discharged, but haven't learned how to "get over the top." If you are a woman who is not yet orgasmic but would like to be, you will have to make a deliberate effort to learn how, and learning to masturbate is perhaps the best approach. There are a number of excellent books available to assist women in learning how to actualize their orgasmic potential, among which is **For Yourself: The Fulfillment of Female Sexuality**, by Lonnie Barbach (Garden City, New York: Doubleday, 1975).

Some women feel they should not have to **learn** how to be orgasmic, thinking that if it were really important, it would "just happen." In a kinder, gentler world, perhaps this would be the case. But the fact is that for many women, what they have learned about the risks of actualizing their sexuality exerts a tremendous block on their ability to derive pleasure from their own bodies. So it takes some "unlearning" in order to restore these women to a state whereby they can claim the right to enjoy this kind of pleasure. And there are some very good reasons in addition to pleasure why orgasm is a desirable conclusion to a state of heightened sexual arousal. I'll discuss these reasons in more detail a bit later in this chapter.

The second category of women are those who readily experience orgasm by masturbating or through manual or oral stimulation, but find it almost impossible to come during sexual intercourse. If you are such a woman, you may be able to develop techniques for enhancing clitoral stimulation during intercourse, perhaps manually or with a vibrator, that permit you to reach a level of arousal sufficient to orgasm. Obtaining this kind of added stimulation requires that you be able to communicate this desire clearly to your partner, and explain exactly what he can do to be helpful. It might be embarrassing for you to introduce a vibrator into the lovemaking scene or even to guide your partner's hand in stimulating your clitoris, but the chances are good that your partner will be highly cooperative in this endeavor, especially if he sees how much you enjoy orgasmic release.

For some women it may be a matter of realizing that intercourse itself just isn't sufficient to produce orgasms, and utilizing other methods of stimulation to accomplish this end. If you are a woman who orgasms regularly through these other forms of stimulation there is no reason why either you or your partner should feel cheated. If it works, do it!

The last category of women who have difficulty reaching orgasm during intercourse are those who are not assertive enough in their own behalf, whose partners are insensitive to their instructions, or whose partners are unable to sustain intercourse long enough to provide them with sufficient clitoral stimulation. If you have spent a lifetime learning that your job is to please men, it's not easy to suddenly feel entitled to a piece of the action yourself.

Taking charge of your own orgasm is something that may sound risky, but to place this responsibility on your partner's penis is just asking too much of the little fellah. He has enough trouble taking care of himself, let alone having to look out for someone else's needs. The person attached to a penis, however, is a different story altogether. Men, too, have learned that they are supposed to play an all-important role in female orgasm, so if you are a male it will take some relearning in order to understand how you can make an effective contribution to your partner's arousal.

If you have difficulty with ejaculatory control, there are several techniques which I will discuss later in the chapter you can employ to increase your ability to delay orgasm, and thereby provide your partner with an amount of stimulation sufficient to reach orgasm. What is perhaps most important for a male whose partner is represented by this third category of women is to recognize that he can make his greatest contribution by listening attentively to what his partner says she wants, and by accepting the fact that she is responsible for evoking her own orgasms.

The Physiology of Sexual Response

I've been talking quite a bit about sexual arousal and orgasm, but haven't said anything specifically about the physiology of sexual response. This was deliberate, since if the chapter began with this kind of discussion you might skip over it in search of the good stuff. The graph below summarizes the major features of the sexual response cycle, using a framework proposed by sex therapist Helen Singer Kaplan.

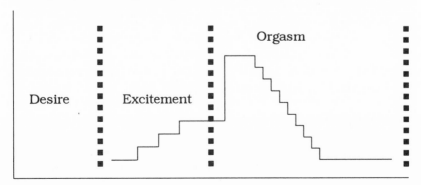

You may have encountered a somewhat similar diagram outlining the sexual response cycle as described by Masters and Johnson, which includes the phases Excitement, Plateau, Orgasm, and Resolution, and omits Kaplan's Desire phase. But it doesn't matter much whose model you favor if you are simply trying to get a basic understanding of what happens during sexual arousal, which is what we are trying to do here.

Desire

Desire is pretty much what it sounds like, which is a willingness to become sexually aroused. It is quite common for both men and women to experience a lack of sexual desire at times in their lives, for reasons that are quite varied. Some people feel so anxious about the possibility of experiencing sexual arousal that they unconsciously turn off their desire switch, which in effect prevents them from becoming sexually excited. Sometimes there is a very good reason why an individual might experience a lack of desire, such as with a partner who was unclean and had a strong body odor, or with someone they really disliked. Severe or protracted illnesses, certain drugs, and depression are all known to suppress sexual desire, as does the excessive use of alcohol. And it is not unusual for one or both partners in an intimate relationship to experience inhibited sexual desire when the relationship is undergoing stress or when one of the partners is feeling controlled by the other.

If you are experiencing a lack of sexual desire you might have a very clear idea of what factor or factors are most likely contributing to this condition. But you may find that it is very difficult to remove the blocks to becoming aroused, even though you can identify them. Sometimes gaining information or doing specific exercises designed to decrease anxiety can be quite helpful, but it is also a good idea to seek help from a counselor or therapist in learning to overcome inhibited sexual desire. If a relationship problem is likely to be an issue, it is important for both partners to be involved in the counseling. It is probably more difficult to "go it alone" with inhibited sexual desire than it is with any of the other common problems that interfere with sexual functioning, so it can make a real difference to have a competent professional help you with this.

Excitement

Most people refer to sexual excitement as "getting hot." Sexual excitement can result from having sexual thoughts or fantasies, from touching yourself or your partner, or from a combination of these two sources of arousal. No matter how excitement is induced, the key physiological mechanism of arousal involves the sending of electrical messages up and down the spinal column, which acts to trigger the engorgement of blood vessels in the pelvic area. The vascular systems of the penis, the vulva, and the vagina usually allow blood to pass through arteries and return through veins at about the same rate of flow. But when the central nervous system responds to sexual stimulation, either through thoughts or touch, it causes the vascular net in the pelvis to react like a sponge and to retain the blood it would normally allow to flow steadily back to the heart. In males, this pooled blood supply results in engorgement of the spongy tissue of the penis, producing an erection. In females, pressure of the blood vessels surrounding and comprising the vaginal walls causes swelling of this tissue, resulting in droplets of moisture being exuded into the vagina. The condition of wetness that results in the vagina is called "sweating," or lubrication. As the level of sexual excitement increases, other parts of the body show signs of this heightened arousal as well.

The amount of time people spend in the excitement phase varies quite a bit according to their individual preferences and the immediate circumstances. Sometimes a couple will reach a high level of excitement very gradually, and then hang out at that place just short of orgasmic release for a long time, perhaps dropping back periodically to a less excited level in order to prolong the build-up of their sexual tension. At other times the same couple might proceed rapidly up a very steep curve toward orgasm, and do little or nothing to elongate the excitement period.

It is also common for only one partner to desire to follow through to orgasm, while the other is quite satisfied with the non-orgasmic pleasures of sexual intercourse. And there are many times in the sexual lives of long-term partners when neither of them desires to orgasm during intercourse. For variety, many couples complete a lovemaking episode that includes intercourse by attaining orgasm in some other way, such as through manual or oral stimulation or by masturbating together. Reaching orgasm by means other than through the direct stimulation of intercourse provides such couples with the ability to do so at the same time, something which I have already indicated is often difficult to accomplish from intercourse alone. Simultaneous orgasm is not something that most couples worry about, but occasionally it serves as a nice way to culminate their lovemaking.

Both women and men occasionally experience difficulties with the excitement phase of the sexual response cycle, although it is more common among men. It's important to mention here that inhibited sexual excitement is different from inhibited sexual desire. Someone experiencing inhibited desire doesn't even **feel** like becoming excited, whereas someone who has difficulty in becoming excited usually **wants** to become lubricated or develop an erection, but has difficulty doing so. A lack of vaginal lubrication may result from ambivalent or anxious feelings a woman has about the sexual experience in which she is engaging, but may also occur during prolonged intercourse. A woman might want very much to have intercourse with her partner, for instance, but in the absence of an effective contraceptive be worried about becoming pregnant, and therefore have difficulty becoming excited. If you are a woman whose lubrication decreases during prolonged intercourse you may benefit by taking a break from intercourse and employing other forms of lovemaking until your level of excitement is heightened. If you desire to continue intercourse, you can use a waterless lubricant like K-Y jelly to provide additional vaginal lubrication.

It is probably safe to say that at one time or another every male has had difficulty developing and maintaining an erection. Most of the time difficulties with erection have psychological origins, often related to performance anxieties. When a male is about to have intercourse with a new partner there may be a question lurking in the back of his mind about whether or not he will be able to have an erection when this is called for. If his partner is being especially assertive his anxiety may be heightened because he is faced with the kind of opportunity all males are supposed to welcome, and he may feel compelled to measure up to an imagined sexual standard. If he has had a similar problem in previous initial sexual experiences his level of anxiety is likely to be even higher, since he knows he has failed in this situation before. When faced with an uncooperative penis, most men are reluctant to admit to their partners that anxiety is the problem, but rather are more likely to attribute their lack of erection to fatigue or an excess of alcohol. Once in established sexual relationships, erectile inhibition is rare, and usually can be traced to angry feelings toward a partner or the actual effects of fatigue, drugs, or alcohol.

There are many non-psychological factors that can contribute to erectile problems, and if you or your partner are experiencing erection problems that don't appear to be psychological in origin, it would be wise to see a physician. Certain medical conditions, such as severe diabetes, kidney disease and infections, as well as the prescription medicines used in their treatment may lead to erection inhibition. Alcohol and illicit drugs also contribute to erectile problems, and in a cruel irony, some men drink with the thought that alcohol will diminish their anxiety only to discover that although their inhibitions **are** decreased, the alcohol has in fact led to an inability to develop an erection. Rather than easing it toward sexual compliance, the use of alcohol renders their penis into a state of semi-consciousness. If you have never been able to sustain an erection with a partner long enough to have intercourse, or if you have frequent and unexplained erectile difficulties, you should see a sex counselor or therapist. Ask your doctor for a referral.

It is important for men to acknowledge that if anxiety and performance worries are at the root of their erection difficulties they will have to be willing to discuss this with their partners, and seek their cooperation in helping them relax sufficiently for an erection to occur. Remember this simple advice: when your penis speaks, listen to it, because it is trying to tell you something about what you are attempting to do with it. You can't fool your penis, or trick it into doing something which it doesn't feel up to doing. Maybe the reason your penis doesn't want to stand up is because it knows that you only intend to use it one time with the woman you are with, and this desire conflicts with a deeper value you hold about the importance of intimacy and caring in sexual relationships. Or maybe it is not eager to enter a vagina that it thinks might transmit some kind of unpleasant consequence, like chlamydia or herpes. Or maybe it is unhappy because you have lied to your partner about important aspects of your sexual past, like the extent of your sexual experience with women. Your penis has a mind of its own, and deserves to be listened to and treated with respect. If your penis fails to measure up to your expectations as you prepare it for a one night stand, you deserve what you don't get. You can't train a penis like a circus lion, expecting it to perform under any circumstance rain or shine. When it feels safe and secure it will provide you with all the pleasures you so richly deserve.

Orgasm

The last and shortest phase of the sexual response cycle is orgasm, which consists of a series of rhythmic muscular contractions that release the vascular congestion built up during the excitement phase. Orgasm occurs when some arbitrary high level of stimulation has been reached, a phenomenon which fires off a series of electrical discharges to the pelvic musculature. In females, these rhythmic contractions take place in the uterus, the outer third of the vagina, and in the anal sphincter muscles. Orgasm in males is a two step process, the first consisting of the emission of seminal fluid into the bulb of the urethra, the second involving the expulsion of semen down through the urethra and out of the penis. Although there are two phases to male orgasm, males don't typically perceive their orgasms as two distinct reactions: things happen so quickly that they can't distinguish between the emission and expulsion phases. The initial contractions of orgasm in both males and females take place at intervals of less than a second, and recur for a period of five to fifteen seconds. Some women like to experience more than one orgasm, and unlike most males can return quickly to a point of peak arousal and repeated orgasm. Men usually experience what is called a refractory period after orgasm, an age-dependent amount of time during which it is difficult or impossible to become re-stimulated to the point of orgasm. This period might be minutes or hours, and is affected by things like fatigue and alcohol, as well as age.

Orgasm is often described as being like a sneeze. Think about what happens when you are about to sneeze. First, your nose begins to itch and you realize that if the itch continues you will sneeze. Sometimes you are able to stifle the sneeze by rubbing your nose firmly, but often this action is ineffective and you proceed toward the inevitable. As the sneeze builds up, blood rushes to your head and nose, resulting in a kind of congestion that is only fully dissipated by sneezing. If you get to the edge of a sneeze that doesn't want to happen it's usually very frustrating, so much so that some people have discovered they can trigger the ultimate release by looking at a bright light. Sneezing usually feels good, because it rapidly releases the congestion built up in your head and puts an end to the itching in your nose. Orgasm acts in a similar way to release all the tension and pelvic congestion built up during sexual excitement, so you might say that an orgasm is to your pelvis as a sneeze is to your nose.

In addition to **feeling** wonderful, orgasm performs a very useful function to the body by releasing built up sexual tension and vascular congestion very rapidly. It's not that the congestion won't subside without orgasm, but it will take much longer to do so, and you may experience some real discomfort if this happens frequently. The term "blue balls" conveys the kind of discomfort felt by males, and although females experience a similar kind of aching condition, I know of no analogous term to describe their pain. In addition, you can think of orgasm as Nature's reward for entering the sexual response cycle in the first place--it feels so good that you want to do it again.

The two most common problems associated with the orgasmic phase of the sexual response cycle are anorgasmia (difficulty in reaching orgasm) in females, and premature ejaculation in males. It is the supreme irony that males and females should have just the opposite problems with orgasm, but it is no coincidence that these problems result largely from similar kinds of socialization. If females have been socialized to suppress their sexuality, including their sexual responsiveness, males have learned to orgasm quickly in order to escape detection. Many early sexual intercourse experiences take place in inherently risky settings, like on the living room couch or the back seat of a car parked in a lovers' lane. In these kinds of situations, although both partners are worried that they will be detected, the outcome of this anxiety leaves one of them orgasmically unfulfilled, the other prematurely orgasmic.

Orgasmic control, whether one is trying to elicit or constrain it, requires that both partners feel safe and secure in their environment, as well as with each other. It follows that the orgasmic experiences for new sexual partners are likely to be less than totally satisfying for both of them, since anxiety is so often a visitor to this kind of sexual interaction. Earlier in this chapter I discussed orgasmic difficulties of women in some detail, so it remains here only to say something about premature ejaculation.

Most sexuality textbooks spend a fair amount of time defining premature ejaculation, perhaps because it is such a subjective term. What one person thinks is premature another feels is long overdue. Definitions of premature ejaculation have included criteria such as these: how many minutes a male's penis is in his partner's vagina before he reaches orgasm; whether the male considers he comes too soon; whether his partner feels he comes too soon; whether he comes sooner than he would like to at least twenty-five percent of the time; and whether **both** partners feel the male comes too soon most of the time. Most people do agree that if a male ejaculates while inserting his penis into his partner's vagina, it is premature, so at least there is some agreement on this issue. Suffice it to say that if you are a male who feels you have little control over when you ejaculate during intercourse or you are a female whose partner frequently comes sooner than you would like to, the problem is likely to be one of premature ejaculation.

Gaining a handle on premature ejaculation requires first that partners provide themselves adequate time and a relaxed setting, so that neither of them feels rushed or compelled to get things over with quickly. Talking together about the male's desire to gain better control over his orgasm is important also, because it acknowledges the issue and allows partners to develop a mutual plan designed to improve things. The goal is to help the male develop better voluntary control over his own sexual excitement, and although he holds most of the cards in this game his partner's cooperation is vital. If premature ejaculation is the most common male sexual problem it is also the easiest one to improve upon, especially if both partners are willing to respond openly in dealing with it.

When they masturbate, males are able to maintain their balance as they tread the precipice between extreme sexual excitement and orgasm. As they approach the slippery slope of what sex therapists sometimes refer to as the "point of ejaculatory inevitability," most masturbating males can usually switch off the mechanism that triggers orgasm, and render control over the explosive forces of their impending climax. To do this, they release hand pressure on their penis, and may quickly switch their cognitive set away from a sexual fantasy to other non-sexual thoughts. Once assured that they have regained their balance, they can continue this cycle of stimulation and retreat until they feel ready to take the final plunge.

There are several simple measures a male and his partner can employ that may help him improve his ejaculatory control. He can use a lubricant when he masturbates, to simulate the sensations of vaginal intercourse; he can ejaculate more frequently from intercourse, masturbation, or from manual or oral stimulation provided by his partner; and he and his partner can experiment with different intercourse positions, such as with her on top, to determine which ones put the least direct pressure on his penis and allow him the most freedom to control their thrusting motions. Many couples make good progress with premature ejaculation by practicing the squeeze technique, in which after manually stimulating her partner to the peak of sexual arousal, and on his signaling her to stop, the woman uses her thumb and forefingers to apply firm pressure just below the glans, or head of the penis. After they repeat the cycle of stimulation and squeezing several times, the male can continue on through to orgasm when he decides the next time is to be the last. This same procedure, with the addition of a lubricant, provides an added level of sensation to the male, and so permits a gradual progression of heightened stimulation culminating with that of intercourse itself.

When his penis is in his partner's vagina, a male encounters a bundle of variables over which he has limited control, so it is easier for him both to misperceive that critical edge of no return as well as slip over it more readily once it has occurred. The trick is for the male to see the caution light in time to apply the brakes, and it helps to realize that the lights change a lot faster in this neighborhood than they do during masturbation. It also helps to be on the lookout for these cautionary signals and not wait until the last moment to hit the brakes. As soon as you sense the light change from green to amber, hold your partner firmly and say "**STOP!**" lovingly but with conviction, knowing that because you discussed this signal with her before, she will understand what you want. Resume the motions of intercourse only after regaining full control over your arousal. A male partner must be assertive both in stopping any thrusting that is occurring, and in communicating to his partner his desire to control his orgasmic response. If premature ejaculation continues to be a problem after applying these basic remedies, it would be wise for both partners to discuss the problem together with a sex counselor or therapist. With the help of such a qualified professional, most couples are able to eliminate premature ejaculation.

There are several conditions related to sexual intercourse that occur infrequently but are worth mentioning in the event that you or your partner may be experiencing them, and may be completely in the dark about how to begin dealing with them. Painful intercourse, called **dyspareunia** in both males and females, can result from infections, lack of lubrication, certain diseases, or injuries to the abdomen or reproductive organs. **Vaginismus** is a condition in which strong involuntary contractions of the muscles in the outer third of the vagina prevent entry of a penis, or perhaps even a finger, into the vagina. A woman with vaginismus may have similar contractions during a pelvic exam or when attempting to insert tampons. And **ejaculatory inhibition**, sometimes called retarded ejaculation, occurs when a male has difficulty or finds it impossible to ejaculate during sexual intercourse, although he is usually able to reach orgasm quite easily with other forms of stimulation. Dyspareunia, vaginismus, and ejaculatory inhibition are all issues that should be discussed with a physician, sex counselor, or sex therapist, because their resolution will be aided greatly with the help of these professionals.

CHAPTER 6

━━━━◄◀♦▶►━━━━

Beyond Homophobia

Of all the topics discussed in my Human Relationships and Sexuality course, homosexuality elicits the most discomfort among students. But homosexuality is also the topic about which my students report they make the greatest gains in terms of understanding, awareness, and insight. Gay and non-gay students alike tell me that by helping them sort out the many issues related to sexual identity they are able to feel more comfortable with their own and the sexual orientations of others. It is my hope that as you read this chapter you too will increase the comfort you feel about your sexual orientation, whether you are a gay male, lesbian, bisexual or straight, and at the same time you will understand better the nature of sexual identity in general.

People who study the topic of sexual orientation know that one of the hardest parts of this work is to identify what questions to ask. I think it is unfortunate that many of the key questions about sexual orientation that were asked in the past have centered on why and how people become **homo**sexual, rather than on how **any** individual develops feelings of desire for any other individual. Many young people, for example, raise questions about homosexuality and bisexuality that they never ask about heterosexuality, which suggests to me that these individuals see the fundamental processes of homosexual development to be substantially different in nature from those involved in heterosexuality.

But homosexuality and heterosexuality are not polar opposites: they are far more alike than they are different from one another, in that each represents a very complex and diffuse set of attitudes, desires, and experiences related to sexuality. Many people emphasize the differences, however, probably because they want to maintain their particular view of homosexuality, which may be that it is abnormal, unnatural and/or sinful. While it is perfectly legitimate to ask how our sexual identity develops, including our sense of gender and our feelings of sexual desire, it is time to stop asking these questions solely about homosexuality. Instead of asking "How do people become homosexual?" it would be more fruitful to inquire into how people come to think of and label themselves as homosexual, heterosexual or bisexual, and identify what the personal consequences of each of these labels are for the individuals who bear them.

Our Sexual Identity

For a number of years now, scholars in the field of human sexuality have asserted that sexual identity consists of three components: core gender identity, which pertains to whether you see yourself as either male or female; gender role behaviors, which consist of all the things you do and say to demonstrate to others that you are male or female; and sexual orientation, which expresses the gender(s) of the individuals you are sexually aroused by in fantasy or sexual acts.

Your core gender identity was established early in life. Ask a three or four year old child whether they are a boy or a girl and they will not only be able to tell you the correct answer, but also explain why they are that gender. During early childhood, boys and girls quickly assimilate the stereotypical behaviors of their genders, although of course individual children display a wide variety of gender roles. Some girls feel free to express what society may label more masculine elements of their gender role, some boys express behaviors labeled as feminine. What children of both sexes learn early is that expressing other-gender roles may lead to disapproval and taunting from peers and adults alike.

Like many other features of human life, sexual orientation is not something that can be categorized as black or white. Let's consider some of the factors that act to richly color the mosaic of sexual orientation through a series of questions and responses. Answers to these questions must sometimes be qualified, because we simply don't have adequate evidence to support a clear conclusion.

✿ How do people go about identifying themselves as heterosexual, homosexual, or bisexual?

You can probably recall the first time you experienced feelings of sexual attraction toward another person, perhaps as early as ages five or six. By junior high school you may have developed sexual feelings toward your peers and begun to think of ways you could act on your desires such as by holding hands or kissing. At puberty these sexual urges may have appeared in fantasies, and you may have actualized them directly. So although it might be difficult to conduct this kind of research, it would be possible to ask young people about the gender(s) of the objects of their sexual fantasies and desires.

If asked this question, most young adults would say their fantasy and real life sexual attractions were for members of the other gender. Perhaps ten percent would say they were attracted by members of their own gender. And a much smaller percentage would describe strong feelings of sexual attraction to both genders, although the intensity of attraction might be weighted toward one or the other gender.

There is one question, however, that you are unable to answer with authority: **How** did your sense of gender attraction develop? You can only speculate on how your attractions for one gender or the other occurred, because the process that shapes gender attraction is diffuse and multifaceted, and occurred without your paying any attention to it. What is crystal clear is that when people feel safe to disclose the nature of their sexual attractions they can describe their present and past orientations, and can often speculate on their future attractions.

✿ Are people born with a sexual orientation, or is this a socialized phenomenon?

This has been the sixty-four dollar question since the beginning of the modern age of scientific inquiry into human sexuality. Research approaches to sexual orientation have been similar to those taken in the investigation of many other areas of human development, which means that some scholars attribute sexual orientation to biology (**nature**), some to socialization (**nurture**), and others to a combination of nature and nurture (**interactionist**). At the present time it is impossible to say which of these theories, if any of them, adequately and accurately explains how sexual orientation develops. And it looks very much like a complete answer to this question may not be uncovered in our lifetime.

✿ Do people have a sexual orientation even if they never act on their feelings of sexual attraction?

Yes, they do. Whether or not people are sexually active, they can tell you which gender(s) they would prefer to interact with sexually if they chose to do so. Many people never act on their feelings of sexual attraction, perhaps because they have taken chastity vows consistent with their religious beliefs or because they simply have never had the opportunity or inclination to do so.

✪ Do people <u>choose</u> their sexual orientation?

No one that I have ever heard about can recall a moment in their childhood when they decided to be straight or gay or bisexual. Our awareness of the gender of the individuals to whom we are sexually attracted tends to appear subtly, rather than as an explicit choice we made on October 16th in the fifth year of our life. On the other hand, we know of many individuals who choose to **act** on their feelings of attraction to someone of the same or other gender after many years of repressing, denying, or being unaware of any urge to do so. It does appear that circumstances and opportunity play important roles in determining whether some individuals act on such desires they discover within themselves.

✪ Can people <u>change</u> their sexual orientation?

This is a tough question to answer. Some scholars are convinced that people have a core or "essential" sexual orientation that remains fixed throughout their entire life. Other researchers suggest that circumstances and opportunity lead some people to adopt different sexual lifestyles at different points in their lives, and argue strongly against this "essential" approach to sexual orientation. I believe there is strong and increasing evidence to support this latter explanation.

But if people's feelings of sexual attraction change or broaden at some points in their lives, this is not a matter of a person saying, "Let's see, if this is Wednesday I must be straight. Or is it that I'm gay on Wednesdays?" Changes in an individual's feelings toward sexual orientation appear to be less like closing one door and opening another than they are like changes that occur in a river as it courses slowly through its natural environment.

So in terms of how your sexual identity develops, it is safe to say at least three things with confidence. First, you acquired feelings of sexual desire for members of your own or the other gender during your childhood years. We don't know how this happens, but it does. If you identify yourself as heterosexually oriented, it is unlikely that you can explain with any precision how or why this occurred. The same is true if you are homosexually or bisexually oriented. Second, you may choose to act on or not act on your feelings of sexual attraction, but you nonetheless always have a sexual orientation. And finally, there is a tremendous emphasis in our culture on being heterosexually oriented. Perhaps because of this fact, many people who have feelings of sexual attraction to members of their own gender limit their sexual expressions to individuals of the other gender, fearful that if they don't they will be subjected to severe sanctions.

The Social Context of Homosexuality

Why are so many people so passionate in wanting to know how homosexual but not heterosexual sexual orientation develops? People who focus on the question of homosexual orientation usually do so because they see homosexuality as abnormal, deviant, unnatural, and/or sinful. They have no interest in how heterosexual sexual orientation develops because they see heterosexuality as "natural and normal," and thus in no need of scientific inquiry. Don't misunderstand me: research into sexual orientation is important and valid. But today's social scientists seeking answers to the riddle of sexual orientation do not proceed from the bias that homosexuality is deviant or abnormal. They study this legitimate question because it is one of many in the field of human sexual identity.

There is a good chance that you may have some bias against homosexuality, and to one degree or another consider homosexuality to be abnormal, deviant, unnatural, and/or sinful. If this is the case, you are not alone. For almost twenty years now polls of Americans have indicated that upwards of 75 percent feel that a homosexual orientation is almost always "wrong." **The central issue of this chapter is not how or why some people develop a homosexual orientation, but rather why this fact is a problem for so many people in this country.**

Why do people like Jerry Falwell and Jesse Helms rant and rave about how homosexuals are responsible for the breakdown of the moral fiber of America? Why are gay men and lesbians the victims of hate crimes to an extent greater than any other identified group in the country? Why are so many people adamantly opposed to gays adopting children or serving as foster parents, or being police officers or teachers? What raises the hackles of folks who feel gays and lesbians should not be permitted to marry or become ministers or priests?

As a young adult in contemporary America, these are the questions you need to be wrestling with, and not with how sexual orientation is established. If you grew up in the United States, you did so surrounded by myths and lies about homosexuality, lies and myths that you may be very reluctant to abandon. Here is a short list of facts about homosexuality and gay men and lesbians: **I urge you to read them and then stop worrying about any need you may feel to protect the world from their influence.**

✿   Gay men and lesbians don't want to be the other gender. They like being male or female, and have no desire to change. Yes, some gay men behave in ways that are labeled as stereotypically "feminine," some lesbians act in ways labeled as "masculine." But individuals who dress or behave in these ways do not do so because they want to be the other gender; they do so because they feel comfortable expressing a range of gender stereotypes. I like very much being male, but I also enjoy behaving in ways that have traditionally been thought of as feminine. My desire to act in these ways has nothing to do with my sexual orientation.

✿   Gays and lesbians are not interested in "hitting on" straights. Why would they want to waste their time? If a gay person is attracted to you and you do not wish to respond to their invitation, the polite thing to say is "Thanks, but no thanks." Incidentally, straight men "hit on" straight women all the time, so it is not like this behavior is unknown in the straight kingdom.

✿   Gay men and lesbians are as interested in forming long term intimate relationships as straight people, and they do so with the same frequency as do straights. Their relationships are durable and committed to the same extent as are those of straight people.

✿   Gays and lesbians don't adopt male and female gender roles in their intimate relationships. In fact, gay relationships are generally much more flexible in terms of gender roles than are heterosexual ones.

✿   Lesbians and gay men make good parents—just as good as heterosexual parents. There is no longer any doubt about this fact.

✿   When lesbians and gays hold hands or show affection publicly they are not doing so to "flaunt their sexuality." They are doing what heterosexual partners do, and for the same reasons.

✿   Over ninety percent of child sexual abuse is committed by straight men, not gays. In fact the extent of sexual crimes gay men commit against children is somewhat less than the proportion they represent in society at large.

✿   In terms of sexuality, gender is a more unifying element than is sexual orientation. In other words, lesbian women have more in common with straight women than they do with gay men; gay men have more in common with straight men than they do with lesbians. These elements involve matters like sexual exclusivity, emotional sharing, and the desire for egalitarian intimate relationships. Gay males, however, are more likely than straight males to want their intimate relationships to be egalitarian.

These facts about homosexuality have been established through careful, well-documented research. In terms of homosexual behaviors, values and attitudes, it is no longer justifiable to rely on stereotypes and biased opinions; the facts speak for themselves.

Homophobia: the Root of the Problem

Given the facts I just presented about homosexuality, why do so many myths and lies persist? To gain insight into this question, we need to examine the ways in which homophobia shapes our national attitudes about homosexuality. Homophobia means an unwarranted or irrational fear of homosexuality. Fear itself is a perfectly legitimate concept in life. There are things that all of us have good reason to be afraid of. But when we fear something even though its actual threat to us is minimal or nonexistent, we have what is called a phobia. So why are so many people afraid of homosexuality?

If you scratch the surface of homophobia, what you will find underneath is a very thick layer of sexism. Homophobia is a dominant theme in our society because we are a sexist society. By sexist I mean that our society considers females to be subordinate to males. By any measure, females in our society fare worse than males. Females earn less; females occupy a tiny proportion of elected government positions (three out of fifty of today's governors are women); women who divorce experience a decrease in their annual income while their former husbands experience a significant gain in theirs; women are denied a role in their churches similar to those afforded men; most women are sexually harassed by men at one time or another, while men virtually never experience sexual harassment; all women live with the fear of being raped and sexually assaulted, a fear that never occurs to most men; and society's major institutions like businesses, schools, churches, and the armed forces systematically impede women's progress in occupying roles of leadership and responsibility.

What is the link between sexism and homophobia? The link has to do with the way females are devalued in our society. Not only are females in general devalued, but all things **feminine** are devalued as well. Through the lens of sexism, that which is feminine is weak, trivial, passive, dependent and shallow. These are hardly the qualities any "self-respecting" male is eager to embrace. Coupled to sexism is a condition called heterosexism, which holds that heterosexuality is society's only acceptable sexual orientation. So the fear of homosexuality is based on the fear that women might become as fully valued as men, a thought that scares the daylights out of a great many men, and believe it or not, some women as well.

Here is the way homophobia and heterosexism work to keep females subordinate to males. When gay men are taunted, called faggots and beaten, the message being conveyed by their aggressors is "You are acting like a woman. Real men don't act like women." When lesbians are assaulted and called dykes, the message is that they are not "real women." If they were real women, they would be sexually attracted only to men. Because homophobes fear the condition of women being equal to men, lashing out at gay men and lesbians is a way to hurt all women, and therefore keep all women in their place.

So if you are homophobic, which is to say that if you feel that homosexuality is abnormal, unnatural, or deviant, your feelings are being fueled by your sexism. There is no scientific evidence to support the idea that homosexuality is abnormal, unnatural, or deviant. In fact, all the evidence demonstrates that homosexuality is both normal and natural. Those religions that consider homosexuality sinful are also sexist, in that their doctrines subordinate females to males.

My guess is that if you feel that homosexuality is abnormal, unnatural, or deviant, you are pretty upset with what I have said so far in this chapter. You may feel that I am biased, that I am not presenting "both sides of this question." You probably resent the implications that if you hold these feelings about homosexuality that you are therefore homophobic and heterosexist. But before you blow a gasket I want you to think very carefully about why it is so disquieting for you to consider homosexuality as normal and healthy, why it is that you feel gays and lesbians are deviant. I firmly believe that if you are willing to think seriously about the views you have toward homosexuality, you will find that all of them are informed by sexism. And it will probably be more difficult for you to acknowledge your sexism than it is your homophobia.

Letting Go of Our Homophobia

A very sad paradox is that even gays and lesbians have difficulty escaping their own homophobia. If you grow up in a world that despises you, it's very difficult to love yourself. It is indeed fortunate that as more and more gays have come out of the closet over the last twenty years that there is now a "gay community" within which gay men and lesbian women can find affirmation and acceptance. I grew up fearful of homosexuality just as you probably did. The question for all of us, gay and non-gay alike, is whether we want to let go of these fears, whether we want to help create a society in which all people feel safe and valued regardless of their gender, race, or sexual orientation. I suspect that you share this vision of a just and safe society, at least to some degree. I invite you to consider why letting go of your homophobia and heterosexism might benefit both you and society.

Getting Started: An Appeal to Fairness and Justice

When I was a boy I learned from my parents and society in general that blacks were inferior to whites in intellect, drive to succeed, morality, and creativity. As a teenager my world began to enlarge and include black acquaintances, and I found the stereotypes I had acquired during childhood difficult to reconcile with my broadening vision of the nature and potential of blacks. But it was difficult for me to overcome the weight of my prejudice because this emerging view of blacks was contrary to that of most of the people who lived in my town (which was all white at the time), and was also contrary to the views supported by schools, businesses and churches.

I grew up with a similar prejudice against homosexuality. Most of my prejudice centered around what I was told was its sinful nature, although I also believed homosexuality resulted from a genetic aberration. My experiences in the U.S. Army brought my racism and homophobia into focus, and interestingly enough it was three boyhood values that helped me begin to unload the baggage of my racial and homophobic prejudices. The values that rescued me were those of fairness, justice, and loyalty. It is a great testimony to the power of these principles of democracy that they were able to move me to consider why my biases against blacks and gays were so destructive to me and others.

I was stationed at a military post in Louisiana during the early sixties, and it was there that I first encountered the terrible results of racism. At this time in our history most facilities like hotels, bars, restaurants, bus depots and so on were still segregated. As a result, my black friends and I were unable to socialize together unless we did so on the military reservation. Black soldiers and their families were relegated to substandard housing in towns adjacent to the post, and the children of black servicemen had to attend segregated schools. Seeing firsthand the pain that these forms of discrimination brought to my black friends galvanized for me the injustice all blacks were experiencing. Because I had never had black friends prior to my military service I had never encountered the effects of racism at a personal level.

In the same way that I had limited contact with blacks prior to my Army tour of duty, I was also unaware of the prevalence of gay men and lesbian women in our society. But a number of the men I worked with in my military hospital assignment were gay, and they told me that there were hundreds of others gays assigned to our post. It was when my best friend Tom told me he was gay and was sexually attracted to me that I began to confront my homophobia for the first time in my life. I liked Tom a great deal and I didn't want to do anything to jeopardize our relationship, but I knew I wasn't interested in being sexual with him or with other men. Fortunately, Tom was able to help me understand that our friendship did not depend on my being gay or on responding to his sexual invitation.

Shortly before our two year tour of duty was complete, Tom and about twenty-five other gay soldiers were "caught" at a party hosted by the assistant to the post commander. Many of the men held enlisted grades, and like me they had been drafted into the Army. Others, however, were officers whose rank ranged from lieutenant to colonel. Several were physicians, two were lawyers, one a veterinarian, one a pharmacist, and several others were field commanders. All these men, who had served honorably and without incident for periods of from two to almost thirty years, were courts-martialed and discharged from the Army. They lost all benefits, like retirement and educational funds available through the G.I. Bill.

Although I was incensed by the treatment Tom and his friends received, I felt paralyzed to do anything on their behalf. Their trial was conducted in private, and within a short time they were all whisked away from the post. Because I could see no way in which their homosexuality interfered with their military performance, their dismissal violated everything I had ever learned about fairness and justice, and because some of these men were my close friends, it also evoked strong feelings of loyalty.

So like racism, homophobia can prevent us from acting confidently in response to issues of fairness and equity. Is this what you want for yourself? If you believe in the rights of blacks or others with a multi-cultural background, can you believe also in the rights of people whose sexual orientations are different from yours? Can you be supportive of gays at this level of fairness and justice? If not, what rationale do you employ to deny to gays those rights you accord to blacks and to yourself? Having learned something here about homosexuality, are you willing to examine your feelings about gays from the perspective of fairness and justice?

If you are willing to think of homosexuality from the perspectives of fairness and justice you have made a wonderful beginning in moving beyond homophobia. You may find that although you feel comfortable with a fairness and justice approach, your gut level response to homosexuality is still one of apprehension and lingering fear. This is to be expected. No one changes their strongly held feelings about anything by simply turning a switch in their heads. The move from tolerance to a fuller acceptance of homosexuality is a mighty big one, and will take time and thoughtful effort.

Beyond Tolerance

What is the difference between tolerating homosexuality and fully accepting it? To tolerate homosexuality means that you may favor gay rights, that you would not vote against someone simply because they were gay, that you believe in an adult's right to engage in consensual sexual acts with other adults irrespective of their gender, that you abhor violence against gays, and that you think a person's sexual orientation should not have a bearing on things like employment and military service.

But there are lots of people who support these basic rights for lesbian women, bisexuals, and gay men without really knowing much about the sexuality or the personal lives of such individuals. In a way this analogy is somewhat akin to the "separate but equal" reasoning applied by those who supported segregation: yes, give blacks opportunities, but keep them separated from whites.

Being supportive of gays in the ways I just described is a first critical step toward broadening your acceptance of homosexuality. You can now work to develop friendships with bisexuals, gay men and lesbian women, learn about gay culture and art, celebrate your belief that diversity adds richness to our culture by joining with friends in gay pride marches, and stand in solidarity with gays at protest rallies and demonstrations.

You may worry that if you do these kinds of things that people will assume you are gay, and indeed they may. Anxiety about being perceived as gay is yet one more element of our homophobia, and conquering this fear depends on our getting to a place where we can say, "It doesn't really matter whether people feel I'm gay, because I consider homosexuality, bisexuality and heterosexuality to be equally legitimate expressions of sexual diversity within a culture. If I can help it, I'm not going to let people use their homophobia as a weapon to hurt me or anyone else."

Imagine what it is like for a gay young person to face the prospect of coming out to their friends and parents. If you are gay, lesbian or bisexual, you already know the terror this task can engender. Although the benefits to coming out seem to outweigh the risks, this is rarely the perspective of individuals who are facing this choice.

There is surely no greater fear than that of being rejected by one's own family, yet this is the central worry of gay and lesbian individuals as they contemplate coming out. How much saner it would be if young people knew that their parents and family would love and accept them unconditionally, that parents would feel comfortable celebrating their children's developing sexuality irrespective of their sexual orientation. By coming out, gays and lesbians lay claim to an essence of their life, which is their sexuality. But coming out also includes identifying openly with the gay community, with gay culture, and with gay music and art and literature.

It takes a lot of psychic energy for a person to maintain their homophobia or racism or sexism. In addition to psychic energy, some people actually spend quite a bit of time fighting to maintain the conditions of homophobia, racism and sexism in our society. It also takes a lot of energy for lesbian women, gay men and bisexuals to obtain and protect their rights to be full citizens in our country, rights that homophobes want to deny them. If you have been working to overcome your homophobia, you know that as you broaden your feelings of acceptance toward diversity, you also experience an increase in your own self-esteem. Being able to value diversity is a key to being able to value yourself. Another way to say this is that those individuals whose homophobia, racism and sexism is most intense are also those individuals whose self-esteem is the most fragile.

Whether you are gay, bisexual or straight, I encourage you to work to overcome your fears about homosexuality. To do this will require that you examine your sexism to see how homophobia and sexism are linked together. As you delve into how you learned from your culture to devalue certain classes of people, you will begin to identify sources of power within yourself that you can harness to overcome these harmful attitudes that drain you and all of us of energy we could put to better use.

CHAPTER 7

Sexual Responsibilities

As you probably know, the publishing industry is a very competitive one, and for an author to get their book published today requires persistence and sometimes just plain good luck. Prior to signing a contract with an author, publishers usually send a manuscript to experts in the field for advice about its merits and market potential. Here is what one such reviewer said about this book:

> "I find this manuscript taking a very open approach to sexuality. I read it very carefully and my conclusion is that it encourages, or promotes sexuality among young adults. While the statistics show that over three-quarters of the men and two-thirds of young women are sexually active, I'm not sure that the posture of this manuscript will be well accepted."

I was not surprised by this reviewer's comment. There are many Americans who think that the simple act of providing clear information about sex and sexual behavior to young people **encourages** them to be sexual. To suggest that parents and other adults might actually **help** young people maintain sexually intimate relationships, as I do in this book, could easily be interpreted to mean that I wish to "promote and encourage sexuality among young adults."

If I am trying to promote anything in this book it is the idea that society should take a more open and responsible approach toward the way it views human sexuality, especially its approach to the sexuality education of young people. Young and old alike in this country are surrounded by conflicting messages about sex. On the one hand, the media, pop music, TV and movies suggest that sex and sexuality is "where it's at." On the other, fundamentalists and other conservative groups insist that education for sexuality is not within the scope of public schools. No wonder, then, that our rate of unwanted pregnancies surpasses those of all other industrialized nations, and the incidence of sexually transmitted diseases (STD's) in the U.S. continues to increase.

Although there are many issues that might fall under the heading "sexual responsibilities," I am going to limit discussion here to the three I consider most important for you as a young adult to confront: failure to use contraception; sexually transmitted diseases; and force used to obtain sex. I will consider contraception and sexually transmitted diseases together since the issues involved in avoiding pregnancy or an STD are related. Forced sex will constitute the final portion of the chapter.

Contraception and Sexually Transmitted Diseases

Did you know that over half the pregnancies that occur among all women in the United States are unintended? Among high school and college women, virtually all pregnancies are unintended. Very few high school or college students consider themselves ready to take on the responsibilities that accompany being a parent. All this might not be a problem if the actual numbers of unintended pregnancies were small, but such is not the case. For each of the past twenty years close to one million teenage women became pregnant, about half of whom carried their pregnancies to term. Most of these young mothers are poor.

Although unintended pregnancies occur in young women of all social and economic backgrounds, a disproportionate percentage are among individuals whose educational opportunities have been cut short by poverty and dismal living conditions. Better educated and economically more stable young women are not only more likely to use contraception to prevent pregnancy, but also are more likely to see that carrying an unwanted pregnancy to term will seriously affect their abilities to control and shape their lives in a meaningful way. Thus these young women abort their unwanted pregnancies.

For the past fifteen years, an average of about twelve percent of the women who take my Human Relationships and Sexuality course have reported at least one unintended pregnancy, virtually all of which were terminated by abortion. Some of these pregnancies occurred while the students were in high school, some during their college years. It is not unusual for a young woman to come to me even late in the semester to seek advice about their unplanned pregnancy. Taking a course in human sexuality carries no guarantee of preventing pregnancy.

The news about sexually transmitted diseases is no more optimistic than it is about unintended pregnancies. It's pretty grim. Chlamydia infections, which have the potential to cause serious and life-long damage to the reproductive tract, are among the most prominent of STD's in the young adult population. The incidence of genital warts is now considered to be epidemic in the United states, with at least a million new cases occurring each year. The current incidence of syphilis is higher than it has been since 1950, having increased twenty-five percent in the year 1987 alone. Gonorrheal infections continue to be among the highest of all STD's, with perhaps three to four million new cases occurring each year in the U.S. alone. And acquired immunodeficiency syndrome (AIDS) stands alone among other STD's in its power to cause premature death.

Many people say that the way to lower the incidence of unintended pregnancies and sexually transmitted diseases is through education. I'm not about to challenge this wisdom here, but I believe that education is only part of our problem. Most young adults know without a doubt that if they have sexual intercourse without contraception they risk beginning a pregnancy. Likewise, they know that having intercourse without condoms and spermicides puts them at risk for acquiring a sexually transmitted disease. Young people know these things. But this knowledge does not keep them from having unprotected sexual intercourse or from engaging in other risky sexual behaviors.

Let's look at some data from a recent survey of my students which reports their use of contraceptives. The first chart reveals that at the time of first intercourse about two-thirds said they used an effective contraceptive.

The Very First Time You Had Sexual Intercourse, Did You Or Your Partner Use an Effective Form of Contraception?		
RESPONSE	FEMALE	MALES
ABSOLUTELY, & I KNEW IT	65	66
I DIDN'T; I'M UNSURE ABOUT PARTNER	1	11
NO, NEITHER USED CONTRACEPTION	34	23

As we might expect, my students' contraceptive use is higher now than on the occasion of first intercourse, which for most of them was when they were in high school. Remember, however, that the most recent intercourse might have been the first time as well.

During Your Most Recent Intercourse Experience, Did You or Your Partner Use an Effective Form of Contraception?		
RESPONSE	FEMALE	MALES
ABSOLUTELY, & I KNEW IT	84	77
I DIDN'T; I'M UNSURE ABOUT PARTNER	0	9
NO, NEITHER USED CONTRACEPTION	16	14

Perhaps the most telling data about contraceptive use among my students appears in this final chart, which clearly illustrates why so many of them are at risk for unplanned pregnancies and sexually transmitted diseases.

Estimate the Percentage of your Total Sexual Intercourse Experiences in Which You and/or Your Partner Used an Effective Form of Contraception.		
RESPONSE	FEMALE	MALES
100 PERCENT	50	42
75 PERCENT	38	38
50 PERCENT	7	11
25 PERCENT	5	9

If less than half of a well educated group of young adults who has benefitted from the best of what their society has to offer have used contraceptives every time they have had intercourse, it should be no surprise that our unplanned pregnancy rate is so high. If only about a quarter of young adults today are using condoms and spermicides regularly, there is little reason to wonder why the incidence of sexually transmitted diseases is skyrocketing.

Why is it, then, that so many smart young adults in the United States behave as if their brains were anesthetized while they were having sex? Why do even those young adults who have the best opportunities to reap the benefits afforded by a good education behave in ways that threaten their fertility and their very lives? Why don't young people act on the sexual knowledge they possess? What would have to happen in order for young adults to stop their risky sexual behaviors, to act consistently on their knowledge?

Of course none of these questions has a simple answer. But not having simple answers to these questions does not mean we should feel paralyzed to respond to them. I believe that, to a large degree, the major themes of this book explain why young adults do not behave sexually in ways that protect their own and the well being of others. They do so because society sends mixed messages about sex and the role that sexual interaction might play in human life. They do so because from the day they were born they have been urged by media and pop culture to be sexy, to dress sexy and to look sexy, while at the same time they have been denied even the most basic opportunities to learn how to express their sexuality in responsible ways. They have not seen condom ads on TV because the media moguls think such ads would offend some of their viewers. They have not had adequate sexuality education programs in their schools because a small but vocal minority of citizens browbeat school boards and administrators into keeping such programs out.

So the failure of young people to use contraceptives consistently reflects the tragic failure of their society to ensure that they put their knowledge into practice. If American adults cannot agree on what messages to give young people about sex, it's easy to understand why we have the problems we do.

Children growing up in America also learn some other things that ultimately contribute to their irresponsible sexual behaviors as young adults. One of the most insidious of these lessons is that **things** can make them happy, that the right products can solve even the most intractable problems. And among the products that are pitched to young adults at an ever-increasing tempo is alcohol, the universal problem solver. **Alcohol is the anesthetic that allows people to separate their good judgement from their risky behaviors, that massages hard facts into distant possibilities, that disengages people from reality and eases them into the fantasy of "perhaps."** It is impossible to escape the message in our country today that alcohol will help you have a better life, be more social, and in general just get it on. It is very hard for young adults not to succumb to the lie of this message, and as a result many young people do indeed have sex while their brains are anesthetized.

If you don't use an effective method of birth control each and every time you have sexual intercourse, and if you don't use a condom lubricated with a spermicide each and every time you have vaginal or anal sexual intercourse, you are not being sexually responsible. It is crucial to use condoms at all times because even the most effective contraceptives, such as the pill and the IUD, offer no protection against STD's. If you are in a committed monogamous partnership and you and your partner have both tested negative for STD's including AIDS, use of a condom may be optional according to the method of contraception you employ.

No one can guarantee that if you use condoms each and every time you engage in some kind of genital sexual activity that you will not acquire an STD. But this risk is minuscule compared to the risk you face if you don't. And since there is no way that you can reasonably expect to avoid an STD by being "prudent" about the selection of your sexual partners, your only choice is to use condoms during every sexual act. While abstinence may represent an option for some individuals, it is not a viable choice for the majority of Americans today; so to suggest that the way to check AIDS and other STD's is to abstain from sex is not only foolish but is also dangerous. Those young people who are **least likely** to use effective contraception and condoms are often those whose families feel that abstinence is the only acceptable sexual option for unmarried men and women.

It will take a lot of courage and determination on your part to swim against the current tide of non-protected sexual intercourse. It's very easy for strong and healthy young adults to think that they are invulnerable to unplanned pregnancies and STD's. It will probably be very difficult for you to imagine that the person you have begun to see socially may have an STD; in fact there is a good chance that if they do have one they don't even know it. So even the direct approach of asking a partner whether they may have an STD is unlikely to be very helpful to you in avoiding an infection. And it also makes no sense to stop using condoms after you have gotten to know a new partner, unless of course you have both been tested as being free of all STD's. Knowing someone well provides no protection against acquiring a disease from them!

As a young adult you are on the cusp of being able to realize your dreams of a future of satisfying work and relationships. In addition, you are also about to complete a tremendous amount of effort you have already put into your life. Fulfilling these dreams may well depend on two things: first, your willingness to address the role that alcohol and other drugs play in your life and the lives of your friends; and second, a desire to assess your self-esteem and develop a plan of action designed to improve it. For many young adults, the real danger of alcohol abuse lies less in their becoming alcoholic (although this is a substantial risk) than it does in diminishing their judgment to an extent sufficient for them to engage in risky sexual activity. Since alcohol abuse is so closely tied to a person's self-esteem, anything you can do to maintain a high level of esteem will help you avoid both unplanned pregnancies and sexually transmitted diseases. Chapters ten and eleven of this book were designed to help you understand the role that self-esteem plays in forming and maintaining intimate relationships. I encourage you to think carefully about the framework presented in these two chapters as a means of assessing and strengthening this central part of your life.

The Use of Force to Obtain Sex

As I have discussed earlier in this book, I think it is fair to say that our society today is in deep trouble regarding human relationships, especially those between males and females. Violence that males inflict on females is at the extreme end of a spectrum of behaviors that range from benign and loving to aggressive and hurtful. Although the data from research reports varies regarding the numbers of women being sexually abused or raped each year, there is unanimous agreement among the experts that the scope of the problem is truly staggering: **in the United States a woman is raped every 2-3 minutes; at least a third of all females are sexually abused before age eighteen; and almost half of all women are the victims of some form of sexual coercion at some time during their life**. Over eighty percent of rapes are committed by someone known by the victim. A 1988 study of students at Arizona State University revealed that 95 percent of the women reported having been coerced into one or more sexual behaviors, and a recent study at Cornell found that 16 percent of the women had been forced to have sexual intercourse against their will.

The term forced sex applies to a range of sexual behaviors, from unwanted touch of some part of the body, to coercion to perform manual or oral sex, to forced sexual intercourse. Whether we use the term "force someone to have sex," or the term "acquaintance rape," or the term "sexual assault," or the term "rape," we are talking about the same thing. If you have intercourse with someone who is too drunk to give their consent, that too is rape. Using force of any kind, whether it's verbal coercion or physical force, in order to have intercourse with someone against their will is rape, and if you employ any of these kinds of force you are liable to go to jail. A 23 year old Cornell student was recently sentenced to fifteen years in prison as a result of an acquaintance rape.

I want to mention a few specific reasons that both males and females cite to explain why force may play a role in an individual sexual encounter. Women report that they sometimes give in to a sexual act because they are worried their partner will dump them; because they feel obligated because their partner spent a lot of money on them; because their partner accused them of being a sexual tease; because they want to be considered popular; because their partner questioned their sexuality; or because they were intoxicated or under the influence of another drug. Alcohol plays a contributing role in over 80 percent of acquaintance rapes. Men say that they use force for similar reasons, and also because they feel they need to live up to a stereotype of what they consider to be real masculine behavior.

And there is another very important explanation for the use of force in sex, especially in relation to acquaintance rape. This is what is called **token resistance** on the part of females. The fact of the matter is, of course, that many females **want** to engage in sexual activities with their partner, but for a woman to openly admit this desire means she runs the risk of being labeled a slut or an "easy lay." So instead of acknowledging her desire openly to her partner, a woman may put up token resistance, which means she initially resists her partner's sexual advances but then goes along with them and responds like a dynamo gone wild. It is estimated that at least 40 percent of college women use token resistance at some time as part of their sexual interactions. The message a partner then gets is obvious: women have to be pushed before they will go along with a sexual advance. When such men encounter other women who resist their sexual advances they may interpret any resistance as being token, and simply not stop before they have forced their partner into a sexual act against her will.

No woman wants to be raped, no matter what myths exist to the contrary. While it is of course impossible to be totally safe from rape in today's world, there are many things that women can do to protect themselves from being sexually assaulted. Andrea Parrot, a teacher and researcher at Cornell University, has developed some excellent strategies which can help women avoid being raped by an acquaintance. The following suggestions are adapted from Parrot's **Acquaintance Rape and Sexual Assault Prevention Training Manual** (Ithaca, N.Y.: Cornell University, 1985).

- ✿ **Self Assessment.** Think about what you really want to do with a partner. Trust your instincts if you are fearful in a particular situation. Ask yourself whether you can say **NO** if you begin to feel uncomfortable during a sexual experience.
- ✿ **Communication.** Be assertive in stating what you do or do not want to experience sexually. Avoid token resistance, and likewise state clearly when a partner has exceeded a sexual limit. **Say what you mean, and mean what you say.**

✿ **Interpersonal.** Don't assume that someone who has done nothing violent before will not do so in the future. Being passive, coy and submissive may set you up for being a victim of sexual aggression.

✿ **Awareness.** Since acquaintance rape is such a common occurrence, it is critical that you be aware that you are a potential victim. It **can** happen to you!

✿ **Control.** Being in control of environmental factors can play a big role in protecting you from assault. Until you know someone well enough to trust them, avoid going to their room or apartment alone or being alone with them in your space. Be sure you always have access to a phone, and have police numbers posted nearby. Attend parties with friends, and make transportation arrangements to get home **before** you go. Take classes in assertiveness training and self-defense.

There are many things that men can do to help stop rape and other kinds of violence against women. The first is to realize that because you grew up in a society that devalues all females, you are at risk for hurting or raping a woman yourself. You probably don't think of yourself as a rapist, but unless you are aware that you have this potential you may force someone to have sex against their will. **Men Stopping Rape**, a group in Madison, Wisconsin, has developed an excellent program to help men realize how they can change their present attitudes and behaviors to help reduce the incidence of rape. The following suggestions for men are adapted from their brochure "Rape Spectrum."

✿ **Confront woman-hating attitudes in yourself and others.** There are so many ways that females are disparaged and put down in our society that such behaviors are easy to overlook. Even teasing a male friend about "throwing like a girl" contributes to an attitude that devalues and diminishes women. Recognize that you probably have been contributing to this process of trivializing that which is female, and stop these behaviors.

✿ **Talk with women about what makes them feel unsafe.** Knowing that many women feel uncomfortable when they hear someone walking behind them on a dark street suggests that you can be deliberate about crossing and walking on the other side. Discovering from your female friends what threatens them will permit you to avoid these behaviors yourself.

✿ **Develop full relationships with both men and women.** By having a wide range of friendships with men and we are more able to meet our emotional needs. When our emotional needs are met through our many friendships, we are less likely to pressure our sexual partners to meet all of them herself.

✿ **Stop telling sexist jokes.** Although it may not appear that sexist jokes contribute to an unsafe environment for women, anything men do to demean females has the potential to hurt them. When men talk about women as objects, as occurs in sexist jokes, it makes it easier for them to employ violence against them.

✿ **Stop pretending submission is consent.** Because a woman submits to a sexual act does not mean she consents to it. If you have any reason to believe that the sexual act you are engaging in is not being done with your partner's full consent, **STOP!** Don't assume that your sexual advances are enjoyable to your partner. Talk together about what each of you wants and expects from your sexual interactions, and then stay within the bounds of these agreements.

In the best of all worlds, no one would need to worry about being coerced into any sexual act. But the real world is loaded with risks to people's safety and well-being. As a young adult it is crucial for you to understand in what ways you are at risk, whether the risks involve being a victim or an aggressor. I hope that the major themes of this book will help you appreciate the many ways in which our socialization can interfere with our having full and satisfying relationships with both women and men. The challenge for all of us is to see that gender equality is an attainable goal that will benefit males and females alike, and that indeed we can overcome the negative influence of our socialized images of masculinity and femininity.

CHAPTER 8

━━━━━━━━━━━━━━━▶◀▮▶━━━━━━━━━━━━━━━

Becoming Autonomous: Laying the Groundwork for Intimacy

One of the most common reasons young people come to see me is to talk about an intimate relationship that has recently ended or is tottering on the brink of dissolution. It is usually the partner who has been left or is about to be left who seeks me out, and it is not a happy scene. Being rejected by someone you love can result in some of the most intense pain you will ever experience, and if this is your first "real" love relationship the feelings of despair can be overwhelming. In situations like these there is nothing I can say that will immediately restore a person's self-confidence and spirit, no window I can open that will let in a whisper of fresh air permitting them to breathe freely. What I **can** do is encourage them to talk about the pain they are feeling, let them know that I believe them fully when they say how much this hurts, and grieve with them for their loss.

After talking a while with such a young person I usually ask a question that initially startles them, but invariably leads them to think about relationships in ways they have not considered before. What I ask them is this: "What has your **partner** lost by not having you as their lover any more?"

The first response I usually get to this question is something like, "What do you mean, 'What have **they** lost?' My partner is the one who wanted to end the relationship in the first place— I don't see how they have lost anything!"

"But they have lost **you**," I reply. "Isn't that a significant loss? After all, you have many fine qualities which your partner will no longer be able to enjoy as a result of ending your relationship. You are feeling now like your loss was greater than your partner's, but if relationships are two way streets both of you stand to lose in equal measures when the relationship ends."

As much as this may be a logical statement for me to make, it usually does little to ease the pain of rejection. And yet it is often the case that when we are spurned by a lover we assume that **we** are the ones who don't measure up in the relationship, that we don't have as much power to hurt our partner by withdrawing our love as they do. This assessment of how important we really are to our partner is often based on how important we assess ourselves to be as individuals, and it is very likely that the less worthy we feel as total persons the more deeply we will feel the rejection of a lover. It is trite but true to say that a strong and healthy self-image is the key to being happy in virtually all aspects of a person's life, and this is especially true of their intimate life.

Before we explore the area of intimate relationships it will be helpful to consider how our self-concept is shaped during the young adult years. In order to understand why we choose one particular person for a partner rather than another and why our relationships develop in certain predictable ways, it will be useful to become familiar with the basic structures that underlie all our relationships. In this chapter I'll discuss some core ideas about human development in general, and then focus in on a few concepts that have special significance for young adulthood. Most of what I describe will not be entirely new to you, but it may be the first time you have considered these ideas in any cohesive way. In a later chapter dealing with long-term relationships I will continue this discussion of the ways in which self-concept affects our intimate relationships.

Let's start with the concept of human development itself. You probably use this term fairly often, but may not give much thought to just exactly what it means. When a person says, "I've experienced a lot of personal growth in the last few years," you have a general sense of what they are talking about, but you would also feel it was appropriate to ask them for some specific examples to illustrate how they have grown. The person might respond by saying they are less possessive in their intimate relationships, they are less likely to procrastinate on school or work assignments, they take a more active role in determining whether or not they are eating properly and getting sufficient rest and exercise, and have become more reflective when responding to personal questions. Each of these responses indicates an increase in the amount of personal responsibility the individual is claiming, often as a result of having made significant changes in their life.

No doubt you could make a similar list of the ways you have grown in the past few years, and in doing so you would be making the judgment that new or changed life processes constituted evidence of your growth. When we say we grow we mean this term to apply to physical, intellectual, emotional, as well as spiritual aspects of our lives, and the term growth most importantly implies **change**.

But if the term growth suggests change, it is important to remember that human development also connotes stability and **constancy**. There are many things about our selves that remain quite constant over time: at age twenty-five or fifty-five we are very much the same person we were at age twenty or even twelve. Examples of this kind of constancy might include the level of care we extend to others, our enjoyment of music, a sense of humor, and the fun we get out of playing games or reading. Although we are continually changing, life for most of us would be too disruptive if we had to reinvent ourselves every few weeks. These elements of our self that change little or not at all provide us with the rudders we need to navigate life with some measure of predictability, and act as useful constraints to keep us from popping apart at the seams.

Over a period of seventy or eighty or ninety years, then, we experience these two major features of life, change and constancy, and taken together they constitute what we call human development. Certain periods in life tend to be liberally salted with changes, while others are blander and more tranquil. The early childhood years, for example, can appear to consist of almost nothing but changes, while old age often seems to be totally static. Neither of these conditions is true, of course, but this often **appears** to be the case. What is clear, though, is that each stage of life brings with it a new set of demands or tasks to be accomplished, and it is primarily these new demands that compel us to change and adapt to the new circumstances of our life. It is also apparent that, within a given culture, the work of some stages in life is almost universally perceived to be more difficult than that of other stages.

Although there is a new set of tasks to be accomplished at each of life's stages, the work of all previous stages remains ongoing, and to some degree never ends. For example, although we complete a major portion of our identity formation by our early twenties, we never get to a point in life where our identity is so fully formed and completely understood that we can say, "There, my identity is complete, I'll have no further questions about it." At fifty we are less likely to agonize over our identity and may feel reasonably secure about it, but the questions of who we are and who we want to be remain with us throughout our life. It is also true that residuals of work we don't accomplish fully at an earlier stage in life tend to permeate all subsequent stages, and in one way or another press to be completed.

As you have gotten older you have probably noticed that developmental changes occurring in one individual have a direct effect on those around them. Another way to say this is that all development takes place within some kind of context, usually that of a family. If you are a young adult, your parents are probably in their late forties to mid-fifties. By this point in their lives your parents are well settled into their middle years, have careers or jobs that are running on course, and are psychologically ready to let go of you as you enter the adult years. But let's say that you are among the growing number of young adults whose parents are in the midst of beginning a second family, and now have one or more infants or young children from their new marriage. It is more likely to be your father who is having another child because he has married a woman many years younger than your mother, and who may not have any children from her previous relationships. If your mother remarries when you are in your late teens or twenties she is less likely than your father to have more children.

In this situation, your father is having to deal with the demands of young children at a time in his life when he is probably more interested in and perhaps better suited to be a mentor than a new parent. He is thus less likely to have the time and energy to nurture his relationship with **you**, just at a point in both of your lives when you are ready to establish a more fully adult relationship. And when your new step-siblings are your age, your father will be in his late sixties or seventies, if indeed he is fortunate to live that long. This example illustrates how the developmental work of one individual affects the lives of those around them. As we are growing up, our own developmental process takes place within the context of the developmental processes of each of our siblings, our parents, and sometimes our grand-parents.

All of this is not to say that there is some ideal set of developmental conditions under which all families should exist, or that people should have their children at some ideal time in their lives. But it is a fact that these different sets of developmental conditions make it easier or more difficult for parents and children to adjust to the varying demands of each stage of their development. This is probably apparent to you if you are the youngest of several children in your family. The way your parents treated you was no doubt quite different from the way they dealt with your older siblings, in part because they had more practice, but also because they had gained a measure of confidence from their earlier experiences.

Before you can establish a satisfying intimate relationship, you need to have a good sense of who you are and also need to be well on your way to being an autonomous or self-governing person. This chapter will examine why autonomy is so crucial to intimate relationships.

Autonomy

Autonomy: (n) 1.) The condition or state of being self-governing. 2.) Independent. Do you meet this dictionary definition of autonomy? If you are like most young adults, you are more autonomous in some areas of your life than in others. Life in college or the military services provides a gradual transition between total dependence on parents and other adults to complete dependence on yourself. At many colleges, for example, students live in residence halls for one or two years and then move off campus to an apartment, which allows for a kind of step-wise introduction to adult living. Even in those schools in which residential living crosses all four years there is often an increasing amount of housing freedom permitted students as they become juniors and seniors, perhaps in the form of town houses or on-campus apartments. And in a similar manner, men and women serving in the armed forces must live on their military posts until they reach a certain rank or have family needs that necessitate off-post accommodations.

When students live on campus they are usually required to purchase a meal plan, which puts some limits on food choices but eases the responsibilities of shopping and preparing meals. As a young adult, you probably wash and iron (just kidding) your own clothes, clean your own room (so to speak), get yourself up, and maintain a checkbook, all of which are examples of increasing autonomy. You may also pay for all or a portion of your living expenses. Financial independence is one of the most frequent marker events that people use to assess their degree of autonomy, but this is by no means a sure sign of this condition.

Autonomy involves a great deal more than simply taking care of yourself. Perhaps the most distinctive attribute of an autonomous individual is that they are **inner**- rather than **other**-directed. What this means in a nutshell is that these individuals actively write the scripts of their own lives rather than live by scripts written by others. For most young adults, the "others" tend to be parents, employers, teachers, and what they perceive to be important societal standards. Two examples should help illustrate the difference between inner- and other-directed individuals.

After working with students for a number of years I discovered that it is quite common for a young person to enter college with the idea that their job is to fulfill a set of requirements, after which they will graduate and take their place in the "real" world. At first this kind of student places almost total reliance on others to determine what they should do, what courses they should take, which parties to attend, and whether or not to join a fraternity or sorority. Such individuals may consult their parents before making decisions ranging from course selections to whether to go to Florida for spring break. While inner-directed persons may well discuss these matters with their parents, unlike other-directed individuals they don't feel obligated to take their parents' advice. Other-directed students tend to feel that they have little control over things like course selection and assignments, often acting as if their only goal is to put in their time and get out.

I often see examples of two extremes of these students: those who come to class every day only because they think they might miss something if they skipped; and those who skip class regularly because they feel no personal responsibility to make the class interesting and vital to themselves, to other students, and the instructor. Students who are autonomous understand that attending class is a voluntary act, just as is attending college, and they therefore treat seriously the way in which they invest their time. For this reason these students demand a lot from their professors, but they also place equal demands on themselves and don't sit around like passive vessels waiting for someone else to fill them up with knowledge. Many students complete their entire undergraduate program without ever gaining this kind of autonomy over their academic life. Some take on this kind of personal responsibility only quite a bit later, perhaps in graduate school or after they have been working for a while.

A second example to illustrate autonomy, and one that pertains directly to the subject of this book, relates to the degree to which young adults feel they own and are in full control of their intimate sexual relationships. Let's say that you were in what you considered a stable, loving, long-term sexually intimate relationship, in which you and your lover slept together most or all of the time. Would you expect to sleep together if you visited your parents for a weekend?

I frequently ask my students this question, and invariably get replies ranging from a simple "Yes" to "You gotta be kidding!" Here are some of the typical responses young people give to explain why they would not expect to sleep with their lover on a visit home:

♣ "If my mother knew I was sleeping with my partner she'd kill me, so what do you think would happen if I tried to get away with it in my own house?"

♣ "If I were to ask my parents whether it would be O.K. for me to sleep with my girlfriend, which I really can't see myself doing, they would probably say something like, 'As long as this is our house you can follow our rules, which means that sleeping with your girlfriend in your own bed is out of the question!'"

♣ "My parents have different values than I do, which don't happen to include pre-marital sex, and I think I should respect their wishes. After all, it's their house."

♣ "My parents probably suspect that I sleep with my boyfriend, but they've never come right out and asked me about it and I've never told them. I think we both play this little game, and as long as they don't have to see it they won't complain about it. But if I wanted to sleep with my boyfriend at home it would probably lead to more of a hassle than it's worth. What's the big deal? It's only for a weekend."

♣ "I still depend on my parents for financial support, and if I asked them about sleeping with my lover they'd say, 'Oh, you just go right ahead and do that, Little Miss Independent. And since you think you're old enough to have sex, you certainly must be old enough to pay your own way in life.' So I can't see risking losing that financial support just to be able to be with my lover for a couple of nights."

These responses say a lot about autonomy, and illustrate the ambivalent feelings many young people have over whether or not to be open with their parents about their own sexuality. I challenge these individuals with the idea that if they are unwilling to be up front with their parents about the fact that they are in loving, sexually intimate relationships, it's not fair for them to label their **parents** as prudes. I suggest that the problem here is not of their parents' invention, but is rather one they create themselves. This analysis is always unsettling to these individuals, probably because they assume I will be on their side in this issue and help rescue them from having to face the matter squarely. Let's look at what lies beneath the surface of this rather common concern of young adults.

We can begin by considering how the parents of these students might **actually** feel about having them sleep with their lover when home for a visit. Many parents would in fact be just as adamant about this matter as their children have said they would be—some maybe even more so. And it might well be that some parents would actually threaten to cut off their financial support over this issue. I have no reason to dispute the idea that some parents get completely bent out of shape over the sexual behaviors of their children. I also know that many parents disapprove of what they consider to be the open sexual climate that prevails within the youth culture, and do not feel it is right or proper for young adults to engage in genital sexual activities unless they are married.

On the other hand I also know that few of the parents I just described have taken much if any responsibility for educating their children about human sexuality, and in fact have often done their best to keep them in the dark about sex. And these are the same parents who make pious statements to their children about the importance of being honest, of feeling free to come to them with their problems, and of the value of establishing relationships that are caring and loving. It is often the case that the very same parents who preach about honesty in general would rather have their children conduct their sexual relationships behind their backs, and look the other way in order to avoid the truth of their children's lives. But just because they are parents doesn't mean they should be able to have it both ways. If your parents act this way toward you they are being hypocritical, something which has no doubt already occurred to you. But because you love them (or fear them) you may let them get away with this manipulation of reality.

I mentioned in an earlier chapter that it's difficult to come down too hard on parents about their rather parochial views toward sex when you realize that **their** parents didn't help them figure this all out, and that they were probably reared much more strictly than you were. On the other hand, nothing prevents children from attempting to drag their parents into the twentieth century. What this means is that rather than whining about how provincial and conservative your parents are, you are free to assert your own position on an issue like bringing a lover home. You are free to seize responsibility for your own development, rather than assume you are incapable of making such a fundamental decision in your own behalf.

If you read between the lines of the rationalizations young people often make about an issue like taking a lover home, it's hard to escape feeling that they are trying to **protect** their parents. It's like, "Oh, our poor parents have so much to worry about, why burden them with one more thing, especially since it's something we can live without." If I believed that young adults' concerns were really as altruistically motivated as they make them sound I might agree with them. But I don't believe for one minute that most young adults feel they are doing their parents a favor by keeping secret the facts of their own intimate lives. I think these people are doing

themselves a favor by avoiding this kind of sexual discussion because they know full well that it might lead to a very dicey confrontation with their parents, something they want to avoid like the plague.

> If you are living in a sexually intimate relationship and you are unable or unwilling to live the relationship openly with your parents, I think you are copping out, and rather than protecting your parents, you are protecting your own butt.

"But," you protest with great indignation, "what are we supposed to do, **demand** to sleep with a lover when we go home? You're probably going to say we should tell our parents we're going to do whatever we want to do, whether they like it or not?" No, I would never advise you to take this kind of immature and selfish approach. But if you are trying to become autonomous, which is to say **self-governing**, you **can** take some very important steps toward asserting yourself as a maturing young adult. The most important way you could begin this process would be to discuss with your parents the substance of your own developing sexuality as it is expressing itself through your intimate relationships. A script for such a discussion might look something like this.

"Mom and Dad, I've been thinking a lot lately about how you have always encouraged us to talk with you when we are concerned about something, and I've been thinking that I'd like to talk with you about my intimate relationships. This is a pretty scary idea for most people my age, and it is for me, too.

"You know that Tom and I have been going out for about six months now, but I've never told you very much about our relationship or how much we both treasure it. You might have suspected that Tom and I have sex, and we do, but it's important for you to understand that sex is only one of a number of significant parts of our relationship. For the past six months we've spent most of our time together, and usually sleep together at Tom's or my apartment. One of the really nice things about our relationship is that we are learning how to combine working with being in an intimate relationship, which we think is an important thing for any adult to be able to do.

"I'm going to be coming home for a visit in a few weeks, and I'd like Tom to come with me so you can get to know one another better and because he's really eager to meet you. I know that you might not like the idea of me and Tom sleeping together while we're home, but I think it's important for all of us to be honest about this relationship, and a very important and natural part of it is that we **do** sleep together. Tom and I both accept full responsibility for our relationship, and since we feel very good about it we don't want to play games with you or anyone else. I'd like to know how you feel about this before I speak with Tom again."

Now in reality you probably wouldn't lay out the issue quite this smoothly, especially if you were anxious about how your parents might respond. But the important idea here is that if you were to say something like this to your parents you would be acting like a responsible adult, and would be doing something that you hoped would strengthen the relationship you have with them. You wouldn't be talking with them like this because you wanted to hurt their feelings or force them to see things your way. A statement like this makes it clear that your goal is honest communication, and it also says that you love, trust, and respect your parents enough to share something with them that you consider to be an essential part of your life. **Having opened up the topic and laid it squarely on the table, the ball is now in your parents' court.**

It's now up to your parents to take up your invitation to dialogue, and how they respond is their responsibility, not yours. Some parents will be totally opposed to this idea, and will lay down the law with the "not in our house" routine. Some parents will say they don't approve of what you are doing, but will agree to go along with the plan and "see what happens." Others will be very proud to hear their child present their case so well, and will be fully supportive of the relationship.

"But," you ask, "suppose my parents just slam the door on the whole discussion. What am I supposed to do then?"

In this worst case scenario I can see why you might feel like you were back to square one, but you aren't. Having given your parents an opportunity to respond to you as an adult, you are now in the position of exercising a range of options related to a family visit. You could cancel your plans to visit. You and Tom could visit, and not sleep together during the weekend. Or you and Tom could visit with your parents but stay together in a nearby motel, much as you might do if you were visiting friends who had limited accommodations. This last suggestion is probably the most disconcerting of the three, because your immediate reaction is probably that if you did that **you would be spiting your parents.** No, that is not what you would be doing. In fact, this approach would allow both you **and** your parents to have what each wants.

This solution allows both sides to maintain their integrity, and to live out their values as they feel they should. What then can be the harm of this arrangement?

Are you thinking that I'm a dreamer to suggest that young adults can realistically be expected to deal this directly with their parents? Maybe. But if this is the case it's not because they are incapable of doing it, it's because they don't feel ready to act as autonomous individuals. You can decide to sleep in separate bedrooms when you visit your parents and still be considered highly autonomous. But if you are unable to even talk with your parents about your sexually intimate relationship, you have a ways to go.

For many of the students that I work with, the university system really works against them becoming autonomous intimate persons. This idea really struck home for me recently as I spoke with a group of students in one of our residence halls. We had been talking about the kinds of problems these students were experiencing related to sex and intimacy, and a common one that emerged was that of sexual privacy. Privacy was a concern both for those students who wanted to have sex with a partner and who had difficulty finding places to do this, as well as for roommates of students whose lovers spent the night, producing an awkward situation for everyone involved. In our discussion I suggested that colleges and universities could be doing a great deal more than they are to help students learn about intimacy and develop satisfying intimate relationships. A major way for this to occur would be for the university to be supportive of young people like Bill and Meredith, and provide housing and programming for couples who wanted to live together in the residence halls. But I argued that the university could take a much broader approach to meeting the intimacy needs of their students by providing the following kinds of options:

❀ All residence halls could maintain some rooms for use by students of that hall who wanted to spend short amounts of time with a partner. These rooms would be available for a modest fee, and might be utilized both by students whose lovers were visiting as well as by those who were in the process of beginning a sexual relationship.

❀ Some halls could be designed for students who wanted to live together but would utilize the university dining facilities for most of their meals. These halls would provide active programming for the residents, and would assist them in developing and maintaining their relationships.

There would also be help for couples who were experiencing stress and conflict, and this would include assistance
in splitting up if this were desired.

✿ A third option would be apartments or town houses in which
couples could live together much as they might if they were
living off campus. An important difference, however,
would be that the university would offer active programming for such students focused on building relationships,
perhaps as a required component of such an arrangement.

In each of these three examples, the university would be
giving sanction to sexual activities and sexual relationships, and
would be acknowledging that it had a responsibility to assist its
students in developing skills for this aspect of life. At the same time
this approach would help validate the idea that it is desirable to
maintain a balance between work and intimate relationships, and
would also help create new norms around what kinds of sexual
relationships are considered healthy for young adults. And these
options would encourage young people in becoming autonomous
because they would lend credence to the idea that it is important
to take personal responsibility for the development of one's
intimate relationships. They would ease the transition between
dependence and interdependence, and perhaps most important,
they would represent a public statement of the value that intimate
relationships bring to society. While the initial reaction of many
parents and the community-at-large to this proposal would be to
go into shock, after such a system functioned for a few years most
people would accept it just as they have accepted co-education and
pre-marital sex.

But if a university does little to foster independence,
beyond its influence lies a much more global set of societal
attitudes that make it difficult for young adults to become self-
governing. Much of American society is very confused over how to
deal with today's young adults. On one hand, you may enjoy the
privileges of voting, serving your country in the military services,
entering into legal contracts, marrying, needing no one's consent
to obtain birth control or an abortion, signing a lease or borrowing
money from a bank. But on the other hand, unless you are twenty-
one you cannot purchase alcohol. And regardless of your age, if
you are a college student or in the military service there are many
things related to your living arrangements over which you have
little control. While a college may look the other way from its
knowledge that its students are having sex in the residence halls,
it draws the line over permitting people to live openly in campus

housing with their sexual partner, unless of course they are married.

So colleges and universities do little more than reflect the values held by the larger society, and most colleges are not about to rock the boat over something like sexual intimacy. The slug-like pace of innovation related to student life on most campuses illustrates the political nature of these institutions, but also makes it clear that universities don't really consider education about intimacy and relationships to be part of their mission. And this is unfortunate, because providing this kind of education would not put a heavy burden on the financial resources of most colleges, and could go a long way toward preparing young people for long-term relationships. But in the absence of such institutional support, young adults will have to seize their own opportunities for becoming self governing with respect to their intimate relationships, an idea I will discuss more fully in a later chapter on intimacy.

How To Tell Whether You Are Sexually Autonomous

You discuss your sexual feelings with your partner before beginning to interact sexually.

You know or are willing to explore the kinds of sexual behaviors that you enjoy participating in.

You can talk with your partner about how you are feeling while interacting sexually.

You engage in sexual activities only when you truly want to. This does not mean your sexual desires must always match those of your partner's.

You can ask your partner for what you want while interacting sexually.

You are able to live out your sexual relationship in a public way, with friends and family.

You accept responsibility for contraception and sexual disease prevention.

CHAPTER 9

━━━━◀◀♦▶▶━━━━

What is This Thing Called Intimacy?

Most of the young people I work with did not come to college with the express purpose of forming an intimate relationship with someone who might become their spouse or soul mate. People may be open to the possibility that this kind of relationship will develop, but most young adults are not consciously seeking such a partner when they arrive on campus.

But because they may not be consciously seeking intimate relationships doesn't mean that young adults don't devote a tremendous amount of energy coping with their **desires** for intimacy and connection to others. One of the most telling indications I have from young people which indicates their wish for intimate relationships is revealed in the results of a survey question that asks whether an individual is now in an intimate relationship whose duration is longer than six weeks. While I don't know whether those reporting they are currently in such a relationship are **satisfied** with them, there seems little doubt that a great majority of these respondents see intimate relationships as something they desire. And considering the fact that we are bombarded with images of intimacy on a daily basis, it's no wonder that so many of us have such a strong yearning for intimacy. In this chapter I will describe the reasons why the roots of intimacy are so deep and have such a pervasive influence on our lives, as well

Are you Now in an Intimate Relationship Whose Duration is Six Weeks or Longer?		
RESPONSE	FEMALE	MALES
YES	51	44
NO, BUT I WOULD LIKE TO BE	43	42
NO, AND I DON'T WISH TO BE AT THIS TIME	6	14

as examine some of the most significant barriers to creating intimate relationships. The following three chapters will focus on how intimate relationships are formed and develop, as well as explore a variety of factors that contribute to their breakdown. The present chapter then deals with the roots of our need for intimate relationships; the next three with the beginnings, middles, and endings of these relationships.

We are a society that is fascinated with intimacy. It may not be too strong a statement to say we are **obsessed** with intimacy. Magazines like **Cosmopolitan, Redbook, Seventeen, Sassy,** and **Ladies' Home Journal** have cover stories in every issue that offer advice on how women can create and maintain more satisfying intimate relationships, and often have little quizzes designed to help readers assess their "Intimacy Quotient." Products from perfume to lawn mowers are advertised with copy that often suggests that the use of these products will enhance the buyer's sex and intimacy appeal. Even cigarettes, whose potential for death and misery are well known, are advertised by models who are beautiful and healthy, and who are posed to convey the idea that their smoking behavior is sexy and likely to lead to intimacy. A myriad of businesses flourish around helping people connect with others who share their interest in forming intimate relationships, and the personals columns of newspapers and magazines are teeming with hopeful, sometimes desperate ads placed by people who seem willing to fish for a trophy catch with small hooks but lots of fresh bait. And while it's true that almost half of marriages end in divorce, most of those who divorce, especially men, remarry, and do so rather soon after the official end of their previous marriage.

What is there about intimacy that drives people to spend such large amounts of time and money searching for it? Why are so many young adults having sexual encounters of short duration and low satisfaction, rather than forming committed relationships that meet their emotional as well as physical needs? Why is loneliness such a prevalent complaint among young men and women? What explains the increasing numbers of young people seeking counseling because they feel isolated, alone, and alienated from themselves and their own personal values? Why, after spending years in troubled and unsatisfying marriages, perhaps struggling for as long as a decade to get out of them, are so many people so quick to enter new intimate relationships? And why is it that so many products are advertised with the promise of increased intimacy?

There is no simple answer to these questions, of course, because intimacy is a complex and multifaceted phenomenon. But I believe that **a central reason why we are so consumed by matters of intimacy is that many of us lack the benefits that intimate relationships afford**, and this absence of meaningful connections to others leads us to suffer in some way. Not having a clear idea of what we need to do in order to establish the kinds of relationships we truly desire, we are vulnerable to quick-fix solutions and the seductive messages of advertising. And in addition to lacking the skills and knowledge necessary to create satisfying intimate relationships, there is a substantial list of reasons that people often cite to explain why they actively **avoid** intimacy. Fears about intimacy range from having to disclose hidden feelings about oneself, to being rejected, to the threat of losing one's sense of personal identity, none of which are minor or trivial concerns.

Living in the midst of a high-tech world, it is very difficult for many of us to accept the idea that intimacy and intimate relationships do not result from the application of technological innovations. The promises of success and wealth exert a very powerful influence on people, especially on those individuals whose educational preparation often provides them access to high paying jobs and high status careers. But life in the fast lane is simply incompatible with satisfying close relationships, because such relationships require a sizable investment of time and energy, factors which compete against rather than complement the life styles of those in the fast lane. What tends to happen in real life is that many people compromise their needs for intimacy more readily than their desires for wealth and status, a choice which predictably results in unfulfilling and problematic close relationships. And this process of compromise begins early in life, and is well established by young adulthood.

In order to understand why our culture is experiencing something of a crisis around matters of intimacy it will be helpful to explore what intimacy means, and what purposes intimate relationships serve for human beings. Then we can look at the youth sub-culture as a means of understanding why so many young people are presently frustrated in meeting their needs for intimacy. At the risk of offending your sensibilities and in order to focus your attention on this issue, I'm going to make the following brazen generalization:

> **Much of the sexual interaction that young people engage in detracts from, rather than enhances, their chances for forming and maintaining enduring intimate relationships.**

I'm going to expand on this idea later in this chapter, but I wanted to introduce it here because for many young people sexual interaction serves as a substitute for what they really crave, which are the benefits derived from intimate relationships. I assume that by now you realize I have no moral objections **per se** to sexual interactions between young adults, and therefore you understand that the statement in the box is not a moral condemnation of non-marital sexual expression.

At the very outset, it's clear that the word intimacy means many different things to different people. For some people, the concept of intimacy is always linked to some form of sexual contact between two or more individuals, whereas for others, intimacy suggests more of an emotional than sexual connection. As a means of opening up discussion about intimacy with young people, I sometimes ask them to brainstorm words that they associate with the terms sex and intimacy. Here is a typical list of these words.

Sex			Intimacy		
hot	action	wet	understanding	touch	warmth
orgasm	intercourse		affection	nurturing	love
performance	spontaneity		vulnerability	trust	mutuality
pleasure	arousal	orgasm	interdependence		acceptance
relief	personal	genitals	communication		caring

The difference between the kinds of words in these two lists is readily apparent: the words on the sex list tend to focus on physical actions or reactions of the body, are goal directed and appear to be genitally and orgasmically oriented; the words on the intimacy list are more diffuse, pertain to the whole person, and suggest that relatedness is a high value.

The word intimate derives from the Latin **intimus**, which means innermost. It stands to reason, then, that intimacy is a process by which individuals try to share and explore one another's thoughts, feelings, and behaviors, and do so in ways that are aimed at getting to the core or innermost levels of these elements. What people seem to be seeking are relationships in which they can make deeply personal disclosures and have trust and confidence that the responses to these disclosures will be ones of affirmation and understanding. When these kinds of disclosures are made, and when there is some kind of verbal or non-verbal response which respectfully acknowledges the nature and significance of the disclosure, an **intimate experience** has occurred. Many individuals feel that if a relationship manifests **recurring intimate experiences over a period of time,** it can rightfully be thought of as an **intimate relationship**.

But anyone who has been in an intimate relationship knows that this kind of relationship requires a lot more than the recurrence of intimate experiences over time. Intimate experiences don't typically happen because partners in a relationship are trying to make them happen, but rather may occur when the many conditions needed for intimacy are present. And even in the most satisfying of relationships, the condition of intimacy occurs only sporadically. Intimacy itself is a very subjective entity; while it has the potential of **strengthening** a relationship, it is not really a central **component** of an intimate relationship. So it is very likely that when people say they would like to be in intimate relationships, they are asking for relationships that do much more than provide them with occasional moments of intimacy.

ACCEPTANCE:
The Core Benefit of Intimate Relationships

I have tried to capture the central benefits of intimate relationships in the acronym **ACCEPTANCE**. To me the word acceptance sums up nicely the spirit of what we seek in an intimate relationship, and the acronym **ACCEPTANCE** delineates how we benefit from this kind of relationship. As you read through the following box, note how each element implies a reciprocal process—that is, not only do **you** benefit when a partner provides you with a particular benefit, but you also benefit when you provide **them** with a similar benefit.

ACCEPTANCE: The Core Benefit of Intimate Relationships

A •	**Attachment.** A feeling of being deeply connected to another human being. Our need for attachment grows out of the earliest trusting connections we had with our parents. The bond we sense through being attached to another person is not easily broken.
C	**Caring.** It feels good to care for others, and to be cared for by them. Caring for someone else allows us to feel competent; being cared for leads to feelings of self-worth.
C	**Companionship.** Spending time with someone who appreciates us and has fun in our company staves off loneliness, and provides us with opportunities to share our thoughts and feelings. Companionship includes doing things actively with another as well as just being in their presence, such as by spending a quiet evening reading together in front of a cozy fire.
E	**Empathy.** When someone empathizes with us they are letting us know that they understand us. Adolescents often say that nobody understands them except their closest friends; the kind of understanding they are seeking is that which helps them feel their ideas, values, beliefs and behaviors are worthy and legitimate.

P	**Practical.** By being able to pool their economic resources, individuals in intimate relationships ease the practical matter of having to pay for housing and living expenses. There is also a practical economy of time derived by not having to search constantly for someone to meet one's needs for intimacy.
T	**Touch.** When another person touches us, whether it is by a kind word or deed or by physically touching us, it not only feels good but also helps reaffirm to us that we exist. Touching another person affirms our own competence, and feels good to us as well.
A	**Appreciation.** People with whom we have intimate relationships recognize our special talents and attributes that others are unfamiliar with, and this recognition enhances our self-esteem.
N	**Nurturance.** Intimate partners nurture our dreams and aspirations, and help us have confidence in our ability to take on new and challenging ventures. They encourage us to live out our vision of the future.
C	**Counsel.** Having a person we can trust for good advice and assistance in solving our day-to-day problems gives us the good feeling that there is an empathic fellow-traveller who has our best interests at heart. Being able to bounce an idea off a good friend is sometimes all we need in order to feel confident that the idea has merit.
E	**Efficacy.** People who function well in intimate relationships feel efficacious—that is, they feel competent and empowered. This kind of empowerment tends to carry over into all other aspects of a person's life, and produces feelings of strength and mastery.

I'm sure there are other benefits to intimate relationships, but to me these are the central ones. It may have occurred to you as you read through this list that these core benefits of intimate relationships also lie at the heart of healthy families and close friendships. Another way of saying this is that healthy families and friendships are ones in which the relationships are intimate.

It is probably safe to say that our desire for intimate connection to another person has its roots in that earliest attachment we had to our parents as infants. Most infants begin learning from the moment of their birth that life is predictable: when they are hungry, they are fed; when they have a dirty diaper, they are changed; when they are cold, someone warms them; and when they want to feel nurtured, someone holds them, talks or sings to them, tosses them in the air, smiles and plays with them. This kind of predictability in an infant's life is a precursor to the development of a sense of trust, which is easy to understand if you consider the idea that being able to trust someone means being able to predict their responses.

Although as we get older we become increasingly adept at caring for ourselves, we retain the memories of how good it felt to be cared for in such a total way when we were infants, and we continue to desire a similar sense of predictable care from another adult. With increasing maturity, however, we also become aware that caring **for** another person is the reciprocal of being **cared for**, and we come to understand that not only did we benefit by being cared for as infants, but also that our parents took great joy in meeting our needs. But unlike infants, who are totally **dependent** on others for their care, adults construct relationships that are **inter-dependent**; two adults, therefore, have the potential for a kind of mutuality impossible in the parent-infant bond. Pretty much irrespective of what happened to us from the time we were infants until we reached young adulthood, most of us live our adult lives in search of that feeling of unconditional love we experienced as infants. Relatively few people are able to create and maintain adult intimate relationships that mirror the way they felt as infants, but this fact does not deter them from trying. It is very important to realize, however, that our desire for intimate relationships is not only normal, but it is also a healthy desire since the benefits we gain through intimate relationships clearly strengthen and enrich our lives in general. So if intimate relationships are healthy and desirable and if most people want to be in them, why are they so hard to create and maintain? Again, a very good question, with no simple answer.

Why Are Intimate Relationships So Elusive?

There are many reasons why some people resist forming intimate relationships, while others have enormous difficulty forming them even when they are greatly desired. At the very outset, it's helpful to realize that there is a basic tension within human beings between individuality and relatedness, a kind of tension that exists throughout our entire lifetime. You can probably recall instances when you were so involved in a project or in attaining a particular goal that you felt very little need for much or any human interaction. You are also aware that during such periods you may have felt very alive and healthy, and were able to carry on your life in all its diverse and responsible ways. Your need for intimate connection to others may have been quite low during such periods. But it is quite likely also true that there have been other periods in your life when what you most wanted were the benefits you derive from intimate relationships, and in general sought out connections with others rather than isolation. And no doubt there have also been times when there appeared to be a comfortable balance between these two basic features of human life, when you felt in harmony with your needs for individuation and relatedness.

But beyond the basic tension of relatedness and individuation that individuals experience throughout their lives lies a set of factors that, taken as a whole, can make the task of forming and maintaining intimate relationships appear to be overwhelming. I'd like to discuss four of these influences, which seem to me to be the ones that are most responsible for creating so many problems for us in this regard. Broadly speaking, these influences are societal values in general, family mobility, divorce, and the changing roles of men and women.

Societal Values

Various elements in society act to color the way we learn about and value intimacy and intimate relationships. Almost anywhere you look you will find individuals or institutions which in some way act to shape the way people learn about intimacy and the conditions under which intimate relationships are thought to be desirable. Social norms, parents, religious organizations, business and industry, and even your peer group all contribute to the images you have formed about intimate relationships.

Adult society in general seems to me to have very mixed feelings about the role that intimate relationships might play in human life. On the one hand, most adults would probably **say** that intimate relationships were important. But on the other, few would be able to tell you much about the benefits they themselves were deriving from intimate relationships, because few adults really are reaping very many of these benefits. Like many other areas of adult life in America, this is another one in which "do as we say" is the guiding principle. It may sound radical, but I believe there is a kind of tacit conspiracy among adults to deny children and youth the truth of what adult life is like regarding intimate relationships.

It should not be surprising that adults are generally ignorant about intimate relationships, given the very short period of time in our history during which intimacy between spouses has been considered a valued aspect of marriage. It has only been within the last fifty years that married couples have begun to discuss openly the possibilities of their relationships being truly mutual, so most adults today did not learn about intimacy from parents who themselves had enjoyed the benefits of intimate relationships. But being ignorant does not seem to me to justify the way society in general, and parents in particular, deceive children about such an important and powerful potential in life.

Consider for a minute some of the things parents and society in general tell young people about intimacy and intimate relationships:

- ♣ A sexually intimate relationship is a wonderful aspect of life, but such relationships should occur only between adults, preferably those who are married to each other.
- ♣ It's a good idea during the young adult years to go out with a number of different people so you will be able to select, not just settle for a partner.
- ♣ It's not a good idea to start going out with one person seriously in your late teens or early twenties, because to do so might interfere with your education or career plans.
- ♣ It's best to defer selecting a partner until you have finished your education; there will be time enough later for intimate relationships.
- ♣ There is a lot more to a good relationship than sex; good relationships take a lot of hard work.
- ♣ Things are different today than they were when your parents were young adults.

I feel strongly that people who make claims like this are terribly misguided. While they no doubt have good intentions, their advice is badly flawed. The fact is that there is no evidence to support most of these claims about young adult life and intimate relationships. If this were not bad enough, many adults insist on repeating these myths even though their own lives give lie to the truth of the matter. The truth of the matter is that many of the people who make these claims are, and have been, living lives virtually devoid of the benefits of intimacy and intimate relationships. They are therefore not reliable sources for advice about intimacy.

I certainly agree that there is a lot more to intimate relationships than sex, and that relationships take hard work. But even in their statements about sex and hard work most parents misrepresent both their own feelings about how sex may contribute to intimate relationships, as well as just what kind of hard work is involved. They often imply that **they** have done the hard work, but in most cases what they may really mean by this is that they have stayed together in an unsatisfying relationship because they were unable to accept or determine an appropriate alternative. In addition, they may never have really enjoyed a fulfilling sexual life with their partner, and still harbor many repressive attitudes toward sexual expression.

Yes, things **are** different from when your parents were your age. But the most pressing issues you face as a young adult today have more in common with those your parents faced when they were your age than they differ from them. The reason for this is that young adults continue to be young adults, and the central issues for individuals this age are developmental in nature. Thus the issues tend to remain quite similar over time.

So why do parents insist on passing on this kind of nonsense? Lots of reasons. For starters, they cling to the idea that maybe they **are** right, even if their own lives tell them they are wrong. It's hard to give up old ways of looking at the world, and this is especially true if you believe that if you screw up in your advice your own child might get hurt. This leads to a second reason: they are afraid that if their children become involved in intimate relationships before they complete their educations they will drop out of school, get married, have four kids, and be doomed to a subsistence lifestyle. Many parents would consider this kind of outcome to be a colossal waste of money. Their money. Some parents probably worry like this because this was the fate they suffered, and they want their children to have a better crack at life. It's hard to blame parents who feel this way, even though they are still misguided in their beliefs of what is needed in order to have a satisfying intimate relationship.

It stands to reason, then, that although they may be criticized for not being able to build a decent automobile, American adults know an enormous amount about how to work hard, and they are eager to pass this knowledge on to their children. Many American parents hope that if their children can obtain the college education they were not fortunate enough to acquire, they will have more options available to them in their work life and will therefore not have to scrape so desperately in order to have a decent life. It is this kind of thinking that informs parents' counsel to their children about the importance of deferring intimate relationships until a work life is well established.

This parental and societal advice is badly flawed, however, because it implies that not only do adults know what is needed for a satisfactory work life, but also that they are equally knowledge-able about the prerequisites for a satisfying intimate life. But they aren't! The evidence for adults' inability to create and maintain healthy intimate relationships litters the landscape of this country, and shows little sign of abating in the near future. The incidence of divorce, a sense of loneliness and isolation felt by many marriage partners, alcohol and substance abuse, domestic violence, sexual abuse and assault, suicide, hate crimes, and demands for psychological services all testify in some way to our inability as a culture to come to grips with the horrendous consequences that result from unmet needs for intimate connection.

Those with the most influence in our society tend to give lip service to the value of close relationships; what they seem to value most is wealth, status, and things. Re-ordering societal values to place intimate relationships on the same level as work will perhaps become the agenda of the next few generations. I hope so. But in the meantime it is vital that as a young adult you begin to look for ways of overcoming what you have learned about intimacy that may make this task more difficult, if not impossible. A good way to start this process is to realize that many adults lack credibility when it comes to good advice about intimacy; their wisdom about work may be useful, but about healthy intimate relationships they are essentially without a clue.

Family Mobility

When I was three years old in 1941 my parents bought their first house in a small suburban town in New Jersey. Like virtually all my friends and classmates, I lived in the same house until I graduated from college and went off into the adult world. Even as a child I knew that "new kids" in town faced some real problems when they tried to break into such a tightly structured and stable community. In hindsight, I can see how much I and my friends benefitted from being able to experience our childhood and youth in such a continuous fashion. Geographic stability provides children and adolescents with a tremendous resource they can draw on in coping with the many changes that are occurring in their own internal lives, and adds a measure of predictability to a world filled with uncertainty.

Families today are in general much more mobile than they were in the era immediately following World War II. My own two children have lived in New Jersey and Vermont in a total of six houses in three different communities. Our family is often described as unusual because we have moved so **infrequently**, and compared to some people this is certainly true. I know a number of young people who have moved fifteen to twenty times before they were eighteen years old, and these were often moves involving considerable distances. The impact of this kind of mobility on American families is substantial, and has a direct bearing on the problems we have in forming close relationships. The effects of mobility take a particularly heavy toll on children and adolescents, but adults, especially women, are also affected by frequent moves.

It remains to be seen whether human beings can fully adapt to the kind of mobility American families have been experiencing since the early fifties, but I suspect that this kind of adaptation will be slow in coming.

How does family mobility contribute directly to the difficulty we have in forming close relationships? In a number of ways. First of all, children look to their parents to provide the ultimate kind of stability to their lives. If parents are uncertain of where they might be living next year, they themselves are not able to count on a sense of continuity in their own lives, let alone provide that continuity for their children. Second, children who move with some frequency learn that there is a danger in forming close relationships which they know will end with the next move. The pain associated with ending a relationship means that many individuals, both children and adults, become much more cautious about getting too deeply involved with new friends, although they may become very good at establishing superficial relationships quickly.

From the perspectives of children and their mothers, moving often appears to be something over which they have little, if any, control. Families typically move because Dad has been transferred or seeks a different job in another part of the country. Although men are not always enamored with the idea of frequent moving, families usually move to accommodate Dad's career development. If mothers and their children are left feeling powerless in the face of such moves they are likely to become depressed or angry, two conditions that interfere tremendously with the conduct of healthy intimate relationships. When they move into a new community, mothers and their children are largely left to their own devices to build new friendships, and frequent dislocation puts such family members under tremendous stress. Fathers experience similar demands in making new friends, but for the most part they enjoy the advantage of moving into a well established network of fellow workers with whom it is easier to create a kind of instant rapport based on shared work values and common backgrounds.

When children have their close friendships severed because of family moves, they lose a form of predictability in their life that can seriously threaten their overall sense of well-being. Predictability is crucial to establishing trust in another person, and in this instance, the predictability is not imperiled by the breach of trust but by the loss of the relationship.

Divorce

The effects of divorce on intimate relationships are similar to those produced by family mobility but are even more intense, and have a far broader sphere of influence. Whether or not your own parents are divorced, as a young adult there is no way you can escape being touched in some way by the effects that divorce have visited on our society. There is an almost fifty percent chance that your parents are divorced. If they are not, there remains a high probability that at some time you will go out with or form an intimate relationship with someone whose parents are divorced. So from this perspective it is not a matter of **whether**, but rather **in what ways** the presence of divorce in our culture will affect your relationships. To the extent that you can understand more clearly what impact divorce has on children and families you will be better able to appreciate the effects that divorce have on the dynamics of intimate relationships.

During the past twenty years there has been a great deal of research on divorce, some of the best of which was done by Dr. Judith S. Wallerstein and her colleagues at the Center for the Family in Transition in San Francisco. Dr. Wallerstein's book **Second Chances: Men, Women, and Children a Decade after Divorce** (New York: Ticknor & Fields, 1989), is one of the most concise and thorough summaries of the ways in which divorce affects children and families, and especially if your parents are divorced, I urge you read this book.

Children of divorce must confront a cruel paradox: as much as they may strive to create intimate relationships that will endure and be healthy they are at substantial risk of developing marriages that are no more successful than were those of their parents. This is not to say that if your parents' intimate relationship failed that yours will, too. But there are many reasons why children whose adult model of intimacy was seriously flawed are likely to repeat this history in their own relationships. This fact helps explain why it is important to have a good understanding of the effects of divorce, whether or not your own parents are divorced.

Children of divorce invariably vow not to make the same mistakes their parents did and are often convinced that, unlike their parents, they will be able to chose a partner with whom they can have a happy, committed relationship. And given what we know about divorce and children, it's easy to understand why they feel this way. But what this fear does for many such young adults is to make them hyper-cautious about forming intimate relationships, and not infrequently leads them to develop standards for a partner that are unrealistic and misguided. In a sense these individuals are in search for a perfect match, yet because they never had a good model of effective intimacy to guide them they really don't know what to look for.

Earlier in this chapter I discussed the whole issue of how flawed parental models of intimacy, even in intact marriages, make it difficult for children to gain a realistic concept of how to behave in an intimate relationship. In divorced families this problem is compounded to a significant degree, because in these families the crucial parental model may be totally absent from the scene. And because of our tradition of assigning custody to mothers, it is more often the father who has been missing. One common manifestation of this absence is that young women whose parents are divorced often seek out older men for partners, men who will care for and nurture them in ways their own fathers never did. And the market for older men being what it is, it is not too difficult for these women to find men willing to oblige them in this respect. Of course there is nothing wrong in wanting your partner to care for and nurture you. But it's one thing to care for a partner as an equal, quite another to care for them as you would nurture a child. Not only is the power of the relationship seriously imbalanced, but equally important the challenge of intimate relationships is to create a loving bond with a peer, not a parent figure.

All of this does not mean that if your parents are divorced or if your partner's parents are divorced, that you are doomed to a life of failed intimacy. But I think that what we have been learning about divorce over the past few years does suggest that all of us are touched in some way by the effects of divorce, and that young adults especially are wise to think and talk about how these effects may influence their own relationships. Although there is a strong tendency for children of divorce to deny just how powerful an influence this event has been for them in terms of intimacy, time spent in discussing with one's partner the whole range of issues related to divorce will be time well spent. It might also be very helpful to share concerns about divorce with a counselor, and to join support groups for young people whose parents are divorced. For some people, young adulthood may be a very good time to work through issues about divorce that remain unresolved, and to gain a better understanding of what constitutes proper caution in partner selection.

Changing Roles of Men and Women

Of all the factors in our society that influence the way we go about forming intimate relationships, our gender role learnings probably have the most pervasive effect, and are the most difficult to overcome. In fact, our gender learnings deeply color the preceding three issues I just discussed, so it is almost as if matters of gender role are the threads that weave together the entire fabric of all our interpersonal relationships. In an earlier chapter on sexual intercourse, I wrote at length about how gender learnings contribute to specific sexual attitudes and behaviors. And in the chapter on childhood, I described in considerable detail the many ways parents transmit messages about gender to their children. So in this section dealing with the barriers to intimacy I need only outline a few significant historical beliefs about gender roles, and then describe some of the ways in which recent changes in these roles directly affect intimate relationships.

Throughout history, males and females have been taught to fulfill certain roles according to their gender. No one knows just why there has been this division of roles, but it is probably safe to assume that some of them may have grown out of human needs, while others took root as a result of the desire on the part of one gender to control the other, or at least for one gender to benefit in ways that the other gender did not. Far back in time it may have been advantageous for the species to divide its human functions according to gender, and given that most animal behavior is based on survival needs of the species, these kinds of roles may have been absolutely necessary to preserve the species. In the opinions of many contemporary scholars of sex roles, however, such a gender division has really not been truly adaptive for thousands of years. But in evolutionary terms, a thousand years is a drop in the bucket.

In talking with young people over the years I have found that they are more defensive about gender roles than any other issue related to human relationships and sexuality. Although women are usually more cognizant of how small the gains have been in this respect, women and men alike become quite upset when I introduce the notion that gender role learnings interfere with their forming and maintaining healthy intimate relationships. Most young adults hold a deep and abiding belief that gender will not negatively affect their love relationships, and they also believe that issues of gender have been largely remediated as a result of the women's movement. Neither of these beliefs could be farther from the truth.

It was the Industrial Revolution that set the stage for the massive changes that would occur in the way human life was organized, and the ways in which men and women would act out their gender roles. Not only did factory work re-shape the American family, it also gave rise to dramatic changes in gender roles. These changes resulted both from the fact that women and men worked side by side in factories, as well as from the evolving technologies that permitted women especially to exercise roles and options they never before could have anticipated.

Of the many changes that would deeply affect men and women, two are central to an understanding of how gender influences intimate relationships.   The first is that most women today have a paid work life outside of the home, a condition brought on by a number of factors. For example, the amount of real work needed to manage a household has been significantly reduced as a result of modern appliances like washers, dryers, dishwashers, and microwave ovens. Coupled to this idea is the fact that in order to purchase these modern conveniences, as well as to afford the basic costs associated with housing, clothing, food, and education is the need in American families for both parents to be wage earners. So it is true that more women are now in the employed work force than at any other time in our history, and this means that for the first time, women have the potential to reap the same benefits that paid work has always provided to men. Some of these benefits take the form of money, while others are represented by things like job satisfaction and intellectual stimulation.

But because of well-entrenched institutional sexism, most women today continue to earn only about sixty cents for each dollar earned by a male worker with similar qualifications. And women's work in general is still considered to be less valuable than that done by men. In Vermont, for example, well over 90 percent of all day care for children is provided by women, whose average pay is less than the minimum wage. No matter what story the numbers tell, however, the important idea to grasp here is that women's roles have broadened tremendously over the past five decades, and this increase in role flexibility presents both women and men with new challenges as well as possibilities for intimate relationships.

A second significant element to unlocking the options of women has been the advent of safe, inexpensive, highly effective contraception. With the introduction of the pill and IUD, women have become able to control their fertility, and as a result have begun to experience a new sense of sexual freedom. Perhaps more than any other factor, effective contraception has given women control over their reproductive lives for the first time in history.

These changes in gender role options for women, brought about by new opportunities in work and by effective contraception, have acted together to create a whole new ball game in terms of intimate relationships. The most important effect of these options is that men and women now have the possibility of building relationships based on mutuality and shared responsibility rather than on the limited choices permitted by traditional sex roles. But for most women and men, these new opportunities have not been accompanied by new insights into how they might be achieved by couples. And there are few models available to young adults who might provide guidance and wisdom to young lovers about how to negotiate the twisting path of mutual intimacy. It takes a great deal of patience and perseverance for couples to overcome what they have learned about their appropriate gender roles, and to develop new expectations of one another based on shared agreements.

A compounding aspect of changing gender roles is that women are permitted more flexibility in roles than are men. Women are freer to exercise a much broader range of roles than men, a fact that most men are aware of and sometimes feel jealous about. Although society in general is not wild about the idea, it is more supportive of this flexibility in women's roles than it is in supporting such flexibility in men's roles.

A tragic consequence of the increased options of women resulting from role flexibility and contraception is that many men have come to feel inadequate in a social system that is supportive of equality of genders. As a result, these men are angry with women and all things female, and their anger often leads to violent acts, frequently carried out against women and children. A basic explanation of why men act violently toward women is that it makes them angry to think that women might have as much power as they have. What kinds of power? Reproductive power. Sexual power. Economic power. Supervisory power. Religious power. In short, all forms of power that up until this point in history have been the exclusive prerogatives of men.

If you are a well-educated person, you will have far more opportunities than most young adults to shed much of the baggage of your sex role socialization that might inhibit the formation and maintenance of a mutual intimate relationship. This is so because you will have more control over your occupational choices, and because you have had your consciousness raised by reading this book! But as I indicated earlier, a good education alone is not sufficient to overcome a lifetime of daily learning. As a barrier to intimate relationships, your sex role socialization will more than likely be an on-going source of concern throughout your lifetime. I encourage you to think about how your own sex role learnings have already influenced your intimate relationships, and to dis-cuss with your lovers and your friends how you might work together to decrease the impact of this influence.

Sexual Expression and Intimacy:
A Dilemma for Young Adults

At the beginning of this chapter I asserted that much of the sexual interaction young adults engage in **detracts** from, rather than **enhances** their chances for forming and maintaining enduring intimate relationships. Even though I qualified that statement with a reminder that I was not opposed to sexual interaction between young people **per se**, you probably have been wondering why I said this, especially given the fact that I spent a great deal of time in previous chapters elaborating on how you might heighten the enjoyment of your sexual expression. In this final section dealing with the roots of intimacy I will try to clarify this issue, and establish a framework for understanding the links between sex and intimate relationships.

Let's begin with two generalizations about young adults in America today, both of which have a certain element of truth about them. First of all, contemporary young people demand a certain immediacy in the fulfillment of their needs and desires. This immediacy applies to the acquisition of things, like stereos and cars, as well as to the enjoyment of sexual pleasure. Whether you like it or not (you probably don't), I'm sure you are aware that many older adults label most young people today as being "gimme oriented," as in "Gimme this, gimme that. NOW!" If American youth are like this, and I think to a degree they are, it is not their fault. They have acquired this insatiable craving for immediate gratification from their parents, who indulged them throughout their childhood and in fact gave them what they wanted, when they wanted it.

But if your parents are in their forties or fifties, they didn't inherit this trait of indulgence from **their** parents. Their parents experienced the deprivations of the Great Depression and of World War II, so the values your grandparents attempted to transmit were heavily laced with the importance of delaying gratification, of saving for a rainy day, of **saving yourself for the right person!** Young men have never been swayed by this kind of advice in terms of their sexuality, but it has only been since the advent of oral contraception that young women have openly begun to seek sexual fulfillment.

A second generalization is that even though they are young and have relatively little experience with life, many young people today have already bought into the broader societal value placed on immediate gratification. There is a heavy interest in vocational education today, and a high value is placed on using one's education as a means of earning lots of money. So even at a time in their lives when it is appropriate to be forming romantic, passionate love relationships, many young people delude themselves into thinking that there will be a better time for such relationships after a career has been well established. But young adults have sexual needs which cry out for satiation, and within a value system that supports immediate gratification they attempt to gratify their sexual needs through encounters that are devoid of romance, passion, and love. And herein lies the dilemma.

In many ways the problem here is a simple one, but it is one that has eluded most young people. The issue here is that most young adults do not take seriously the critical role that sex plays in forging an intimate bond between two people. They engage in sexual activities even when the anticipated outcome does not include the expectation that they will form such a bond. This kind of interaction places sexual expression in with all the other kinds of things that people do with little consideration to the meanings or consequences of the behaviors. For many young adults, having sex appears to be as common and ordinary and lacking of special meaning as yawning or grocery shopping. People are usually more eager to have sex than to yawn or shop for groceries, but in terms of the way they conduct their sexual business, it is no big deal.

But sex **is** a big deal, and intuitively, people know this. When you fully expose your body for the pleasure of you and your partner, **that's a big deal!** It's a big deal because people know intuitively that they experience a sense of sexual ecstasy only when their partner is someone with whom they have a passionate, romantic relationship. It's a big deal because people know intuitively that in order to participate fully in a sexual act one must be willing to expose oneself at the deepest psychological levels, something that people are unwilling to do unless they feel safe and secure and loved by their partner.

Your parents may have counselled you that sex is something very special, something to be reserved until you meet the "right" person, and you might have felt that this advice was informed primarily from the perspective of their morality. And in some cases it is probably true that the special nature of sexual expression for your parents is linked primarily to issues of morality. Some parents might hope that you would save your sexual self for the person you marry, but I think that most parents today would be reasonably happy if you reserved your sexual expression for those individuals for whom you had deep, passionate feelings of love and commitment. This would be a person with whom you had an intimate relationship. I realize, too, that if you are gay or lesbian that your parents are unlikely to have given you any support for being sexual in any way.

It is very important that you not misinterpret the idea that the specialness of sex is tied up exclusively with the issue of morality, or for that matter that morality is even the central consideration. You don't have to look to religious or moral beliefs in order to understand the power that sex plays in human life. Sexual expression generates its own set of meanings, has its own intrinsic purpose of maintaining both the biological and psychological well-being of the species. The biological purpose of sex needs no explanation; but you may not have thought much about what role sex plays in the psychological functioning of human beings.

If I asked you to make a list of the qualities you most value in your best friends, your list would probably include words like understanding, trustworthy, supportive, non-judgmental, sense of humor, accepting, fun to be with, caring, and so on. When we are with our friends we feel an overall sense of comfort, an ease about being in their presence. We often use expressions like "letting our hair down" to describe how free and open we feel in their presence, how safe we feel to be the person we most want to be. With our closest friends, we feel no need to be on guard, to worry that they might misinterpret something we do or say. The reason we feel so comfortable and so much at ease with such friends is that we have arrived at this safe place through a mutual process of relationship building over time. We feel we can trust a friend because we have learned that their behavior is predictable. We have disclosed our deepest feelings to them in a gradual and progressive way, and have evidence of the ways these feelings were respected and protected by our friends.

The specialness of sex has the same origins and provides the same rewards as the specialness of friendship: it originates through a shared process of mutual bonding, and it provides lovers with a sense of well-being unobtainable from persons they do not know. When we are in the bosom of a friend we not only feel safe, we experience a sense of pleasure, pleasure whose roots lie in our own ability to craft a successful relationship. The deepest kind of pleasure that sex provides results from that same feeling, from the feeling that our competence as human beings is being rewarded by the good sensations that accompany sex with a loved partner. Our best and most fulfilling sexual experiences are with those individuals with whom we feel most free to be the sexual person we truly want to be, and by definition this can only be an individual to whom we feel a profound attachment.

If you compare these conditions of fulfilling sexual expression with the typical sexual experiences of young adults, you will see immediately a major discrepancy. I think that for most young people it's very much a matter of feeling trapped between a rock and a hard place. On the one hand, the prevailing ethos of immediate gratification, combined with the general acceptance of genital sexual expression between young adults, leads most individuals to interact sexually. On the other, an equally powerful ethos devalues committed, romantic relationships between young people. But what young adults want and need are intimate relationships, which for many of them would include sexual intimacy. The result is a clash between these opposing value systems, a contest that has devastating effects on a large percentage of these individuals.

Counseling centers are filled with young people who are experiencing the effects of restraining their emotional attachments to a romantic partner. When you attempt to dissociate sexual expression from intimacy and emotional involvement, you set yourself up for feelings of inner confusion and turmoil, for feeling alienated from your sense of self and from your own body. If you restrain yourself from experiencing the kind of sexual passion that can only occur if you are emotionally connected to your partner, you are denying to yourself the most fundamental need you have as a human being, which is to be intimately attached to another person.

For many young people, the ability to interact sexually appears to represent a new kind of freedom, brought about by effective contraception and the women's movement. **It is a cruel irony that instead of liberating people, the prevailing ethos of sexual freedom has had just the opposite effect on many young adults: it has held back their growth, eroded their self-confidence and self-esteem, diminished their ability to feel competent as partners in an intimate relationship, and led to distance rather than emotional closeness between young adults.**

When I discuss with young people this idea about the link between sexual expression and intimate relationships the response is typically a combination of denial and shocked recognition. It startles people when I suggest to them that they are hurting themselves by engaging in casual sex, not because it is immoral but because casual sex is contrary to the basic nature of human relationships. I understand very well why young people are caught off-guard by my approach. If you think about what adults have been telling you about sex for as long as you can remember, it has probably been something like this:

✿ Don't have sex until and unless you are married.
✿ If you must have sex, be careful. Be careful about pregnancy, be careful about sexually transmitted diseases, be careful about your reputation.

What adults have probably not said to you is this:

✿ Sex is not a trivial, inconsequential behavior. Sex has its own intrinsic meanings, and these meanings are profound and tied directly to the very nature of human existence.
✿ Although religion and morality play a heavy role in shaping the way many people view sex, they are not the most important considerations to take into account when contemplating what role sexual expression is to play in your life.
✿ Because sexual expression plays such an integral role in human life, it warrants the highest form of respect and responsibility one can muster. These responsibilities include matters like contraception and disease prevention, but equally important, being responsive to the emotional needs of yourself and your partner.
✿ Sex without passionate emotional engagement not only goes against the natural inclinations of human beings, it also carries serious psychological consequences for the participants. The consequences include profound feelings of alienation, lowered self-esteem, and a diminished capacity to feel an appropriate zest for life and all its pleasures.

So does all this look like just another list of Shoulds and Oughts? I hope not. The wisdom of these guidelines doesn't simply reflect my own particular bias—it is based on hard evidence we have accumulated during the past ten years from contemporary American young adults.

It appears to me that much of the sexual interaction young people engage in is not very rewarding, primarily because it is not taking place within a committed intimate relationship. What to do? Well, you have only a certain number of options.

✿ You can do what most young adults do, which is to "date around" casually and engage in various forms of sexual expression, from petting to intercourse and oral-genital sex.
✿ You can meet some of your needs for sexual release by masturbating, and deliberately avoid sexual contact with others.
✿ You can actively seek to establish an intimate, sexual relationship, reserving genital sexual expression until you and your partner have built a firm foundation of friendship, trust, and commitment.

I'm sure you know by now that I consider the last option to be the most desirable, the first to be the least. What I hear from young people most often is that this suggestion is unrealistic. These individuals say it is just as unrealistic to expect them to refrain from sex because it has some negative consequences as it is to expect them to refrain from drinking because they are not of legal age. "Give us a break," they say. And given the prevailing attitudes about sex, I think young adults are entitled to feel stymied by this possibility. But that is precisely the problem this book addresses, and I would not have written it if I thought for a minute that it was impossible to change the sexual climate of today's young adult social environment. If you have read this far it means you are a prime candidate to help change the sexual ethos of young adults and to create a new and healthy one under which you, and ultimately your own children, will thrive. The task, then, is to learn something about how intimate relationships are constructed, and determine what steps you can take to create them for yourself.

CHAPTER 10

Body and Mind

In the last chapter I described the roots of intimacy and outlined a number of barriers that interfere with our ability to establish intimate relationships. The next task is to consider what factors contribute to the process of building intimate relationships, and examine the thoughts, feelings, and behaviors of people who are involved in this process. As I was organizing my notes for these next two chapters it occurred to me that I had an awesome job on my hands. Trying to sort out and assemble the many pieces that comprise the puzzle of intimate relationships is like bringing order to a Rubic Cube: it looks a lot easier than it is, but you discover very quickly that each time you move one piece you change the relationships of many other pieces.

The way I have chosen to approach this problem is to devise several avenues of inquiry, each designed to open up broad sets of issues related to a major element of intimate relationships. The range of experiences and attitudes represented by the readers of this book is immense, so I must be aware that while some have never been in an intimate sexual relationship, others are or have been deeply enmeshed in this kind of relationship for a number of years. What makes this all the more complicated is that each person comes to this work with a different set of relationship circumstances, which means in a sense that each reader enters at a different point on the learning loop.

In the next two chapters we will explore two fundamental issues related to building relationships. The first deals with our self-concept, which constitutes the basis for everything we do or don't do in behalf of our needs for intimacy. The second represents the behaviors we employ as we set out to act on our intimacy needs, using our self-concept as a rudder for guidance. We will follow the development of a relationship until the point where one or both of the partners wishes to increase the level of their commitment, a condition which often results from feelings or thoughts of love. Chapter 12 will explore some of the meanings and consequences of love and commitment in a sexually intimate relationship, concluding with a discussion of relationship breakdown and dissolution.

Before proceeding, however, let's look at the range of relationship circumstances represented by young adults in order to appreciate how these circumstances influence the approach a person will take when considering whether or not to pursue an intimate relationship. Remember, too, that this entire discussion of intimate relationships applies to people whether they are straight or gay or bi-sexual; sexual orientation **per se** has little bearing on why or how one goes about becoming an intimate partner.

What Is Your Relationship Status?

It is important for the work of this chapter for you to be clear about your present relationship status. On the surface this question may appear simple and unambiguous, but my experience suggests that for many people it is not simply a matter of being coupled or not coupled. Let's see why.

The two most obvious categories of relationship status are that one either is, or is not, presently in an intimate relationship. We can sub-divide each of these categories, however, as follows:

Category A: Presently in an Intimate Relationship

1. Your partner is in the near environment, you see this person regularly, and perhaps live with them.
2. Your partner lives away from you, with the result that you have frequent periods of separation. You are in what is called a long-distance relationship.
3. You are mostly satisfied with your relationship, and would like to maintain and develop it.
4. You are mostly unsatisfied with your relationship, and may want to improve it or end it.
5. This is your first intimate relationship.
6. You have had one or more intimate relationships prior to this one.

Category B: Not Presently in an Intimate Relationship

1. You have never before had an intimate relationship.
2. You have had one or more intimate relationships in the past.
3. You presently desire to be in an intimate relationship.

4.   You feel you have the social skills and/or self-confidence needed to create an intimate relationship.

5.   You feel you lack the social skills and/or self-confidence needed to create an intimate relationship.

6.   You understand clearly why you are not presently in an intimate relationship, even though you desire this kind of relationship.

7.   You are unsure about why you are not presently in an intimate relationship, even though you desire this kind of relationship.

8.   You presently do not desire to be in an intimate relationship.

There are probably some additional categories I haven't included on this list, but I have found that most young people can be located somewhere along this continuum.

It should be apparent that your relationship status has a great deal to do with how you live out your relational life. What I find amazing is that many young adults are often not aware of precisely where they fall on this continuum. Of course they know whether or not they are in an intimate relationship. But when questioned intensely they frequently indicate that they **don't want to think about** things like whether or not they are satisfied with their partner or whether or not they are well prepared to create an intimate relationship. As a result of this confusion and ambivalence, at least in terms of intimacy, it is not unusual for young adults to feel like their life is living them, rather than that they are living their life. Not only are they often not in control of this aspect of their life, they are frequently unsure about **whether or not they really want to be in control!**

There are two important sets of reasons why young adults feel they have little control over their intimate life. The first set is represented by all the barriers to intimacy I discussed in the last chapter. The overall pressures against forming intimate relationships lead many young people to identify intimacy as something that will just have to wait until a better time in their lives. The second reason, however, is bound up in the individual, personal interpretation an individual makes concerning whether or not they are **entitled** to be in such relationships. A person's feelings of entitlement are based on a host of factors, but most of them have to do with how worthy they feel they are to be the beneficiary of the rewards of an intimate relationship. Surprisingly enough, this idea of being worthy applies not only to those who are not in an intimate relationship but also to those who are. Strange as it may seem, because a person has an intimate partner does not mean they feel entitled to the benefits intimacy affords.

For the most part, people do not deal with this issue of relationship entitlement at the conscious level. If you ask them why they are not presently in an intimate relationship, they will rarely volunteer the fact that they don't feel entitled. Rather, they will cite the reasons I mentioned earlier. But if you were to probe them more deeply or were to talk with a psychotherapist, you would discover that these personal apprehensions account for a major portion of the reasons young people avoid intimacy.

Nor is it a matter of young adults feeling generally inadequate; the feelings of inadequacy are related to intimacy. A person may be quite confident about their academic or athletic abilities, but they may feel these kinds of attributes have little to do with whether or not they are entitled to intimacy. In fact, some people consider their intellectual ability to be a **liability** in terms of their potential for intimate relationships. **Almost always, young people keep these personal assessments of their intimacy entitlement a secret,** something that is not hard to understand. It's much easier to say you don't have time for an intimate relationship than it is to say you don't feel entitled to one.

So the place to begin any consideration of intimate relationships is with the way you feel about yourself, and this is true whether or not you are presently in such a relationship. Your self-concept is a very complex thing, especially because it is always changing. For example, self-confidence as a component of self-concept can fluctuate on an almost daily basis, and is influenced by everything from the weather to your levels of steroid hormones! Let's proceed, then, to a more thorough look at how self-concept relates to intimacy.

In an earlier chapter on young adult development, I indicated that being autonomous is critically related to the ease with which you are able to form intimate relationships. In that same chapter I described self-concept as a combination of our personal attributes and social identities, and self-esteem as an estimation of how worthy we consider these personal attributes and social identities to be at any given point in time. Now we need to expand considerably on the specific ways in which aspects of our self-concept directly influence our choices related to intimacy, and to become aware of how we can increase our feelings of self-esteem. Our self-concept consists of the pictures we have of ourselves as physical, intellectual, emotional, and social beings, so we can begin by addressing each of these elements in detail.

Physical Self-Concept

As an element of a written project tracing their sexual development, students in my human relationships and sexuality course are asked to describe their feelings toward their bodies in general, and to comment specifically on various sexual parts such as breasts, vulva, clitoris, penis, testicles, and scrotum. On the basis of reviewing thousands of these projects with my teaching assistants over the years, I feel safe in making three generalizations about how my students feel toward their bodies, illustrated by the graph that follows.

- ✿ Students are more satisfied than dissatisfied with their bodies.
- ✿ Males are somewhat more satisfied with their bodies than are females.
- ✿ Both females and males are more satisfied and accepting of the sexual parts of their bodies than of their bodies as a whole. Breasts and penises are commented on most frequently. Typically a female will say something like, "I like my breasts a lot, although I wish they were a little bit bigger/smaller," and a male will indicate that, "I like my penis the way it is-—none of my partners have ever complained about its size!"

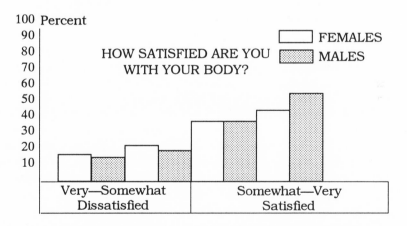

Our physical self-concept embraces much more than our appearance as we perceive it, and includes much more than a simple catalog of how we feel about our various body parts. For example, how we think others see us contributes to shaping our self-perceptions as physical entities just as it does to our intellectual, social, and emotional self-concepts. In addition, we judge our body not only in terms of appearance, but also from the standpoint of how it functions. In other words, we describe our physical selves with words like attractive, unattractive, handsome, pretty, ugly, cute, and beautiful, but we also speak to matters like strength, coordination, dexterity, athleticism, grace, cardiovascular condition, flexibility, and our ability to move creatively.

We have varying measures of control over the appearance and functions of our body, although both features are of course mediated by genetic contributions or limitations. It's also true that in many areas of our physical self, appearance and function are related to some degree. While we can't control the natural color of our eyes or whether we go bald, regular vigorous exercise usually helps us appreciate and feel better about our body, no matter what its appearance. Conversely, such exercise may allow us to reduce or maintain our weight, so that our body appears quite attractive to us and to others.

What all this means is that when people talk about being physically attracted to someone, they are usually talking about a great deal more than surface appearance, although this is central to such a statement. But when I ask young adults to describe their first impression of a partner and what drew their attention to them, they almost always refer to some action element, such as the following examples suggest.

- ✿ "Paul gestured with his hands in such a descriptive way, it was almost as if he were creating poetry in the air."
- ✿ "I watched Maria dancing with a friend, and her body moved in such an uninhibited and spontaneous way, like she wasn't even thinking about what she was doing. I just knew there was this free spirit inside her, something I really could identify with."
- ✿ "I was just frankly impressed with how **strong** Jack was, because my initial impression of him was that he was this gentle, teddy bear type. But when I watched him play tennis, I got goose bumps seeing how powerful and confident he was, how his body seemed to be in complete command of what was going on out there."
- ✿ "I went to an all male prep school and hadn't really had a chance to be around athletic women very much. One of the first things that attracted me to Amy was that she was in excellent shape, and that in terms of running, she had no trouble keeping up with me."
- ✿ "When I first saw Mark he was throwing a small vase on a potter's wheel at the ceramic co-op, and I couldn't keep my eyes off his sinuous fingers as he drew the clay up and shaped it so skillfully. It was almost as if his fingers had a mind of their own."

What interests me about each of these descriptions is that the individuals being described may not be aware that others perceive their physical attributes in such positive ways. Indeed, they themselves may not feel all that enthusiastic about these aspects of their physical self, considering other elements to be much more significant. The point of all this, however, is that our bodies send off powerful messages to others about our sense of self, and it is important not only to transmit the messages we want to, but also to ensure that they are received accurately.

It is well worth your time, then, to make an inventory of your physical attributes, noting how appearance and function are interrelated. Those aspects of your physical self about which you feel most comfortable are likely to be the ones you can employ in attracting potential partners, because they are representative of the person you feel most confident about. Seeking feedback from friends is a good way to discover which attributes others may identify as attractive about you that you yourself don't see.

There is no question that physical attraction plays a crucial role in the initiation of an intimate relationship. It should also go without saying that we reject most potential partners because they don't meet our standard of physical attractiveness, whatever that standard might be. It's almost as if we each had an "attractiveness sifter," whose grade of mesh determined whether or not someone fell through into the arena of possibility. Most of the time the holes in the sifter are fairly small, allowing only certain individuals whose physical attributes we admire to get through. At other times, perhaps toward the end of a party which includes much drinking, the holes are so large that almost any warm body will fall through.

In any event, the perception we have of our own physical attractiveness actually determines who gets through the holes in our sifter in the first place, because this self-assessment measures our feelings of entitlement. I remember well how this principle of physical attraction influenced my dating behavior during high school and college. During that time I would have rated myself on the "somewhat-to-very dissatisfied" side of the body satisfaction graph presented above, closer to the "very" than "somewhat." I was not very muscular, wore unfashionable glasses that forever slipped down my nose, and had a severe case of acne on my face.

Since I felt so unattractive physically it made perfect sense to me that young women I considered to be very attractive would not be interested in me as a dating partner. And I certainly was not about to ask them to rate my attractiveness. As a result, I would simply rule out many women as potential partners, assuming that my looks were not powerful enough to attract them. And it was not until about twenty years ago that I realized that not only had I held this perception of myself as being physically unattractive during high school and college, but that this view of my physical self persisted until my late twenties. Since about age thirty it has never occurred to me to rule out a very attractive potential partner because I was worried that she might not consider me to be physically attractive enough. This doesn't mean that I now think of myself as a gorgeous hunk, but rather that I feel very comfortable with my physical self-concept. In talking with friends, I have discovered that many of them had similar feelings about their physical self-concept, and began to feel physically attractive only after they had developed an overall sense of confidence and competence, which was well after their college years.

This insight has helped me understand how young people are feeling when they describe themselves as being physically unattractive. I am often startled at how different my impression of a person's physical attractiveness is compared to their own assessment. But I realize that a major reason for this discrepancy is that I tend to formulate a physical image of a person that extends well beyond conventional good looks. I use the term "conventional good looks" to describe individuals who look like the attractive models found in popular magazines, movies, and catalogs like J. Crew, Lands End, and Victoria's Secret. The stereotypes of these women and men are well-scrubbed, have nice teeth and smiles, and exude an educated, middle-class quality. This is probably because I have developed a broader and more comprehensive stereotype of physical attractiveness, which incorporates many more attributes than surface appearance. But it is difficult to convince a young person that they are attractive if they themselves feel unattractive.

Much of the research related to physical attractiveness tends to support the idea that young adults prefer dating partners who they assess to be equally or somewhat more attractive than they consider themselves to be. Even a casual observer can find support for this phenomenon by simply rating known dating partners on the basis of their attractiveness complementarity. But if you set out on this kind of research mission you will discover very quickly that there are abundant exceptions to this rule, and you will be faced with trying to determine how such an obviously miss-matched couple could have come about. Your explanation may be that other attributes overpowered the physical ones, permitting one or both partners to make a compromise in the domain of physical attractiveness.

As a teenager I mowed the lawn of a family whose next door neighbor was someone I considered to be the most beautiful and sexy woman in our town. At the time I simply could not fathom how she could have married her husband, who I viewed as a dumpy, balding, slug-like person. My friends and I concluded that he was either very rich or had a very big penis, or was very rich **and** had a very big penis! In neither of these cases, however, did we think that such qualities were sufficient to entitle him to this woman. As I think about this couple today, two things occur to me. First, while the wife was attractive in conventional terms, I realize that I would not be attracted to her if I saw her today. And second, my picture of the husband has improved dramatically as a result of hindsight, and if I were to see him today I would rate him as being well within my present standard of physical attractiveness.

Another research finding about physical attractiveness I find especially interesting is that there is something of a reversal in how an individual's attractiveness is perceived over time. Those people who are rated by their peers as being very physically attractive during their high school and college years are rated by these same peers during their forties as being less attractive than are individuals who were rated as less attractive during high school and college. Conventional good looks do not appear to hold up well to the test of time. But of course there is the other factor which I just discussed, which has to do with how we change our standards of physical attraction over time, typically broadening the scope of what we consider desirable.

When I ask young people to list those features of their appearance that they dislike or that they feel detract from their physical attractiveness, I find the categories that arise encompass virtually every part of the body. Here is a brief, top-to-bottom catalog of unfavorable ratings students typically give to various body parts.

Body Part	Typical Comments
Hair on head	Too thick, thin, flat, curly, greasy, drab.
Nose	Too big, small, crooked, pointy, flat.
Eyes	Pale, offset, wrong color, need glasses.
Lips	Too thin, too thick.
Teeth	Crooked, buck, braces left tracks.
Face	Bad skin, beard too heavy, beard too light.
Chest	Too big, small, not-enough, too-much hair.
Stomach	Too fat, too skinny.
Legs	Too heavy, too scrawny.
Feet	Flat, smelly.
Body Hair	Too much, not enough, in the wrong places.

All this looks very much like a matter of feast or famine, doesn't it? To make matters worse, coming to terms with their body parts and with their entire bodies for some people is as easy as crossing Main Street, while for others this kind of acceptance involves a long and drawn-out process. Unfortunately, many people never fully accept their bodies, probably because in our culture there is such a tremendous emphasis placed on achieving a very narrow standard of physical attractiveness.

What do people who accept and feel comfortable with their bodies do that contributes to their achieving a healthy physical self-concept? I have talked with many young adults about this question, and have been impressed with how consistent the responses have been. While the advice is not all that profound, it reveals a level of self-awareness these individuals have attained, largely through their own experience. In its distilled form, the list of suggestions looks like this.

✿ **Take ownership of your body.** Your genes had a lot to do with how your body looks, and so did your family's attitudes about physical health. You can't change any of those things, but you can work to let go of any anger you harbor about these factors and try to understand that ultimately you are the only person who can take full responsibility for your body.

✿ **You are what you eat.** Almost all young people would benefit from improving on the nutritional patterns established in their families. Good nutrition is now at the forefront of the nation's awareness, and for good reason. The good news is that sound nutrition is not that difficult to achieve, and brings with it rewards that people feel almost immediately.

✿ **Eat less.** This advice is controversial among nutritional specialists but it usually appears on the list of people who feel good about their bodies. Eating less is not a matter of dieting or starving oneself. Rather, the advice pertains to what these individuals consider to be "extra" eating, such as snacking and eating just because food is present. Food is available in a number of situations, and many people eat simply because it is there.

✿ **Limit alcohol consumption.** Young people often drink for the same reason they eat: because the alcohol is there. Alcohol not only is very high in calories, but perhaps equally important in terms of this issue, it is usually consumed with snack foods. A few beers and munchies can provide a person with as much as a third of their daily caloric needs, equivalent to a full meal.

✿ **Avoid tobacco.** Although the rate of smoking among young adults has declined steadily during the past fifteen years, there has been a recent upswing in the use of tobacco products by teenagers. This includes both cigarettes and so-called smokeless tobacco, which people refer to as chewing tobacco. People who feel good about their bodies don't smoke or chew, both for health reasons and because they feel that the smell of smoke, as well as chewing and spitting, detracts from an individual's physical attractiveness.

✿ **Exercise.** Especially when they are under stress of any kind, people find that maintaining their exercise routine is more important than almost anything else they do. And it doesn't matter what the exercise is, as long as it is aerobic and is done consistently. For some people, having a regular exercise partner is a key to staying on schedule, while for others it is a matter of developing the self-discipline to work out alone. Regular exercise tends to make people feel better about their bodies, no matter what their bodies look like.

✿ **Know how your body works.** Knowledge of how their body works, especially in terms of its biological sexual functioning, seems to be an important contributing factor to people feeling good about their bodies. Young adults can gain a very important source of information by having routine physical examinations, and developing a trust in their health care providers. Many young people report that working with both same- and other-sex physicians has helped them feel more comfortable with their bodies and in discussing very personal sexual matters more openly.

✿ **Establish a regular pattern of living.** Human beings are creatures of habit, a concept that is tested to the limits during the young adult years. People who are able to follow a regular pattern of living are less likely to become stressed out, or to reach the point where they feel they need to abandon things like exercise in order to keep up with their work.

To this list of excellent suggestions provided by young adults, I can add one more gained simply by living as long as I have:

✿ **Sign up for the duration.** As I have gotten older, I have realized that maintaining a healthy physical self-concept grows increasingly difficult over time. Although people generally tend to be more accepting of their attractiveness as they age, maintaining physical fitness and appearance become much harder. Two factors typically work against you as you get older: first, your body is less efficient, so it requires less fuel and higher levels of exercise just to maintain a steady state; and second, people's work often becomes more sedentary as they get older, leading them to move their bodies less in their day-to-day routines. My own experience has been similar to that of my age-mates in that the advice found on the list above is just as applicable to us at fifty to sixty as it is to you at eighteen to thirty. If you want to feel good about your body throughout your life, you will have to be willing to invest a lifetime of effort in order to achieve that goal. The good news is that through regular patterns of daily living, most adults are able to accomplish this task if they want to.

It may be possible, of course, to change a bodily feature you feel diminishes your physical attractiveness. These kinds of changes are not typically trivial attempts to become "beautiful," but rather are thoughtful acts of self-assertion. The kinds of changes that come to mind include wearing braces to straighten teeth and improve one's bite, switching from glasses to contact lenses, having cosmetic nose surgery, and removing moles and warts. In each of these cases, what seems to be most important is that the individual actively chooses to make a change in their appearance, and the person usually feels better about their physical self as a result of that action. This is true whether or not others agree with this assessment. But short of changes which require some kind of professional intervention, a person who wants to feel good about their body is pretty much faced with the task of working with what they have, and employing the sugges-tions on the list above.

There are some people whose physical self-concept is greatly affected by a disability, chronic illness or disfigurement, who face a much more difficult than average task of feeling good about their bodies. Not only do they have to deal with their personal feelings about their disability, but they live in a world that is quick to produce stereotypes of disabled individuals, just as it creates stereotypes of what is conventionally attractive. And similar to non-disabled people, the feelings disabled individuals have about their bodies are experienced within the context of their emotional and social self-concepts. Disabled young adults I work with present a range of disabilities, which typically include multiple sclerosis (MS), cerebral palsy (CP), blindness, deafness, severe scarring from burns, and spinal cord injuries.

It is true that many disabled individuals, especially during their adolescent and young adult years, become resentful and bitter because they are unable to enjoy a full, active life like their non-disabled peers. When a disability results from a serious accident during adolescence, the psychological effects can be devastating. Spinal cord injuries, which frequently occur during the high school and college years, are an example of this kind of traumatic impairment. An injury like this could not come at a worse time in a person's life, since this is when they are deep into the process of building intimate relationships and expanding the frontiers of their sexuality. As with all other physical disabilities, spinal cord injured young people are faced with learning two crucial lessons about their physical self-concept: first, to come to accept their bodies as they are, not as they would like them to be; and second, to broaden their understanding of human sexuality beyond that of genital arousal. Exploring one's **sensuality** through fantasy and sensual touch are just two examples of this kind of enlargement of the definition of human sexuality.

Many disabled individuals feel that support groups are a wonderful way for them to feel better about their bodies. Being able to compare notes with people who face the same kinds of barriers to forming intimate relationships provides individuals in these support groups with the feeling that there are fellow travellers out there who can appreciate their vision of the world. One young person I know who has cerebral palsy joined just such a support group, only to discover that most of the other group members did not have what she considered physical disabilities, but rather were dealing with bulimia and anorexia, two of the most common eating disorders seen in young women today. At first she did not see how her disability might relate to people with eating disorders, but within a short period of time she discovered that the central issue for all the group participants was body image and the mystery of physical self-concept. Support groups are not for everyone, however; some people report that associating with other disabled individuals has a negative impact on their sense of self, and only tends to increase their feelings of self-pity.

Whether we are disabled or non-disabled, all of us must reconcile our body image if we are to share it freely with another human being. What I have tried to do in this section on physical self-concept is to open up several issues to think about, and to highlight two inescapable facts. The first is that your personal view of physical attractiveness is highly colored by cultural standards, standards which are shaped by society's prevailing attitudes toward gender, power, race, and money, to name just a few of the most influential factors. Second, your assessment of your **own** physical attractiveness plays the biggest role in determining how attractive a partner you think you deserve. And most of the time, the way you feel about your physical attractiveness is as much related to the way you feel about your emotional and social self as it is to the way your body actually looks. When your friends tell you they think you look terrific they are not usually kidding you, but rather are giving you a more objective reading of what you tend to take very personally. The zit on the end of your nose always looks much worse to you than it does to your friends.

Intellectual Self-Concept

> "Boys don't make passes at girls who wear glasses."
> Ogden Nash

Although we are usually attracted to someone because of their physical appearance, the outcome of that initial exchange depends entirely on how we have assessed our personality as a whole. We typically feel better about some aspects of our self-concept than others, and whether or not an initial meeting grows into something more substantial is directly related to these more global assessments we have made of ourselves. We don't carry lists of our strong and weak points around with us, of course, but these lists exist somewhere in our conscious or unconscious mind. Since the sorting process during the acquaintance stage of a relationship operates at lightning speed, we are not usually aware of opening or closing the gates regulating the progression of a developing relationship. But whether or not we are aware of it, becoming acquainted with a potential partner involves a predictable matching operation, in which each person mentally checks their own list of attributes against what they perceive the other person's list to be. This check-off process is not random, but rather proceeds down lists which each individual has rank-ordered according to how important they consider each attribute.

Just as we have a sense of how accepting we are of our body, we have similar feelings about our intellect. Since the mission of colleges and universities is to deal with the life of the mind, a student's intellectual self-concept is under constant scrutiny, with always the wonder of whether it measures up. Grades are the most conspicuous indicator of how powerful a student's intellect is, but quite often grades are not congruent with the way a person rates their own intellectual abilities. As a professor, I typically hear two stories regarding the match between the grades a student achieves and their private assessment of intelligence.

Most of the students I work with believe that their grades are **not** an accurate reflection of their academic ability. They maintain that, although they are very good at doing many things requiring intellectual rigor, that the testing and grading system of the university is an ineffective tool for measuring this ability. A variation on this theme is that students feel they have the basic intellectual ability, but lack the skills needed to produce top-grade work. The other category of students, which is much smaller and goes almost unnoticed, consists of individuals who get very good grades but who nevertheless don't feel very "smart." These are students who work very hard, have well developed academic skills and employ them effectively, and are rewarded with good grades. But something is missing, they say. They worry about things like a shortage of creative ability, or that maybe they should have broader interests, or, like the girls Ogden Nash was referring to, that their brain power scares away potential partners. In any event, they feel constrained from experiencing a sense of freedom about their intellect.

The grades students receive, then, tell only part of the story of their intellectual self-concept, although it's a very important part. At most colleges there are grading cycles which correspond roughly to the way the academic calendar unfolds. My testing schedule is pretty common for our university, and includes three class exams spaced about four weeks apart, with a final project due during the last third of the semester. From a student's point of view, this evaluation pattern produces regular cycles consisting of a buildup period, followed by the test event, the results, and a psychological response to the grade received. The more courses a student takes, and the more cycles involved, the more potential there is for intense stress during each buildup and testing period. An especially disastrous grading cycle can plunge even the most confident student into a state of panic or depression, and can strain the individual's intellectual self-concept to its limits.

To make matters worse, there is yet another feature to this grading cycle issue which I refer to as the paradox of intellectual uniqueness. The paradox is that **virtually all** students think they are unique among their peers, believing that their peers are not only doing much better academically but also that their peers are not struggling with the issue of intellectual self-esteem to the same degree that they are. If I had not experienced this paradox myself as a college student I don't think I could ever believe the stories of intellectual inferiority I hear, from even the most academically talented students in the university. Students cope with this private view of their intellect in a variety of ways, most of which reflect the negative vision they have of their academic abilities. The students who receive the best grades often diminish the quality of their work by moaning about how they filled **only** three blue books on their exam, whereas so-and-so, whom they assume to be much more skilled than they are, wrote **five** blue books, if you can believe that! Are they dumb, or what? (Of course they end up getting an A+ on the exam, and so-and-so gets an A-.) Students who generally get average and poor grades take a different approach, which interestingly enough is as likely to involve **exaggerating** their test performance as it is disparaging it. These students might say they think they did pretty well on an exam, which reflects either their private delusion of how much they knew or an unrealistic assessment of how their performance compares with what the professor expects. This group of students gets "blown away" when they receive low grades, and are often truly stymied as to "what happened," since they felt they really "knew this stuff" going into the exam.

What fascinates me about all this is that students from both of these categories play a lot of games around issues of their academic performance and ability, games that ultimately have significant consequences for their close relationships. I feel I'm in a good position to understand and appreciate these games, however, since I am well in touch with memories of my collegiate intellectual self-concept, and the maneuvering I did in an attempt to keep together all the parts of my personality. Like the students I have been describing, during my college years I believed I lacked the capacity to be a powerful intellectual person, someone whose ideas and words would be heard and valued by peers and professors. I was the Scarecrow from the **Wizard of Oz,** thoroughly convinced I had no brain. But like the Tin Man and the Cowardly Lion, I had a great abundance of the very quality I thought I lacked. What I had a short supply of was self-confidence, and in this respect I was like most of my peers, and many of the young people I work with today. The wizard I sought to confirm my own intelligence was residing within me all along, but I discovered it only after many other pieces of my self-concept began to fall into place.

So the traditional system of assessing academic worth through grades leaves a high percentage of students feeling less than fully worthy about their intellects. And since students have been graded continuously throughout their school years, they accumulate such evaluations over a period of twelve years or more. The process of learning that you are a Scarecrow may take place gradually, but by the time you graduated from high school you had this concept well integrated into your personality. It is therefore unlikely to change over night, but rather will yield only to a gradual reconstruction of yourself as a thinking person.

It should be no surprise to you at this point to learn that a private assessment of your intellectual abilities plays a critical role in shaping the way you interact with a potential intimate partner. As soon as you meet someone to whom you are attracted, you begin using words and ideas to present a picture of yourself which you think will sustain the meeting long enough to make an impression. Usually you are not conscious of this process, but you do it nonetheless. An important aspect of the "sizing up" stage of acquaintanceship, then, consists of seeing how your intellectual self-concept fits with that of the person you have just met. If you think the person is a lot smarter than you are you may hold back your ideas, and play more of an interviewer role. If you feel pretty confident about your intellect you might take a more active role in this initial exchange, eagerly offering your ideas so that the other person can gain sufficient information about you that will permit them to make an informed judgement of what you are like. Problems are likely to occur when you present an inaccurate picture of your intellectual self, or are unable to gain an accurate reading of your new friend's intellectual self-concept.

The "opposites attract" notion has been around a long time, and some people still believe in its power even though there is little evidence to support the idea in real life. When people make reference to opposites, what they are usually talking about are things like choice in music, movie tastes, and especially temperament. One partner is high strung, the other laid back. One is outgoing, the other reserved. One likes quieter, more cerebral activities, the other enjoys physical activity and challenge. When potential partners talk positively about one another in these terms, they usually do so without realizing that their model of partner selection is most likely going to come crashing down on their heads, typically very soon into the relationship. The school of complementarity asserts that partners "complement" one another, so, for example, one partner's dominance needs are complemented by the other's needs to be submissive. Each partner contributes their own special flavor to the mix. Like its companion "opposites attract," complementarity is a flawed model, although is has a grain of truth in it that lends it an element of credibility.

The basic problem with both the opposites and complementary theories is that neither recognizes the special importance of each partner being a whole unto themselves, nor that people's needs change over time. Partners who at the beginning of a relationship exhibit a complementarity related to nurturance and a need to be nurtured, for instance, are likely to move beyond this particular complementarity as the events and circumstances of their lives change. While people are sometimes attracted to a potential partner because of qualities they see as being different from those which they would use to describe themselves, in general people who advance beyond the acquaintance stage do so because of their commonly shared values, interests and attitudes. Nowhere is this more apparent than it is in the realm of intellectual compatibility.

Satisfying and healthy long-term intimate relationships result when partners are able to solve problems together, and when mutuality characterizes all the processes the couple employs to maintain and develop their relationship. When partners value one another's ideas, thoughts, and words, they are more likely to be able to attain this sense of mutuality, which reflects the shared goal of developing their relationship as it runs its course over time. This is why it is so important to understand and feel more accepting of your intellectual self-concept. Easier said than done, you say.

True, but as a young adult you are in a very favorable position to explore this concept with your friends and potential lovers, probably more so than at any other time in your life.

CHAPTER 11

Social and Emotional Self-Concept

I was an undergraduate student at Rutgers College well before it became co-educational. At that time it was customary for "Rutgers Men" to date women from Douglass College, Rutgers' sister institution located on the other side of the city. A common way that Rutgers men met women at Douglass was to cruise their student center and strike up idle conversation with anyone who looked like a possible date. I spent many hours at the Center, but my time was devoted to watching other men move in on women I thought were quite desirable but felt paralyzed to approach. I was born about twenty-five years too soon, because when I went to the Douglas student center I did so with the fervent hope that one of the women would pick **me** up, since I was petrified to initiate the kind of idle chit-chat necessary even to begin a conversation, let alone ask for a date.

Part of the difficulty I had in making contact with women can be traced to my physical and intellectual self-concepts, but these concerns I had about myself were compounded by my lack of social skills. While it's true that if you don't feel very good about yourself in general it will be more difficult to initiate contact with others, it is equally true that even **with** a healthy self-concept a person requires certain basic social skills in order to function well in the company of others. As an undergraduate it never would have occurred to me that some day I would be able to walk into a group of strangers and feel comfortable introducing myself, making small talk, and getting to know people who were very different from me. As I reflect on my college years, I find many examples to illustrate the discomfort I felt in initiating contact with others in social situations, and I have discovered that many young people today experience similar self-doubts. Here's a list of just a few of the social concerns I had as a young adult.

- ✿ I couldn't phone someone for a date. Would I say, "Hi, this is a guy you may have noticed at the student center on Sunday, but you probably didn't notice me, but I noticed you, and wondered whether you'd like to have coffee some night?" or "Hi, you don't know me, but I'm a friend of Bill, who told me he thought I'd like you, and maybe you'd be interested in going to the movies or something." No script I could think of seemed even remotely credible.
- ✿ I didn't know how to dance. This eliminated what would otherwise have been an excellent opportunity for me to make contact with women. But in the fifties dances actually had steps to them, none of which I knew; it wasn't like today, where you need only go out on the dance floor, face your partner without touching them and move your body rhythmically.
- ✿ I had little knowledge of the social conventions and etiquette practiced by families whose economic status was higher than mine. For example, I didn't know even simple things like which fork to begin with when a place setting offered three of them to choose from.
- ✿ Since I had not been exposed to much cultural or ethnic diversity as a child, I was reluctant to sample foods I regarded as being strange. I therefore avoided going to Chinese and Mexican restaurants with friends, for example, because I worried that I would not understand the menus and would dislike the food.
- ✿ I had no skills related to entertaining, and would never have attempted to invite a group of friends over to my apartment for a cookout or party.

You may be thinking from this description that I was a pretty pathetic soul who, like Charlie Brown, sat wistfully on the periphery of the social scene hoping that some sweet red-haired girl would see through the veneer of my shyness and recognize the treasure that lay beneath. In some respects this would be an accurate assessment of my social self-concept at the time, because I really did feel powerless to act in my own behalf. Had I possessed more of the basic social skills one needs in order to make contact with others I might very well have been able to cultivate a wider range of relationships, which in turn would have helped me develop a better view of myself as a whole person. It is quite apparent to me now why I lacked those skills: my parents never taught them to me, nor discussed why it was important to become familiar with the basic conventions of social life. My parents never entertained, never coached me on how to make introductions, couldn't afford to send me to dancing class and taught me only the most basic kinds of manners and etiquette. I don't blame my parents for this deficiency in my upbringing, because their parents offered no better models. But over time I've come to appreciate the fact that acquiring basic social skills is very much like learning multiplication tables, in that this ability will come in handy throughout one's entire life.

Small Talk

Of all the social skills that might help a person during the acquaintance stage of a relationship, that of making **small talk** is probably the most important. Small talk is the universal lubricant of human relationships, so it will be well worth your while to understand what this kind of talk is all about and what role it plays in human interaction. While the very term "small talk" suggests that this kind of communication is superficial and trivial, nothing could be further from the truth. To the extent that small talk creates most of the possibilities for "big talk," it is much more significant than people think it is. At a recent meeting I had with a group of young people to talk about the ways relationships begin, we brainstormed the following list of situations in which small talk takes place. These are simply examples, and don't include all the possible instances in which this kind of talk occurs.

> ✿ A student I have never seen before knocks on my office door, pokes his head in and sees me working at my computer on this very manuscript, and says, "Hi, Dr. Barbour, are you busy?" I realize immediately that this person knows I **am** busy, but I say, "No, come on in—I was about to take a break. Why don't you sit down so we can chat for a bit. Would you like some coffee or a soda?"
> ✿ A meeting of the Yearbook Council is scheduled to begin at 2 P.M. By five after two, three-quarters of the council has arrived and are sitting around a conference table talking in groups of twos and threes. The talk ranges from how hard it is raining to the fact that one of the group members was in an accident recently and totaled her car. When the council chairperson arrives, she jokes about parking in a reserved spot so she could get to the

meeting on time. Several council members tease her about her special connections with the security police, which, with a smirk, she denies. She then calls the meeting to order.

✿ At a party, Angela and Todd are introduced by a mutual friend. During the first fifteen minutes of their conversation they share the following information with one another: their names, where they live, their ages, home towns, the number of siblings they each have, the number and variety of pets owned by their families, the marital status of their parents, their shared respect for the mutual friend who introduced them, the fact that most parties they have been to recently are pretty dead because there's no alcohol, and in the case of Todd, that he wears contact lenses.

✿ After their class in 19th Century American Literature, Marian approaches Louise, whom she does not know, to tell her how impressed she was by the analysis Louise made of one of the assigned short stories. Louise thanks Marian for her comments, and asks her if she would like to borrow a book of literary criticism that she found particularly useful in developing her analysis. Marian responds affirmatively and recalls that her former roommate, Helen, who is also an English major as is Louise, had used the same book and found it helpful. Louise asks Marion if the Helen who was her roommate is Helen Perkins, from Philadelphia. Indeed she is, and Louise then states enthusiastically that she and Helen have taken many classes together and that she admires greatly Helen's writing skills.

In each of these cases, small talk served either to reunite a group of individuals and center them on their task, as it did for the Yearbook Council, or to open the possibility for new relationships, as in the other three examples. Many people assume that small talk just happens, but individuals who desire to enlarge their network of relationships understand the purpose of such communication and employ small talk that is intentional and thoughtful. They have learned the kinds of things to say that help break the ice in new situations, and are able to explore effectively and economically the potential of a new relationship or the enhancement of an existing one. You may distinguish between the kind of small talk that takes place before a meeting is to start from that which occurs at a bar or a party, but the purpose of all this kind of talk is the same: **people use small talk to determine whether or not they want to continue a relationship.**

Small talk typically begins with biographical data about each individual, probably because this kind of information is well known by each person and is also non-controversial. Most people can handle basic small talk like "Hi, I'm Jim Barbour," and "Where do you live?" but they often choke when they have exhausted the name, rank, and serial number part of the conversation. This is because people are not clear what they want to learn about the other person, nor what they can say about themselves that will likely advance the relationship beyond the superficial level. The questions then become, **What can I say that will reveal something of my uniqueness?** and **How can I discover the special qualities of the person I just met?** As I have already indicated, some forms of small talk are much more likely to be effective in answering these questions than are others. Let's explore what this kind of talk looks like, as well as consider some of the personal behaviors that tend to facilitate small talk.

I'll begin with the example I described above, in which a student comes to see me at my office. You probably can identify with this situation, having no doubt had similar conversations with teachers. The first thing to mention about small talk is that the **environment** plays a very important role in fostering or inhibiting dialogue between two people. The environment of a party, for instance, with loud music and the noise of people trying to be heard above the crowd, can make it almost impossible to carry on even small talk, let alone get into a substantive conversation. And when people are milling about before or after a meeting, it can also be very difficult to feel there is enough privacy to carry on a meaningful conversation. In situations like these it is important to move to a quieter place, where it will be possible to talk more freely. The same environmental principle applies to my office space. Since I want people to feel comfortable in establishing a relationship with me I have designed my office to be warm and inviting, and utilize a similar approach in talking with each person. The behaviors and small talk involved in such a meeting look like this.

When someone appears at my door I assume they want to talk with me in order to have a form signed, to check on a matter related to my course, or to discuss in depth a personal matter that is troubling them. At the outset, of course, I really don't have a clue about their concern, but I realize that they didn't walk all the way over to my office for something trivial. Therefore I treat their appearance as a unique opportunity to get to know them, and for them to know me better as well. Rather than simply looking up from my desk and saying, "Yes, may I help you," I invite the student to come into my office and sit down. My "visitor chair" is placed near my chair, and since my desk is against a wall there is no furniture between me and the student. As the student sits down I close the cabinet door over my computer screen, slide the keyboard into its hidden compartment, turn down the volume of my stereo and swivel on my chair in order to directly face them. These deliberate behaviors on my part signal the individual that I am both physically and psychologically present for them.

The first thing a student usually does is to comment on my office, indicating how unusual it is compared to most professors', and especially how much they like my desk. I thank them, indicating that I made the desk out of wood taken from a giant old walnut tree I found in eastern Pennsylvania. You **made** the desk? is the student's next statement, to which I reply that, yes, cabinet making is one of my two non-sexual passions, the other being cycling. I then ask the student whether they have hobbies they can pursue while here at school, and most of them reply that they do. After they describe what their hobbies are I usually say something like, "That's a great hobby," or "That sounds like a lot of fun." My intent is to establish some common ground with the student before we begin talking about whatever it is they came to see me about.

With the student now a bit more at ease I turn to the business at hand by saying one of two things, both of which seem to be equally effective in getting things going. The first is, "So, what's up?" The second, "So, what would you like to talk with me about?" If the student was seeking simple information, we can usually dispatch with things rather quickly, and if it appears to me that the person needs to move on to another appointment I round off the conversation and bring it to a close. If the student seems in no hurry to leave, I move back into another small talk mode by asking questions like, "So how are things going for you in general so far this year?" or "Tell me something about your experience as a political science major—do you feel we have a good program in this area?" or "How satisfied are you with your overall experience here at UVM—are you getting your money's worth?" These kinds of questions not only give us both an opportunity to share more substantive ideas in depth with one another, but also acknowledge to the student that I am interested in their welfare beyond the immediate scope of my course. And it's not unusual after I have asked how they are in general for a student to unload on me a heavy story of how the world seems to be caving in right under them.

So in the case of my work, the setting, small talk, and my

attending behaviors all serve to help people feel more comfortable sharing with me something about who they are, and at the same time allow me to disclose aspects of myself to them. When the information that each of us acquires is mutually valued, we will then often decide to meet again to follow up on what we talked about. A new relationship is born, largely because small talk helped each of us move efficiently from an initial level of superficial contact toward substantive issues that really mattered to both of us.

We can now turn to a situation more relevant to your concerns about meeting a potential partner. Recall the two basic questions that underlie any first encounter: **What can I say that will reveal something of my uniqueness?** and **How can I discover the special qualities of the person I just met?** The key to both of these questions lies in how you utilize information you already know about yourself, and how you assist other people to disclose important things about themselves. Sometimes a hobby or experience a person has is so unique that as soon as this information enters the conversation it sparks a lively, almost predictable discussion between the two individuals. If a person is fluent in six languages, for example, their new acquaintance is very likely to want to know how and why this skill was acquired. If another individual spent a year living in Peru, their new acquaintance will undoubtedly want to learn more details of their visit. But in both these cases what is important are not the facts themselves, but rather how these facts affect the individuals, and in what ways each person is different because of their unique experiences. Knowing what a person did or saw in Peru, for example, is less important than what they **felt** about what they did and saw. Being fluent in six languages is in itself less important than knowing why this skill is significant, and valuing the way it enriches one's life.

There are a several techniques you can employ as you are becoming acquainted with someone that will help accelerate the process of determining whether you wish to continue beyond the superficial level. If you utilize these strategies each time you meet someone, I think you will be pleasantly surprised by how quickly you are able to determine the potential for a new relationship.

Strategies for Moving from Small Talk to Substance

✿ **Remember the central goal of small talk: to determine whether or not you want a relationship to continue.** Although many young people feel that if a relationship is going to happen it will happen, such an approach tends to have an extremely unpredictable outcome. People who say you can't deliberately seek out an intimate relationship have been influenced by the myth of the magical accidental meeting, in which fate, not considered action, is thought to bring lovers together. In fact, it is not fate but rather **you** that controls the course of a developing relationship, and the deliberate strategies you employ during the acquaintance phase is what will actually make a difference. Like the old cliche asks, if you are not aware of where you want to go, how will you know when you have arrived?

✿ **As much as possible, control for the way in which the environment may influence the encounter.** Even simple things like taking off your sunglasses so that the person you are talking with can see your eyes, or moving your position so the other person is not looking directly into the sun are environmental influences, and when you are deliberate about these behaviors, others will usually notice and respond in kind. You can also remove your Walkman headphones, move next to a person instead of sitting on the other side of a wide table, suggest that you move to a quieter location to talk, put down heavy packages you may be carrying, and do other things that will foster a focused conversation.

✿ **Talk about fifty percent of the time.** Some people are oblivious to the fact that they dominate virtually all initial conversations, while others are unaware of how little they say in similar circumstances. Individuals who observe the fifty percent rule are generally viewed much more favorably than those who either dominate or say little. You can control your side of the equation by monitoring your own verbal contributions, and encouraging similar participation from the other individual. While you are talking you also need to be an observer of the process of your conversation, doing as much as you can to ensure that it proceeds equitably.

✿ **Move the talk toward a discussion of values.** While it is important to learn something of the breadth of a person's interests in order to discover potential areas of compatibility, learning and sharing values is what permits relationships to escalate to a more substantive level. In long-term relationships, partners have far more difficulty dealing with one another's deeper values than they do with personal habits or common interests, so the sooner these values can be identified the more likely it is that each person will use the information in behalf of the relationship. If I discovered during small talk that a person was a racist, for example, I would consider that information crucial to deciding whether or not to continue the relationship. If you understand what you value in a relationship you can utilize these value disclosures as a kind of litmus test for determining which way it might go.

✿ **Acknowledge and affirm instances in which you either share or are repelled by a strongly held value.** When you acknowledge a strongly held value disclosed by the other person you can not only say you agree, but go a step farther by indicating **why** you agree. This lets the person know **your** reasons for embracing the value, and demonstrates your willingness to take a stand on your own. Saying you do **not** share the value will help you to remain true to your own personal code of conduct, as well as give the other person accurate information about you that they need in order to complete their side of the equation.

The most important ways you can improve your social self-concept, then, are less related to things like honing your dancing skills than they are to increasing your ability to reveal yourself to others, and discovering what others would like you to know about them. Although most of us are interested in broadening our interests and enlarging our life skills in general, each person already has many qualities that others are likely to value. The trick is for people to engage in small talk that will provide the opportunities needed to share and obtain this kind of information.

My problem in meeting women at the Douglass student center was compounded significantly by my not realizing how much I would have benefitted by getting to know women regardless of whether they appeared to be potential dating partners. If I had known that most people are introduced to their dating partners by mutual friends, it might have occurred to me that becoming friends with Douglass women in general would enhance my possibilities of finding one I would be attracted to romantically. But I didn't know this, and even if I had I'm not sure my emotional self-concept would have been able to do very much with the information.

Emotional Self-Concept

I placed emotional self-concept last in this general description of how our sense of self affects the initiation of intimate relationships for two reasons: first, it is probably the most complex of the four elements of self-concept I discuss here; and second, because our emotional self-concept is the gate keeper of the physical, intellectual, and social views we have of ourselves. In the world of young adulthood the emotional self is undoubtedly the one least discussed. For many young people, talking about their "emotional selves" is either scary or hokey; scary because they are afraid of identifying feelings they have long suppressed, hokey because they associate the term with a "touchy-feely" mentality. For those who understand and appreciate the role that emotion plays in their lives, however, being in touch with feelings is a basic principle that shapes everything they do.

Although it doesn't sound very scientific or precise, I think for the purposes of this book it is sufficient to say that emotional self-concept refers to the way we feel about our self, and how those feelings influence our day-to-day activities and long-range plans. Sometimes we experience these feelings at a very low level of intensity, while at other times the feelings are so strong they dominate our life to the point where we become convinced they will overcome us. Common discourse about the emotional self usually emphasizes the words emotion or emotional, so an expression like "being emotionally involved" connotes an involvement of one emotional self with that of another. What we need to do here is explore the ways in which a person's emotions or feelings are affected by the events of their life as well as their personality, and conversely, how one's feelings influence how one thinks and behaves.

I sometimes joke with my classes about how there are always a few students who come to every session, but within ten minutes have fallen sound asleep. I wonder aloud why someone would walk all the way across campus just to doze in an uncomfortable lecture hall chair when they could more easily take a nap in their own bed. I acknowledge to the class that my lecturing has been known to induce sleep, but that the students I'm referring to have a pattern of sleeping even when the rest of the class is deeply and obviously engrossed in what I'm saying. But I conclude these remarks by saying that a student who sleeps in class seems well-adjusted compared to one who sleeps virtually the entire day, which is what I did during my senior year in college. During that year I not only averaged perhaps nine hours of sleep at night, but also managed to get in another four hours or so during the day.

Although I didn't realize it at the time, I wasn't sleeping thirteen hours a day because I was tired, but rather because I was depressed. It was only several years later that I discovered that sleeping was one of the most common ways in which people cope with emotional stress, and that I was able to clearly identify what had constituted the stresses during that particular time in my life. Since it was uncommon for people in general to talk about psychological well-being during the period of my college years, I had no awareness that something about my emotional self was out of order. We had no counseling center at Rutgers in the late fifties, nor were resident hall preceptors trained to provide even a modicum of psychological assistance to students assigned to their floors. So like most other students, I simply lacked an awareness that I **had** an emotional life.

Most young adults today are very aware of the fact that they have an emotional self, but only a few are well in touch with the details of this part of their life. The fact of the matter is that many young people experience significant difficulty in dealing with their feelings, to such a degree that their lives are often in deep turmoil. Evidence to support this assessment has been well documented during the past ten years, and comes in many forms. The following three conditions, all very common among young adults today, serve to illustrate the difficulty people have in maintaining a healthy emotional self-concept.

_ **Depression.** I just mentioned that sleeping is a common response to being depressed, but it is only one of the many ways that a person accommodates to the psychological stresses that build up within them. Because depression involves the whole body, including one's thoughts and feelings, the symptoms take many forms. Insomnia, persistent feelings of anxiousness, loss of interest in hobbies and once-enjoyable activities, restlessness and irritability, difficulty in concentrating and making decisions, feelings of helplessness and worthlessness, headaches and stomach disorders, and thoughts of death or suicide all may be symptoms of depression. Most people experience some of these symptoms only occasionally, while for others they represent a rather constant theme in their life. And young people also use the term depressed to describe what is most often a temporary feeling of guilt or worthlessness, such as when they say, "I'm totally depressed because I didn't get the job I applied for."

The most difficult step for people to take in terms of understanding depression is to recognize that most bodily responses that include pain or discomfort have their origins within the emotional self-concept of the individual. While it is always important to see a health provider to check out unexplainable pain, it is equally important to comprehend that when your body speaks, it's a good idea to try to understand what it is saying. Using antacids to relieve the symptoms of a chronic stomach ache without trying to understand what is causing it will serve only as a stopgap measure in alleviating this constant pain. What is likely to help relieve these symptoms of depression are changes in your overall behavior, perhaps made with the assistance of a trained professional.

The most important thing to realize about bodily pain whose origin is psychological rather than physical is that, with some exceptions, making it go away will entail making changes in the way you view your self and live in the world, rather than taking medicine. Some forms of depression do respond very well to medications, which emphasizes the need to see a competent counselor or therapist in assessing the source of your psychological discomfort. But for most young people it is a matter of changing the way one thinks about life that enables them to gain control over the factors that contribute to their pain.

_ **Alcohol abuse.** Drinking in order to get drunk is a dysfunctional behavior, no matter how absurd you think this idea is. Getting drunk regularly is normative behavior for many young adults, **but this kind of behavior always signals underlying doubts the individual has about their sense of self.** People who feel good about themselves not only have no need to get drunk, but more importantly, they consciously avoid this behavior because they know it is self-destructive. The very term "got wasted" captures the essence of this behavior, although young people often use this expression as if it were a positive experience. Alcoholism is one of our nation's most serious illnesses, an illness that for many well educated-individuals has its roots in and is fostered by the culturally approved abuse of alcohol during the young adult years. This is not to say that there are not many other factors including family patterns and heredity that contribute to the development of alcohol addiction, but social norms surrounding alcohol use play a significant role in this process.

When people desire to get drunk they are saying that they do not want to have control over themselves, that they wish to enter a state of mind in which some external factor controls them. Unlike sleeping, which is also a coping mechanism for the stress or dis-ease people feel about themselves, the regular use of alcohol is likely to create an addiction. The reasons why young adults abuse alcohol are identical to those of the population in general, but young people often argue that drinking is just good fun and part of the young adult experience. Many people identify excessive drinking during their young adult years as a phase of social development, something they will grow out of after they get out into the real world. But make no mistake: alcohol use among young adults mirrors exactly its purpose in the larger adult society, and the fact of the matter is that a very large proportion of young people who are considered problem drinkers will not grow out of this pattern of drinking.

It is not a sign of poor mental health when a person gets drunk in the process of experimenting with alcohol. If one has never had a drink before one has no concept of what their limits might be. Getting drunk the first time, with all the trappings of vomiting, spinning rooms, pounding headaches, and unconsciousness can serve as a harsh but relatively innocuous lesson in this search for limits, but to seek to return to this state in order to experience the euphoria of being high is to laugh (puke?) in the face of Mother Nature.

My perspective on alcohol is that of health, in this case psychological health, so if there were no detrimental effects to getting drunk I couldn't possibly argue against it from the standpoint of health. But alcohol abuse not only affects the individuals who are drinking, but also contributes to bad (and sometimes tragic) consequences for others as well. My taking a stand against alcohol abuse has nothing to do with a moralistic desire for you to behave as I do. If you are steamed up at this moment because you can see yourself in the descriptions I just gave, and are angry because you don't consider your drinking behavior to be either dysfunctional or suggestive of a low self-esteem, I can understand why and appreciate your feelings. **People who abuse alcohol invariably deny both that they may be addicted to the substance and that the consequences of their alcohol use may be counterproductive.** And one of the best ways for you to determine whether you actually have a drinking problem is to ask yourself whether or not you are annoyed or angered by what I said; if you are, you have a problem. Trust me.

_ **Problematic responses to angry feelings.** Oscar the Grouch, the Muppet character in the TV show **Sesame Street**, seems always to have something to complain about, whether it be people making noise around his garbage can or the simple inability of others to see things his way. Oscar is often angry and reveals his feelings by shouting, banging things around, and withdrawing from the scene of his discomfort by retreating into his garbage can and slamming the lid. The creators of **Sesame Street**, as do the producers of other children's programs like **Mr. Rogers Neighborhood**, know that anger and angry feelings are part of every child's life. These shows therefore attempt to help children both identify and respond to anger in productive ways, which run the gamut of naming the feeling within oneself to expressing it in a healthy way to another person. It is no accident that the subject of anger occupies such a prominent role in these TV programs, since the producers are all well aware that the cultural consequences of our inability to recognize and deal with anger are truly staggering.

People respond to their angry feelings in myriad ways. Some keep their rage bottled up inside, resulting in depression, or in the case of females, conditions like bulimia and anorexia. Others attempt to escape their anger through drugs or alcohol. Still others act out their anger sexually or aggressively. We learn many of our strategies for coping with anger from our parents and other family members, as well as from societal influences like advertising and the media. TV and movie violence, for example, is one of the most prominent and persistent images in these forms of media, which both reflects and contributes to the way males in our culture respond to their angry feelings.

You are probably aware that anger is experienced and expressed differently by males and females. This has nothing to do with biology, of course, but rather results from the different ways in which females and males are socialized to deal with anger. It should be no surprise, then, that eating disorders like bulimia and anorexia occur almost exclusively among young women, and that excessive drinking and violence are more prominent among young men. The message about expressing their feelings that females acquire is to "stifle," as Archie Bunker would say to his wife Edith or their daughter Gloria. Keep quiet, keep your opinions and feelings **inside yourself.** Eating disorders in young women in which they **withhold food from their bodies,** is to a large degree an expression of the anger they feel toward their father because he **withholds his love and approval from them.** In a similar way, young women who "sleep around" are often acting out sexually the angry feelings they have over the lack of attention their father pays them, and his lack of involvement and caring in their life.

What males learn about feelings is to deny them at all costs, to remain cool and under control. But since men **have** feelings, and many legitimate reasons to feel angry, their strategy of attempting to contain their rage through denial is fruitless. Alcohol and drugs may allow them to escape the pain of their anger temporarily, but in the long run only makes it worse, since the cycle of escape and guilt becomes more intense over time. Aggressive and violent behaviors are ways in which men act out their anger over being denied the love and care of not only their fathers, but of men and women in general. Destructive and aggressive behaviors among males, whether it involves putting a fist through a wall or murdering a drug dealer or raping a woman, grows from the frustration and anger they experience over not being able to control the emotional part of their lives. If you are taught from childhood that simply because you are a male you should be free from feelings and emotions, you will inevitably become angry when you experience those feelings and see no legitimate way to express them.

From Acquaintance to Lover

Having considered some of the ways in which self-esteem contributes to the vision we have of ourselves as potential partners, we can now look at exactly what happens in the process of getting an intimate relationship off the ground. We will be concerned with three general questions: How can you meet a potential partner? What can you do when you feel good about the relationship and want it to continue? And, what factors move a developing intimate relationship toward stability and commitment?

A healthy self-concept paves the way for developing relationships, so anything you do to feel better about yourself will increase your chances of making new friends and meeting a potential partner. This is why it is so important to assess your intimacy status as I suggested earlier, and to understand that throughout your life maintaining satisfying intimate relationships will depend on your ability to continually nourish your self-concept, and to keep growing as an individual. **Most of the problems that partners have in intimate relationships have less to do with the relationship itself than with the issue of personal growth for each individual**, an idea I will expand on in the next chapter.

So if you would like to meet someone who might become an intimate partner, the place to begin is with an assessment of your self-concept, and by acknowledging that although there may be parts of yourself that you don't feel terrific about, you consider yourself to be worthy of someone else's affection and love. Another person's love can never be a substitute for self-love or self-esteem, so seeking a partner to give you what you are unable to give yourself will be a hopeless and painful journey. If you don't feel entitled to an intimate relationship, you would be wise to concentrate on improving your self-esteem before venturing out into the world in search of a partner.

So how did young people who are currently involved in an intimate relationship actually meet their partners? At bars? An ad in the personal column of the local newspaper? At parties? Through friends? All the above? Yes, all the above. But of the many ways that people meet new partners, friends most often help us make this kind of connection, and it doesn't take a lot of deep thought to understand why. We tend to be attracted to people who are similar to us, so it stands to reason that our friends are an excellent source of new referrals for our social life. From this point of view, if we want to increase our chances of meeting a partner we will find desirable we need to increase our friendship network. The more opportunities we have in which a friend introduces us to someone new, the more chance there is that one of these new acquaintances will be someone we can grow close to.

You can make new friends by joining groups that have a specific social purpose, but making friends can be accomplished just as well through the day-to-day contacts you have with other people. One of the most effective approaches to making a new friend is to tell someone that you liked something they said or did, as Marion did when she complimented Louise on her English essay. As a rule we tend to pay attention to someone when they compliment us, and in this process of attending to the other person we usually feel receptive to learning something about them. Because we feel good about being complimented, we often become conscious of a desire to reciprocate the interest shown to us by trying to learn something about the other person.

If you talk with lovers about their first impressions of one another, you will find a wide assortment of stories. In some cases each person experiences an immediate kind of electricity, which leads to a rapid build up of the relationship. The electricity may be expressed sexually almost from the outset, and the partners may feel totally absorbed with one another. In other cases the relationship develops quite slowly, with each person moving cautiously and deliberately toward deeper levels of interaction. In still other instances partners may initially feel no attraction whatsoever, only to discover over time that what they share in common represents the basis for developing an intimate relationship. But regardless of the particular pattern in which a relationship begins, there are common threads that run through all relationships during the acquaintance stage, because all relationships require certain kinds of processes in order to begin functioning. Perhaps the two most important of these processes are what I sometimes refer to as the "M & M's" of developing relationships: matching and meshing.

Matching and Meshing

A crucial way potential partners determine whether they have sufficient grounds for building a relationship is to identify similarities. When two people discover they have many things in common they often attach special meaning to this fact, even though they may share these similarities with thousands of other people. The matching process is an expedition in which two individuals attempt to discover as many similarities as possible, and after finding a multitude of them conclude that it is no coincidence they have so much in common. Matching is a natural and predictable way that people discover common ground, and serves as a useful screening device in developing relationships. There are, however, two hazards to matching: first, individuals frequently stretch unrealistically the closeness of a match; and second, meaning is attached to matches that exaggerates the actual power the match has for contributing anything substantial to the relationship.

Two students who meet at the University of Vermont and discover they both grew up in Topeka, Kansas, for instance, do indeed have something in common. But Topeka is a pretty big place, and had the same two students met while **in** Topeka it would be unlikely for them to attach any significance to this particular match. Potential partners tend to search for special meaning in their similarities when they are uncertain of the value of their own individuality. I won't be eager to give away something of myself in order to create a match with you if I feel very good about who I am, because I won't be worried about the possibility that you will find me unacceptable as a partner. I am only going to be concerned about creating a match if I think you might reject me outright if you knew something about me that didn't correspond to your idea of a perfectly lovable person. And while two people may have something in common they both feel is a very important aspect of their individuality, it is unlikely that this similarity will in itself provide the entire foundation for the relationship.

As individuals get to know one another over time they invariably attempt to mesh their interactions in order to operate more smoothly as a pair. At first, potential partners may feel they are just one big bag of similarities, with never a care that some behaviors or features of their personalities will inevitably clash. If the two individuals are to become a pair, they will need to integrate these differences into their relationship when they occur, and they do this by meshing their interactions. If most interactions between the pair were unmeshed, there would be constant turmoil and little chance the relationship would survive. During the acquaintance stage, potential partners tend to be willing to accommodate their individual needs to the demands of the developing relationship, and they do this by working to establish smooth chains of interaction. The meshing process is only a problem if one or both partners compromise the true vision of themselves in order to appear lovable to the other. In this case, an interaction that is meshed today is likely to become mashed tomorrow.

As relationships develop, one partner is usually a bit ahead of the other, either in knowing the relationship is advancing or in **wanting** it to advance. Most couples can pinpoint turning points in their relationship, or at least can identify markers along the way that illustrate the developmental nature of their relationship. A marker point that many young people have talked with me about occurs when a long period of separation is imminent. As a new couple approaches this kind of separation, many of the unspoken issues of their relationship come to the surface as they begin thinking about what rules might apply during their separation. Facing a separation often forces partners to have some explicit discussions about these matters, and in doing so they may advance the stature of their relationship by making certain commitments to one another.

Sometimes a marker point is established when one of the partners says "I love you" to the other. There are lots of ways to say "I love you," aren't there? For some people, saying "I love you" is as natural as tying their shoes, while for others these words carry such great weight they only say them if they **really mean them!** These three words spoken in the right sequence are so powerful for some individuals that they are **very** careful **not** to say them unless they feel able to carry through with some specific kinds of behaviors and agreements.

If I say "I love you," you might wonder what I mean by these words, especially if I don't tell you what I mean by them. Think of all the different things I might mean.

- ✿ I could say, "I love you, and what I mean by this is that I really **like** you, and would love to hop into bed with you and ball our little eyeballs right out of their sockets!"
- ✿ Or I could say, "I love you, and what I mean by this is that I'd like to be in a sexually exclusive relationship with you, but don't get the idea I want to get married or move in together or really have to spend all our time with each other or anything like that."
- ✿ Or I could say, "I love you, and what I mean by this is that **I really do love you,** I mean you're the first person I've ever felt this way about, and I know it's something special, and since I've never felt this way about anyone else in my life it must really be love, and **that's** what I mean when I say I love you!"

So as you can see, love means different things to different people, and of course it means different things to the very people who say they love one another. I can mean one thing when I say

"I love you," and you can mean something else when you reply "I love you, too." And as you're aware, two individuals don't usually arrive at a point where it occurs to them simultaneously that they love one another—one person says it first, and the other is then confused, pleased, or panics over the possibility of their having to respond in kind.

Saying "I love you" is not the only way partners can tell their relationship is developing. Their day-to-day actions give evidence they are growing closer, as can be seen in this list of loving behaviors.

Behaviors Indicating Developing Love

- Partners express their affections verbally.
- Self-disclosure increases as partners feel more trusting toward one another.
- There is an increase in the non-material evidence of love, such as by giving emotional and moral support, showing interest in the other's activities, and respecting one another's opinions.
- Partners feel happier, more secure, and more relaxed when the other is around.
- Gifts are exchanged as material evidence of love.
- There is an increase in physical expressions of love...hugging, kissing, kissing, hugging, etc., etc.

I used to be surprised when I would ask a young person whether or not they were in an intimate relationship, and they would respond by saying that they were not sure. Not sure? How could you not be sure about something like love? In a case like this the problem is usually that the partners have not explicitly acknowledged they are a couple, although their friends may consider them to be one. A good way to tell if you are in an intimate relationship is to examine whether or not when you use the term "we," your friends understand who you are talking about. If they do, you are probably in an intimate relationship! Your friends may know all about this phenomenon, having heard you go on and on about how "We did this and then we did that."

When partners begin to form agreements related to their intimate behavior with others, they have escalated their developing relationship to a new level of commitment. These agreements are typically both implicit and explicit, often moving from the former to the latter when a violation of an implicit rule occurs. As partners increase their feelings of loyalty to one another they begin the process of forming commitments, which in turn acts to strengthen the pair bond.

CHAPTER 12

━◀♦♦▶━

Long-Term Intimate Relationships

Every relationship has a beginning, middle, and end; an all too obvious statement, perhaps, but one that is worth thinking about at the outset of this chapter on long-term relationships. How partners navigate each of these phases can tell us a great deal about each individual, as well as give us some insight into the meanings of a relationship. Some relationships are of such short duration that it is hard to determine where the middles of them were, since they may have consisted mainly of brief but passionate beginnings, followed almost immediately by abrupt endings. And given the fact that some partners mourn the ending of their relationship for years after its actual collapse, it can sometimes be difficult for an outsider to determine whether in fact the relationship has truly ended.

This chapter will focus on the middles and endings of intimate relationships, an agenda hefty enough to warrant a whole book. But given the book's larger purposes I think a chapter is sufficient to present the concepts about long-term intimate relationships most important to young adults. In deciding what to include and how to shape this chapter I tried to account for the wide range of experiences young people have with intimate relationships, realizing that some have never had a single such relationship while others have been in several. My task was eased considerably by the realization that since I am dealing with only the young adult years I do not have to address some of the more profound issues that often arise later on, such as the ways that children affect an intimate relationship.

While there are some important variations between homosexual and heterosexual long-term intimate relationships, most of the variation can be attributed to gender considerations rather than sexual orientation. Irrespective of sexual orientation, all partners in long-term relationships must deal with issues of love, work, and money, as well as the myriad component pieces that make up each of these three elements of human existence. The core elements of all intimate relationship are similar: friends, family, time, sex, a home, commitment, fidelity, mutuality, communication, problem solving, equity and fairness, power, the effects of gender, recreation, personal growth, and more.

About three-quarters of this chapter deals with "middles," or long-term relationships over time; the remaining portion concentrates on conflict and breakdown. Four central questions about an intimate relationship provide a framework for our discussion:

❧ Where and how does an intimate relationship fit into the life of each partner?
❧ What constitutes the life of a relationship? What do partners **do** that make the relationship intimate? What distinguishes people in this kind of relationship from those who are not?
❧ What are the philosophical elements that form the basis for an intimate relationship? How do partners measure the growth of the relationship? What are the characteristics of a healthy intimate relationship?
❧ What is conflict? What factors most often precipitate the breakdown and dissolution of intimate relationships?

We begin this inquiry by attempting to visualize where intimate relationship fit into each partner's life.

Visualizing Intimate Relationships

In the last few chapters we discovered some of the factors that draw people together, and examined the critical role that self-image plays in the attraction phase of intimate relationships. We can now consider what happens within such relationships over time. Although partners may feel they share a great deal in common in terms of traits, values, and interests, two very important facts remain: first, an intimate relationship never arises from the same blueprint; and second, it doesn't exist in a vacuum. In other words, each partner brings to a new relationship a vision, conscious or unconscious, of what the relationship might look like. And once established, the relationship exists within the context of each partner's social network. Social networks consist of family, friends, co-workers, employers, acquaintances and other groups and organizations.

Most couples, however, are not very deliberate in the way they construct their intimate relationships. So what happens most often is that questions about the extent of each partner's investment in the relationship don't surface until it has actually been in place for perhaps several months. In addition, during the attraction phase it is uncommon for couples to pay much attention to the ways in which their social networks might be influencing their developing relationship. So a very good and fundamental question a couple in a developing relationship can address is, **Where and how does this relationship fit into our lives?**

This may seem like a very simple issue, one whose resolution would appear self-evident to most couples. Yet in working with young adults I have discovered that major discrepancies frequently exist between how individual partners visualize their intimate relationship and the role it plays in their lives. Not infrequently one partner is more invested in the relationship than the other, or one partner's social network has more influence on the relationship than does the other's. **Personal investment** and **social networks**, then, represent tangible elements of a relationship that partners can discuss as a means of examining where and how the relationship fits into their lives.

The following three questions will help you get a better sense of how an intimate relationship fits into your life.

1. **How much "space" do you want an intimate relationship to occupy in your life?**

This question is usually harder to answer than it appears, because it requires that partners be explicit about their commitment to the relationship. There are a finite number of hours in a day, and therefore just in terms of time a relationship must compete with all the other things each partner wishes to do in their life. While one couple may consider their intimate relationship to be but a small part of their lives, another may see it as the very focal point of their existence. In thinking about the "space" an intimate relationship occupies in your life, it is important to consider not only the amount of time you spend with your partner, but also its psychological contribution to your overall sense of well-being. When both partners agree on the relative importance of their intimate relationship this particular feature of their relationship can be said to be **symmetrical**, or in harmony. On the other hand, if one partner considers the relationship more important than the other the relationship is then **asymmetrical** or unbalanced.

As surprising as it may sound, many couples will have considerable difficulty just agreeing on what their relationship looks like, let alone describing what they would **like** it to look like. Why is this so? For several reasons. If you are less invested in your relationship than you think your partner is, you may be reluctant to specify how much less, because to do so raises the risk that your partner's feelings will be hurt, and perhaps will consider withdrawing their love and attention from you. And even if your levels of investment were similar, you might be reluctant to discuss this question if your individual social networks were both strongly opposed to your relationship. Under such a heavy burden of negative influence, you might well choose to avoid close scrutiny of your commitment, lest the worst predictions of your friends come true. Likewise, examining your investment levels might lead to the conclusion that neither of you is sufficiently committed to the relationship to justify continuing it, but you realize that the energy required to end it is greater than that needed to sustain it. Thus it endures.

The remaining two questions focus on the role that each partner's social network plays in their individual lives and in their life together as a couple.

2. **Irrespective of the "size" of your relationship space, how large and varied is the influence of your individual social networks on you as individuals?**

Whether or not we like to acknowledge it, all of us are influenced to some degree by individuals or groups that comprise our social network. Our first such social network was our family, and for many young adults, family members remain an ever-present source of influence, even if they live far from home. This is not to say that these young people are forever calling home to consult or gain approval for a developing relationship, but rather to suggest that one of the inescapable questions that arise in our minds as we begin to develop a relationship is, **How will my family, especially my parents, regard my partner?** This question may never present itself explicitly, but it is tucked somewhere in the recesses of our unconscious. And given that we spent much of our childhood attempting to gain the approval of our parents, it should be no surprise that we would wish for their approval of our choice of an intimate partner. This despite the fact that we may feel we have totally written our parents out of our life. Parents have a way of maintaining their presence in our psychological lives even when they are dead!

Friends, housemates, and social groups may constitute the main framework of your social network, and the role these individuals and groups play in your life may be large or small, the range of your interactions with them may be narrow or diverse. The point to make about social networks is that because they are in fact a part of our life we are in some way influenced by their attitudes, values, and advice. This means that when we create a new intimate relationship we do so within the context of our social networks, and the partner we choose and the way we go about building our relationship are subject to the influence of these networks. A relationship does not exist in a vacuum.

It is also true that some of us have very large and diverse social networks, while others have small networks with narrow and limited forms of interaction and influence. This does not suggest that having a small social network means that one is less subject to being influenced by the individuals who comprise it. It is often the case that a person with a small social network is in fact influenced tremendously by the need to be accepted by those few people who form their network. An individual with a domineering parent, for instance, can operate as if they were a robot, so powerful can be the influence of just one person. Whether one's network is large and diverse or small and narrow, what is important to keep in mind is that when two people come together and form an intimate relationship, they bring their social networks with them.

The final two-part question about where your intimate relationship fits into your life flows naturally out of the second.

3. **How large and varied is the influence of your individual social networks on you as a couple? To what extent do your networks overlap one another?**

Just as we are influenced as individuals by our social networks, so too is our developing intimate relationship. And as you might suspect, the influence can be large or small, limited or diverse. We can begin to appreciate the complexity of intimate relationships when we consider how many kinds of factors are involved just in the matter of the effects of social networks. Not only do our individual networks influence our relationship, but they usually do so at varying degrees, perhaps yours having more influence than your partner's. Sometimes the influence is symmetrical, sometimes asymmetrical. Sometimes our social networks overlap, meaning that members of each partner's network interact with members of the other's. In other cases members of one partner's network never have occasion to interact with those of the other's. And to compound matters even further, the relative amount of influence played by one's social network changes over time, resulting from geographical changes as well as from developmental growth within each individual. Since many of the problems that intimate relationships encounter arise either from the place the relationship occupies in each individual's life or because of the influence of their social networks, there are good reasons why partners would find it time well spent to discuss these issues openly.

Life Within An Intimate Relationship

Partners in love relationships don't typically think of their relationship as consisting of a bunch of tidy little categories, each with its own set of meanings and purposes. Rather, most partners consider their relationship life together as comprising a whole entity, in which the various constituent parts interact with and overlap one another. Having had decades of experience as an intimate partner, I know well that the ecosystem of a close relationship is fluid and dynamic, and cannot easily be teased apart into precise and finite components. But as a student of close relationships I am also aware that it is possible to describe the various elements of a relationship, and to place these elements within some kind of structural framework. When working with young people who are experiencing difficulties in their intimate relationships I find it especially helpful to utilize such a framework as a means of illustrating where the source of their problems may lie, and what they might do to bring about improvements.

For the purposes of this section dealing with the life of an intimate relationship, I am going to concentrate on describing not only what partners **do** with one another, but also **why** what they do helps to make the relationship an intimate one. Let's begin with some obvious but important ideas about what partners do within the framework of their intimate relationship.

- ✿ Partners do some things with just one another; they do other things as a couple with individuals and groups outside their relationship.
- ✿ Many times within a relationship partners do individual things in the presence of their lover. Reading, watching TV, studying, and walking to work are examples of these kinds of behaviors. While partners do indeed usually interact during these kinds of activities, interaction is not the primary purpose of the individual behaviors.

- Some things partners do together have as their primary purpose the maintenance of day-to-day routines. Shopping for groceries and preparing food, for example, have the central goal of providing nourishment to each partner; these routines must be accomplished whether or not an individual is in a relationship. This is not to say that a relationship does not benefit because partners do this kind of work together.

- A major form of interaction between partners centers around joint planning and problem solving. Planning might involve deciding where and how to spend a vacation, what colors to paint the apartment, the menu for a dinner party for friends, and what nights to play racquetball. Problem solving often concerns matters like money and the division of household tasks.

- Partners take care of one another. This caring takes many forms, from picking up stamps for one's partner, to asking about their day, to actually taking care of them when they are ill. Sometimes caring consists of simply listening and being attentive to a partner.

- Most partners spend time together engaging in recreational activities. In some of these activities, like tennis and cards, partners actually interact directly with one another. In others like skiing, partners share the same general space but don't necessarily depend on one another's direct involvement in order to enjoy the recreation. Going to the movies or to sporting events are other examples of partners engaging in recreational activities together that don't require much interaction.

- Virtually all partners devote considerable time to "working on" their relationship. This work tends to include arguing about how the relationship is failing to meet one or both partners' needs, disagreements over what each partner can and cannot do with friends, outbreaks of jealousy, and long discussions over whether or not the partners "really" love one another. The work partners do on their relationship is often stimulated by conflicts they are having, and not infrequently conclude with agreements to approach problems differently or change specified behaviors. Sometimes partners work with counselors or therapists who assist them in understanding the dynamics of their relationship, and help them improve their problem-solving and communication skills. Partners whose relationship is functioning well may engage in developmental work together, attempting to enhance what is already good, so "working on" includes far more than simply reacting to problems.

♣ And finally, certain things partners do together are designed specifically to celebrate their relationship. I use the word celebrate in its widest meaning here, suggesting that such celebration might take the form of a special picnic on a hilltop overlooking the sea or a plan to spend Saturday afternoon in bed making love. The critical point about these kinds of activities is that they are planned, and have as their only purpose the enjoyment partners derive from interacting directly with one another.

If you think about the various things that partners in long-term intimate relationships actually do with one another you realize that each behavior, either positive or negative, contributes something to the overall relationship. In addition, whether reading in the presence of one another, engaging in passionate sexual encounters or fighting about personal dispositions, **intimate partners are shaped by their relationship**. This quality of being influenced by a relationship is one that distinguishes intimate partners from their non-partnered friends and acquaintances, and especially during the initial stage of a developing relationship can present problems for both the couple and their friends.

The creation of a new intimate relationship inevitably leads to changes in the relationships each partner has with members of their social network, changes which can be confusing and disruptive to everyone involved. It is probably safe to say that living within an intimate relationship is more complex than living single. And by extension, living within several intimate relationships, as parents do with their children and with one another, is even more demanding. But as I discussed in an earlier chapter, people benefit from intimate relationships, and therefore tend to see the return to be well worth the effort.

Even a casual inspection of the preceding list of things partners do with one another should reveal that dynamic intimate relationships require an enormous amount of good old-fashioned hard work. And in this respect, intimate relationships are no different from anything else we value in life: to do something well requires knowledge, skills, values, determination, energy, and work. Good relationships do not run on cruise control, but rather are tended and nurtured continuously. To work well they need at least as much effort and commitment as demanded by one's occupation, and may require as much investment of time as does a job.

At this point you may be wondering how any young adult could possibly create a reasonable balance between time spent in their job as a student or worker and time spent with their love partner. If you are a student, your job involves attending classes, studying, and completing the various assignments related to your curriculum. In addition, you may work part-time in order to pay for college and living expenses, and have additional obligations to clubs, athletics, music, and other campus activities. If you work full time, your life is similarly complex and varied. You lead a busy life. But remember that many things that partners actually do with one another represent behaviors that they would carry out independent of their intimate relationship. If you add up the time you devote to meal preparation and eating, recreation, attending social events and sleeping, you will no doubt discover that the total hours at least equal the hours you spend attending classes or working. This time is available for you to spend with your partner, and thus you have the opportunity to balance your love life with your work and personal life. Your life as an adult is not likely to be less busy than it is now. Being able to strike this balance, however, requires that partners solve problems effectively and communicate clearly, perhaps the two most important skills needed for a successful intimate relationship.

Solving Problems Together

During the early part of a developing intimate relationship, partners typically pay little attention to how well or poorly they solve problems together. Caught up in what often is a rather overwhelming sense of romance and passion, the last thing on these lovers' minds is how effective they might be at joint decision-making. But as time goes on, partners discover that the ability to traverse even a single day in a satisfying way depends on their problem-solving skills. As a relationship begins to gel, the "real" life of each partner begins to assert itself, at which point the couple starts to feel the effects of their long-held individual ways of operating in the world. No longer are partners willing to submerge their true feelings about even the most mundane matters, such as what movie to attend or where to go for dinner. So an exchange at the beginning of a relationship that looked like this:

Jack: What would you like to do tonight, Jill?
Jill: Anything's fine with me, Jack, what would you like to do?

| Jack: | It doesn't matter to me, honey, whatever you'd like to do is fine with me. How about a movie? |
| Jill: | A movie sounds fine with me, Jack. What would you like to see? |

now looks more like this:

Jack:	What would you like to do tonight, Jill?
Jill:	Anything's fine with me, Jack, what would you like to do?
Jack:	It doesn't matter to me, honey, whatever you'd like to do is fine with me. How about a movie?
Jill:	Well, that would be OK, I guess, but it seems like all we've done together the last few weeks is go to the movies. Wouldn't you like to do something else for a change?
Jack:	Sure, that's OK with me. What would you like to do?
Jill:	Well, I don't know, maybe we could go dancing at Sha-Na-Na, or get together with Bill and Meredith.
Jack:	I'm not really in the mood for dancing, especially at Sha-Na-Na—it's so smokey and loud in that place I can hardly stand it.
Jill:	I thought you liked Sha-Na-Na! The first time we went there you said you hadn't had so much fun in ages. Were you making all that up just to impress me or something?
Jack:	Of course I wasn't, it's just that after a while that whole club scene gets to be a drag.
Jill:	Well, then what would you like to do instead? Would you rather just go to a movie? Because if you would, I guess it would be alright with me.
Jack:	OK, let's go to a movie. Maybe we can go dancing somewhere else sometime soon. What movie would you like to see?
Jill:	I don't really care, what would you like to see?

Partners in a developing relationship don't invent brand new ways of interacting with their new lover; they bring to their relationship a combination of effective and ineffective ways of interacting, and employ these techniques just as they have in other intimate and non-intimate relationships. Perhaps because competition is so central to our way of life, most American men and women are not very good at solving together the kinds of problems that arise in the day-to-day life of an intimate relationship.

Being able to solve problems together represents one of the more pragmatic aspects of intimate relationships, quite remote from romance and passion. Yet partners who develop good problem-solving skills are far more likely to enjoy the romantic and passionate aspects of their relationship than are those who do not. Many factors act to influence the way partners go about solving problems. Among the most important are power, gender, family modeling, and the extent to which individuals have been exposed to and practiced various decision-making strategies. Improving your joint problem-solving and decision-making skills involves three basic steps.

Three Steps to Improved Problem-Solving

1. **Identify your present strategies**. Most of what you learned about joint problem-solving resulted from observing your parents, so the place to begin is by examining how and how well your parents solved problems together. Was the process a mutual one? Did one parent usually get their way? If so, what strategies were used to accomplish this end? What methods do you typically employ to influence a decision to benefit you? What do you know about your strengths and weaknesses related to joint problem-solving?

2. **Recognize when you and your partner are involved in joint problem-solving**. Deciding what movie to attend or whether to live together utilize the same processes, although these decisions are obviously of a different magnitude. What is crucial to realize is that it is as important to be able to solve the former kind of problem satisfactorily as it is the latter. Recognizing that you are in a "decision-making mode" is a key to being able to behave in a way quite different from what you may be used to.

3. **Use each opportunity to make a joint decision as a time to practice making good joint decisions**. If you have recognized that you and your partner are in a decision-making mode, you are more likely to be able to practice effective problem-solving. A good joint decision has the following characteristics:

* It is mutual. This means that both partners agree with the decision outcome, although each may not get entirely what they want. Neither partner feels they "lost" anything in the decision.
* The decision was not determined because one partner exerted power over the other. Power involves getting someone to do something that they don't really want to do.

❁ It is one that reflects the basic values and beliefs of each partner. Decisions that violate core values and beliefs usually lead to troubled waters in the future.

❁ It is subject to change. Quite often a decision about what to do tomorrow becomes inadequate in meeting needs that arise next month or next year. Thus a good decision is resilient, and can be returned to for modification at a later time.

❁ A good decision often has a back-up decision built into it. Deciding to see a certain movie can also include a decision of what to do if the movie is sold out upon arrival at the theater.

❁ Alternatives have been carefully examined and rejected. A good decision does not leave partners yearning for one of the rejected alternatives, hopeful that if something changes the alternative will be attainable. Although a good decision may include a provision like, "If X happens, we will then be able to do Y," if X never does happen partners will be able to live comfortably with that reality.

One of the most important reasons for practicing joint problem-solving early in a developing relationship is that during this period partners have not had sufficient time to build up their repertory of dysfunctional interaction behaviors, and therefore are more willing to try new ways of relating to one another. Early in a relationship partners are still trying to please one another, still trying to cooperate in reaching mutual goals. It may sound cynical to suggest that most intimate partners are not very good at solving problems together, but this happens to be one of the basic characteristics of a disproportionately large percentage of long-term intimate relationships. So the more willing you are from the outset to carefully work through decisions about all matters affecting your relationship, the less likely you will have to spend time and energy later on undoing the problems you have created for yourselves.

Communicating Clearly

Many times throughout this book I have described how important it is to be able to communicate clearly your thoughts, feelings, desires and intentions, especially to a partner, but also to family and friends. It would be hard to believe that a person could get beyond high school without having had some kind of training or education about the importance of clear communication. I can't imagine a young person not including "good communication" on a list of criteria needed for a satisfying intimate relationship, so well embedded is this concept in our consciousness. Hundreds of books have been written to help people communicate more effectively, and a large industry thrives on assisting corporations and other organizations improve the communication skills of employees. Yet despite the fact that most of us have been exposed to **ideas** about its importance, good communication represents a major stumbling block for many intimate partners.

What does it mean to communicate clearly? In a nutshell clear communication involves sending a message to someone else, who in turn receives the same message thought to have been sent by the sender. Sounds pretty simple, doesn't it? And of course, many messages **are** sent and received accurately. If I ask you "What time is it?" and you reply "Three-thirty," we might well have completed a successful communication transmission. But what if, in response to that same question you reply, "What do you want to know for? Do you have to leave now?" What initially sounded like a very simple question could turn into quite a protracted discussion, which illustrates that much more than words are involved in communication.

We can think of messages as having three important elements: the first represents the **content**, which in this last example would be that I asked you the time; the second consists of the **surface feelings**, which here might be a panicked look on my face, perhaps because I suddenly realized it was later than I thought; and the third element embodies those **underlying feelings** I have about the content of the message, such as what might happen if I'm late to my four o'clock appointment. As the receiver of the message I send, you are exposed to the content and surface feelings in the message, but can only guess about what my underlying feelings might be. The degree to which you are able to perceive accurately all three of these elements allows you to respond in a way that will help or hurt my cause. Because we usually communicate at a very rapid rate, the likelihood that the content or feelings of a message will be miscommunicated, misunderstood or misinterpreted is quite high.

The two way street metaphor for good communication means that as a sender we have the ability to deliver our message in a way that clearly expresses both its content and feelings, and as a receiver we are able to perceive accurately the content and feelings of messages directed our way, **and respond appropriately to those messages.** Remember, too, that non-verbal communication is often as significant a part of our interactions as is communication involving words. Smiles, smirks, shrugs, raised-eyebrows, scowls, rolling eyes, hugs, pats on the shoulder, playful pinches of the cheeks, nose-thumbing, middle-finger gestures and tongue poking are just a few of the ways we communicate without words.

It is usually the underlying feelings of a message that interfere with intimate partners being able to communicate clearly with one another. Underlying feelings are the source of our problems here for two important reasons. First, we are often unaware of just what it is we are feeling or are unable to label quickly and correctly a strong feeling we have. And second, even when we have accurately identified our feelings we may be anxious about acknowledging them as an explicit part of the message, fearful that if we do our partner will misunderstand or be hurt. Whether the reason we do not account for our feelings before sending a message to our partner is because we are unaware of what they are (or for that matter that they might even exist) or because we are afraid to express them, the result is the same: our partner is left to their own devices to interpret them. Identifying feelings and being willing to express them, then, constitutes the real work of improved communication for intimate partners, so let's look at these two issues in more detail.

We can begin by considering some of the words commonly used to describe feelings.

angry	bitter	depressed	furious	lonely
annoyed	concerned	distressed	happy	mad
anxious	confident	elated	hurt	pissed
apathetic	confused	enraged	indifferent	puzzled
assured	dejected	frustrated	irritated	sad
offended	troubled	unloved	upset	worried

There are many more, of course, but this list should give you a sense of the flavors feelings come in. Notice that these words describe both positive and negative feelings, an important point to be aware of. While we usually think that negative feelings are more difficult to locate and express than positive ones, this is not always the case. There are times when we are feeling very good about something, but because we are not feeling trusting toward our partner at the moment we are reluctant to have these feelings bubble over into our conversation.

Learning why we have difficulty identifying and expressing our feelings is one important step toward improved communication with our partner. Once we know **why** we respond a certain way, such as because of our gender learnings, we must then be able to act on this knowledge. This is where the hard work really begins.

Perhaps one of the most satisfying ways that partners can entertain this work is to devote some time talking about what each learned about this whole issue of feelings while growing up, reviewing histories and highlighting some of the strongest messages each received. A second part of this discussion can focus on what each partner knows to be **their** personal history related to identifying and expressing feelings, both within intimate love relationships they may have had in the past as well as with friends and family. Finally, partners can talk about the role that feelings play in their own relationship, noting how both positive and negative feelings color their communication.

During their conversation about communicating feelings, partners can practice some specific skills related to good listening and responding, skills which will aid immensely in helping them identify and express their feelings. Active listening involves far more than occasionally re-phrasing what your partner says, although this technique does tend to allow you to interact without changing the direction of the conversation. Re-phrasings beginning with

"So what you are feeling is..."

"What I heard you say is..."

"It's clear that you feel strongly about..." "

"So if you had to do things differently you would..."

will usually be seen by your partner as evidence that you are interested and involved in what they are saying, and also help you maintain your focus when your partner is talking. Active listening also includes saying and doing things, **as well as *not* saying and *not* doing things**, that facilitate communicating feelings clearly. Especially during a discussion related to feelings, what partners need most is to be warmly appreciated, understood, and respected.

Partners who learn how to help one another locate and express strong feelings will have made a major advance in the development of their relationship. This is one of the most difficult interpersonal skills to acquire, but especially if partners are willing to work on it **early** in their relationship there is real hope that it can be attained. Here are some things to keep in mind as you work toward identifying and expressing your feelings.

✿ When you are aware of a feeling you have while you are talking, make every effort to acknowledge this to your partner. Saying that you are feeling upset, angry, confused, anxious or elated, without assigning the blame for these feelings to either you or your partner, will help you feel more honest about what you are saying and will give your partner essential information.

❀ Be respectful of surface feelings you observe in your partner, especially when they may conflict with the content of their message. When affect and content conflict, many partners use this discrepancy as an opportunity to attack rather than be supportive of their lover. A respectful response might be to simply ask how your partner is feeling at that moment. To offer a diagnosis of how they are feeling would not be helpful, although it would be a typical response in such a circumstance.

❀ Work to understand better and explain the underlying feelings of your own communications. Resist the urge to search for and explain the source of your partner's underlying feelings. Avoid playing therapist.

❀ Let your partner know how much you appreciate their identifying and expressing feelings. Saying things like, "I can see how hard it is for you to talk about this, and I admire you for working so hard," or "I really love you for helping me deal with the way I feel about this," will let your partner know that you value them and the care they are showing toward your relationship, hard as it may be. Encouragement yields better results than discouragement.

❀ Encourage one another to talk about the feelings they have toward friends and family members. Young adulthood is often a time when relationships between children and parents undergo significant changes, changes that are usually accompanied by strong feelings. Asking your partner to talk with you about how such changes may be affecting them promotes the value of disclosing feelings, and also allows opportunities for practicing this skill. It is frequently easier to be objective with our partner in discussing their feelings toward family members than it is to discuss feelings related to one another.

If clear communication and effective joint problem-solving represent the functional means by which an intimate relationship is maintained, love and mutuality are its rewards. But like communication and problem solving, love and mutuality are complex ideas and don't yield easily to simplistic explanations. In this next section we will examine some of the deepest and most fundamental elements of intimacy, matters that speak to the very meaning of intimate relationships.

The Philosophical Elements of Intimate Relationships

At the very core of an intimate relationship resides a system of values which governs the way partners live out their lives together. This system of values results from the combining of the individual value systems of each partner, and becomes a new entity unto itself. The philosophical elements of an intimate relationship can be seen as the principles, values and beliefs that guide it, the underlying moral, ethical, spiritual, and conceptual fibers that bind it together. Included here are matters of love, commitment, fidelity, trust, mutuality, equity and personal growth, to name some of the most significant ones.

These philosophical elements act to give shape to an intimate relationship over time, and often determine whether or not it will endure. Especially when under stress, partners turn to these underlying principles for insights into how to reconcile the turmoil in their lives. Like many other aspects of close relationships, however, these philosophical elements are not always made explicit, and may become known only when they are violated by one or both of the partners. A critical goal for partners, then, is to identify and agree on just what these elements are, and to draw on them as a source of energy to help sustain their relationship.

As a means of helping partners examine the interiors of their intimate relationships, I have developed an inventory they can use as a framework for opening up a discussion about the philosophical elements that guide their relationship. You will find this inventory at the back of this book. Of the many elements that comprise the philosophical basis for an intimate relationship, I believe two are important enough to warrant special attention. **Mutuality** and **fidelity** stand as the hope and promise of an intimate relationship, and are intertwined and reciprocal. Let's consider why these qualities are so significant.

Mutuality

In a relationship that is mutual, partners value one another as they value themselves. While in theory this may seem to be a reasonably moderate goal to accomplish, in practice it presents quite a tall order. Mutuality is much more substantive than matters like equity and fairness, which pertain to issues like the equal distribution of household chores or the sharing of financial resources. Partners may be able to divide money and tasks quite easily and fairly. But mutuality asks whether each partner is truly valued in the relationship, and whether the valuing is reciprocal. It is not unusual in intimate relationships for one partner to feel that he or she is not mutually valued by their lover, that in some fundamental ways they do not measure up.

For heterosexual lovers, it is more common for the female partner to express this lack of value; in gay and lesbian relationships, the partner who feels less valued is frequently the one whose job or status is considered to be less significant. What this suggests is that despite the good intentions of lovers to love and appreciate their partners as equals, their socialization makes this extremely difficult to do. There are many subtle and covert ways that partners collude to perpetuate what they have learned about gender, education, and wealth and status, all of which interfere with the condition of mutuality. Learning to solve problems together and communicate feelings clearly go a long way toward assisting partners who desire mutuality to attain this goal, but there are several other strategies lovers can employ.

- ✿ Discuss together the specific issue of mutuality in your relationship. If one partner is feeling less valued than the other, make this known.
- ✿ Avoid assigning blame to the "more valued" partner for "making" the other feel less valued. The quantity of learned attitudes and behavior partners bring to their intimate relationship is staggering, and it is unrealistic to think that it can be jettisoned merely by labeling it as dysfunctional.
- ✿ Write out lists of what partners have learned and come to believe over time that may help explain why they perceive themselves to be either more or less entitled to being valued mutually in an intimate relationship. Include as many examples of specific learnings that might account for such feelings.
- ✿ Identify behaviors that may help each partner gain increased value in the eyes of their lover. For the partner considered to be more valued, this could include exploring their lover's world outside the relationship in order to discover how and why they are valued by their social network. It might involve asking their partner to teach them something they themselves are unfamiliar with, or asking for and following their advice. For the partner who feels less valued, volunteering to take responsibility for some aspect of the relationship currently being accomplished by their partner will allow that individual an opportunity to demonstrate their competence.

For many couples, real mutuality seems to lie beyond their grasp, and its absence as a cornerstone to the relationship is felt and acknowledged by both partners. Attaining and maintaining a mutual intimate relationship requires a high level of agreement on its philosophical elements, as well as a commitment to treasure one's partner. Unfortunately, however, most youth today simply have not been exposed to the kind of adult love model which would prepare them for their role as a mutual intimate partner, so most partners must struggle to incorporate this element into their relationship.

Fidelity

In its application to intimate relationships, fidelity means faithfulness. Being faithful connotes keeping one's word or vows, fulfilling one's duties and obligations to the relationship. We often think of the word fidelity in relation to **sexual** faithfulness, but it pertains as well to the more general conditions of a relationship and how one treats one's partner. Sexual fidelity is a good place to begin this discussion, however, since many young people express concern about this aspect of their intimate relationships.

I have spoken with quite a few young adults over the years who have come to me to discuss stories that sound like the following. They have been in an intimate relationship for six months to a year, really love their partner and would not for the world want to hurt them. On a recent visit home, however, they "hooked up" with an old friend or the former partner of a friend, and, "Well, one thing led to another, and before we knew it we were having sex." They are overwhelmed with guilt and fear, distraught over the possibility of having to confess the indiscretion to their lover. What should they do?

A variation on this theme is that, while the young person has not engaged in any sexual experiences outside their primary relationship, **they have been thinking about it.** A young man told me recently that he was in just such a situation, and since his partner lived many miles away from him he hoped he might be able to rationalize "having sex" with a local friend who, like him, wanted to keep their relationship "strictly at the friendship level." Was this a good idea, he wondered?

Both these situations reveal two very common features related to sexual fidelity. First, strange as it may sound, most partners do not make explicit agreements about whether they are free to have sexual experiences outside the relationship, and if so, under what conditions. Even among married couples, sexual fidelity is typically not discussed by the partners, although they may vow in their wedding ceremony to be faithful to one another.

It's wise, I think, for partners to include just such an explicit discussion at the outset of their relationship, and if you have not had such a conversation with your lover, now is the time. While at some later time you may have feelings of sexual attractions to someone other than your partner, you can promise to tell your lover of these feelings before you act on them.

And second, perhaps in part as a result of the first feature, it is not uncommon for people to think they can have their cake, and eat it too. In the sixties and seventies, some scholars studying close relationships suggested that lovers could have primary and "satellite" sexual relationships, and that it would be beneficial if people could develop responsible sexual relationships with more than a primary partner. As appealing as this idea was, it is apparently very difficult to bring off in actual practice. What is clear, however, is that if you are considering sexual experiences with someone other than your love partner, you will be well advised to talk about this with them. It may be that, perhaps because of the distance between you or other factors, you and your partner can agree on such an arrangement.

To violate an explicit agreement about sexual exclusivity is probably the most destructive act a partner can commit against their lover, and against the promise of fidelity in their intimate relationship. From a practical standpoint alone, exposing yourself and your partner to the risks of diseases may be lethal to both of you. From a psychological point of view, the broken trust resulting from such a breach of fidelity may be irreparable.

Beyond sexual faithfulness, fidelity also includes being true to the philosophical foundations of your intimate relationship. There are many principles and values that shape a relationship, and if one or both partners work to undermine those principles they are not being faithful to one another. Some partners, for example, agree that the inner workings of their relationship are to be kept private and to be shared with others only with permission. A partner who violates this agreement has indeed been unfaithful.

Problems over matters of fidelity illustrate the great importance of making explicit the underlying structures, beliefs, values and agreements of an intimate relationship. This is especially true in contemporary America because we lack a clear and definitive set of norms governing the workings of such relationships. Although some would argue that if people "really love each other" they have no need for such clarity about fidelity, the real world that I am familiar with has very few such residents.

Having briefly explored some of the issues central to the life of intimate relationships and considered the philosophical elements that shape them, we are ready now to conclude our work on love partnerships by examining the factors that contribute to their decline and eventual ending. Discussing the breakdown and dissolution of relationships is not something I relish, but since most people go through such an experience during their young adult years, this is a topic we cannot omit.

Conflict, Breakdown, and Dissolution

Picture the following situation. You and your partner have agreed to meet at a local coffee shop at 4 P.M. You arrive at ten after four, get a cup of coffee, sit at your usual table and begin reading the paper. Absorbed in your reading, you are startled when you check your watch and discover it is four thirty. You are momentarily puzzled, thinking that your partner would have arrived at the cafe first. You go back to reading the paper, but increasingly check your watch as the time inches toward quarter of five. Several things are likely to be happening inside you at this point. Think about which ones might apply to you.

- ✿ Your primary feeling is worry about your partner's whereabouts, your only concern being their safety and well-being.
- ✿ Your primary feeling is one of a strong desire to strangle your partner as soon as they arrive, if indeed they do arrive.
- ✿ As you become increasingly agitated over their lateness, you realize that your partner's pattern of being late is inherited—from every member of their family. You are certain that not a single member of their family has been on time for anything for at least two decades.
- ✿ You begin to wonder whether you misunderstood the time on which you agreed to meet your partner. You begin thinking about where they might be, and plan to begin phoning around if they don't show up in (you fill in the blank) minutes.
- ✿ You realize that your partner's habitual lateness fits in well with other character disorders you feel they have, such as their inherent sloppy approach to housekeeping and their habit of procrastinating.
- ✿ You decide to say nothing to your partner about their tardiness, but rather to greet them as if it never occurred to you that they were late. You also resolve to be late on the next four occasions on which you agree to meet at a specified time as a means of helping your partner gain a more empathic awareness of how this particular behavioral trait of theirs affects you.

217

My guess is that you can identify with at least one of these descriptions. It is probably also true that the longer you have been in an intimate relationship the easier it was for you to pick out one or two, or hurriedly scribble down a couple of your own that weren't on this list. Being late is often one of the first real tests for a developing relationship, and how partners deal with such an incident says a lot about their conflict resolution skills.

Conflict is an intrinsic part of all intimate relationships, and it would be foolish to think otherwise. Conflict can take the form of occasional rumbles once or twice a year which are quickly and readily resolved or can characterize the entire relationship, as in those labeled "conflict habituated." And almost always, relationships that are in the process of dissolution undergo heavy and protracted periods of conflict. In this final section I will discuss briefly what conflict is, what kinds of events typically lead to conflict, the course that conflict follows as it plays itself out, and how conflicts are resolved. I will conclude with a few strategies for dealing with conflict when it arises.

In the case about being late that I just described, one partner's action interfered with the actions of the other. The interference created by the late partner was direct, in that the partner was unable to do anything but wait, worry, or fume. If the tardy partner was delayed because of an accident there would be less likelihood of conflict.

But conflict also includes the kind of indirect interference that occurs when one partner criticizes the other. If you criticize my tennis serve, your comments are likely to interfere with my already fragile tennis self-concept. If you roll your eyes at my explanation of what causes conflict in intimate relationships, you interfere with both my cognitive and emotional sense of myself. And if you physically block the door of my room making it difficult or impossible for me to leave, you are interfering with my wishes and desires. So **interference** is the key element in defining conflict.

Categories of Conflict

Here is a **very short list** of things young adults have told me they disagree/argue/fight about.

- ♣ The allocation of time for the relationship.
- ♣ Money.
- ♣ Sex—how much, when, where, who initiates, etc.

♣ Individual rights and personal freedom.
♣ Communication—"He/she just doesn't understand me!"
♣ Issues of fidelity and commitment.
♣ Abuse of trust.
♣ Friends.
♣ Partners' personal habits.
♣ Religion.
♣ Being late.

It would be quite easy to double or triple the number of items on this list, so many are the things that produce conflict between lovers. You don't have to listen to intimate partners talk about their conflicts very long, however, to realize that most of the specifics can be divided into several categories. Let's consider what these major categories are, see which ones yield readily to fairly simple resolution strategies and which are more intractable.

1. **Habits reflected in simple behaviors**. Some such habits include knuckle cracking, burping, farting, squeezing tubes from the wrong end, leaving the toilet seat up/down, sprinkling while tinkling, spitting, not cleaning up dishes, cleaning up dishes before meal is over, not opening doors for others, rushing to open doors whether or not they need to be opened, interrupting others, wanting to stay up late and sleep late, wanting to go to bed early and arise early, reading while eating, watching TV while eating, and eating junk food. Each of us has a million habits well in place before we meet a partner, and we bring these habits to our relationship.

2.**Norms about the relationship**. Being late, **per se,** does not necessarily lead to conflict. It is most likely to have this effect when the partners' rules about what to do when late are violated. If a rule about lateness includes a standard set of procedures to follow and each partner follows the procedures, no conflict should result. It's when such rules are broken, or more often the case, when norms governing this kind of situation have not been established, that problems arise.

While it is impossible to set up rules for each and every class of behavior within an intimate relationship, it certainly is wise for partners to develop these agreements on the occasion of the first such problem. A major quandary in many relationships is that partners are reluctant to make explicit just what these norms are to be, and thus diddle with the edges of agreement rather than construct clear norms.

Normative violations also occur when one partner fails to carry out a particular agreed-upon behavior necessary for the relationship to function smoothly. If it's my job to take out the garbage and I don't, my violation of this norm is likely to produce conflict. If it's your job to initiate sexual interaction and you don't do so, this lack of behavior on your part violates a relationship norm.

3. **Personal dispositions**. Features of our personalities get played out in particular behaviors, and when these individual behaviors become aggregated they may constitute what can be called personal dispositions. Personal dispositions include things like being neat or sloppy, being generally aware or unaware of others' feelings, noticing or not noticing what one's partner does to enhance the relationship, thinking ahead and being a planner or encountering each experience as if one had never had a similar experience, tending to be aware of or oblivious to the aesthetic environment, being a loner or generally seeking the company of others, and so on. These personal dispositions frequently act to trigger conflict, in part because they represent clumps of behavior which serve as prominent targets for criticism by one's partner. A single behavior such as not hanging up one's towel can easily be conglomerated with other behaviors into a general pattern of sloppiness, providing considerable fodder for an attack.

4. **Beliefs, values, and attitudes**. Our values and beliefs typically have deep roots and are intertwined with our family and childhood. During the young adult years these values are often tested pretty strenuously; some of them prevail, while others fall by the wayside. When our deepest values clash with those of our lover's, conflict is almost certain to ensue. Religious beliefs can present just such a problem, and because religious beliefs call for a "leap of faith" they cannot be easily negotiated away or compromised.

Other conflicts central to the lives of many young adults involve attitudes toward the importance of competitive sports, the use of alcohol and drugs, the relative value of going to college or working, and so on. The point of all this is that most individuals have a certain number of strongly held views that clash with at least some people, and when these views are contrary to those of a lover the conflict may be intense.

Blaming and Cross-Complaining

Once initiated, a conflict plays itself out toward some point of resolution. How quickly and efficiently partners are able to resolve their disputes depends a lot on their negotiation skills, as well as the strength of their commitment to maintain the relationship. Two of the most typical early responses in a conflict are **blaming** and **cross-complaining**. Blaming can take many forms, but is essentially designed to focus the responsibility for the conflict on one partner or the other. In conflicts involving relationship norms and personal habits, such attributions may be warranted and appropriate, and can frequently be dealt with quite expeditiously, especially if the offending partner acknowledges their responsibility. Blaming someone for being generally messy or having imperfect values, however, is quite another matter and is much more likely to lead to an escalation of the conflict.

Cross-complaining looks like this:

Jill: Jack, you never take a new can of orange juice out of the freezer after you use up what's left in the fridge. I mean is it really so difficult to open the freezer, pick up a can of orange juice and put it in the refrigerator or on the counter?

Jack: Well, Jill dear, if you want to talk about orange juice, why don't we just bring up the matter of how you **always** leave your dryer and curling iron plugged in and I **always** have to wade through a maze of wires so I can plug in my razor. What about that, huh?

Needless to say, cross-complaining does nothing but inflame a conflict. You should see blaming and cross-complaining as big red flags, signaling a need for immediate attention to the strategies you are employing to resolve your conflict. Blaming and cross-complaining tend to increase the resolve of each partner to cling to their individual positions in a dispute, and are more likely to set back creative negotiations than advance a solution.

As you might suspect, it is usually easier for partners to modify personal habits and create clear norms than it is to reconcile differences in personal dispositions or core values and beliefs. Conflicts that arise over habits and unclear norms often yield to simple agreements or compromise, while those rooted in personal dispositions and core values may take years of deliberate and caring negotiations to work out, if indeed they are ever fully resolved.

Conflict Resolution

The range of conflict resolutions is quite wide and diverse, and includes the following kinds of possibilities, as well as others.

1. **No resolution**. Lovers engage in quite a few disputes that never really have an explicit ending or agreement to them. The energy that was expended around the disagreement just peters out and drains away slowly. People being human and infallible as they are, there are often times when partners simply do not have the energy or personal resources to solve their conflicts. Although "no resolution" would not be recommended as an effective conflict strategy, it is important to acknowledge that this "non-solution" is a common response of partners.

2. **One person "wins."** It is not at all unusual in long-term intimate relationships for one partner to have more power when it comes to resolving conflicts. The partner with more power wins by effectively crushing their lover's argument or overwhelming them by a direct or veiled threat to withdraw their love. The less powerful partner then gives in, and feels compelled to bury their angry and hostile feelings.

3. **Compromise**. It is certainly better to compromise than to fail completely in reconciling a conflict. In a compromise both partners settle for less than they would like, which produces something of a diluted agreement. In a sense, compromise is akin to a majority vote by a group in which over fifty percent agree on a solution.

4. **A new, integrated agreement**. Much more difficult to design than compromises, agreements that include a fresh and new approach to a conflict allow each partner to hold onto their most deeply cherished needs or feelings. They must, however be willing to give up certain benefits about which they have less intense feelings. Whereas compromises are most likely struck over less significant matters such as habits and relationship norms, new agreements tend to be forged around more significant elements. Forming new agreements requires a high degree of negotiation skills by both partners because to form them they must be able to hold on fiercely to their deepest needs or values, while being willing to freely let go of less meaningful goals. Within groups, consensus is the corollary of new agreements made by lovers, because unlike a majority vote, consensus implies that each group participant truly gets what he or she wants, although they may not gain a full measure of satisfaction.

5. **A change in the structure of the relationship**. Changes in the basic way each partner conceptualizes their intimate relationship typically are made only when the equilibrium of the relationship has been rocked to its very core. When lovers attempt to build a new order to their relationship it means they have come to realize that certain fundamental premises under which they have been operating must be changed if their partnership is to survive.

They have reached a precipice so dangerous to the integrity of the relationship that no amount of simple tampering will suffice to save it.

New structures typically emerge when the relationship is in a state of crisis. Quite often these new agreements are able to be formed because one or both partners discover something new about their lover, a discovery they make while smack in the middle of impending disaster. They see qualities in their lover they had never noticed before, and this revelation gives them hope for reconstructing their relationship on a new framework. And it is not uncommon for partners who remain together for many years to go through many such periods of crisis and renewal, each time thrown to the bottom of despair only to be saved by new insights and inspirations.

6. **Separation**. When one or both partners withdraws from the relationship, there is at least a temporary resolution to the conflict in which they were engaged. There are times when a brief separation may very well be a reasonable way for partners to cool off and reconsider their positions. A short period of separation sometimes gives each lover new insights into what they appreciate about their partner, and allows them to reexamine the strength and nature of their commitment. But separation is as likely to precipitate the final breakdown of a relationship, especially if one of the partners has been considering this option over a period of time.

Effective conflict management may not spare lovers from the ultimate collapse of their union, but because it is such an integral component of all satisfying intimate relationships, conflict warrants great respect. Here are several things to think about that may assist you in dealing with disputes that arise in your relationships.

- ✿ Know that conflict is a part of life, and that in itself it has equal power to improve or weaken an intimate relationship.
- ✿ When a conflict erupts, try to quickly identify how you are feeling. Are you angry, afraid, anxious, guilty? If you can, let your partner know what your feelings are.
- ✿ Apologize. Saying you are sorry when you have caused the disagreement will often serve as a conciliatory act sufficient to bring the conflict to a quick conclusion.
- ✿ Timing can play a role in resolving conflict. When conflicts occur late at night, for example, both partners may be too tired to consider the issues in a thoughtful way. While it

is usually good to deal with a conflict directly when it arises, there will be many occasions when it is better to postpone this discussion to a later time, perhaps to the next day at a specified hour.

✿ Limit the scope of the conflict to the immediate problem. Before partners can take on aggregations of their problems they must be able to solve simple problems. Cross-complaining often enlarges the scope of a dispute, which is another reason to avoid this tactic.

✿ Develop a plan. As best as possible, leave the conflict with a clear idea of how the same or similar problems will be faced in the future.

✿ Having made a plan, monitor its progress. Check back with one another in a few days or weeks to determine how the resolution is holding up. Re-open negotiations if necessary.

Ending a Relationship

At the beginning of this book I mentioned that many of the young adults who come to talk with me have recently experienced the ending of a love relationship. There are few kinds of pain that rival that which arises from the rejection of a lover, and it tests the limits of my own counseling skills to serve these young people well. One of the most difficult aspects of such endings is that the partners are almost never at the same place in the evolution toward breakdown. One partner is further ahead in the process, having developed plans for leaving for perhaps a period of months. This helps explain why the partner who is "left" is often taken completely by surprise by an event they simply did not see coming.

Before one or both partners decide to end their long-term relationship they usually proceed through a systematic examination of the pluses and minuses of remaining where they are. In business terms this process might be called a costs-benefits analysis. In other words, partners pose questions to them and must feel reasonably confident that they have adequate answers to these questions before they leave the relationship. Here are some of the questions such individuals grapple with.

1. Why can I no longer stay in this relationship? What rational reasons will I offer my lover to explain my leaving?
2. What consequences are likely if I stay in the relationship even though my reasons for wanting to leave remain unchanged? How will my staying under these circum-

stances likely affect me and my partner?

3. If I leave the relationship, how confident am I that I will be able to enter another relationship in the future that holds the promise of being more satisfying than my present one? A lover who has already begun a covert intimate relationship with someone else has already answered this question to some degree.

4. How will my leaving the relationship affect my self-image? Do I feel sufficiently strong to manage as a single person?

5. What effect will my leaving have on my own and my partner's social support networks? Will leaving require that I sever important relationships in either of these networks? Can I break these ties?

A lover who is contemplating leaving their relationship does not necessarily identify each of these questions explicitly, but they must go through some kind of mental analysis before they withdraw. They are unlikely to leave unless the reasons for doing so outweigh those for remaining. What this means is that many lovers stay in very distressing relationships because they perceive that the pain or consequences of leaving will be greater than the anguish of staying. Not a happy set of circumstances.

When an intimate relationship is finally over, each lover is faced with having to reconcile their loss and move on in their lives. Easier said than done, to be sure. Lovers coming from failed relationships might best begin this healing process by asking themselves this core question: "At the beginning of our relationship, what did I seek in my lover that I could not find in myself?" Answers to this question, and there will probably be many, are likely to provide both partners with insights into the genesis of their problems and will also serve as beacons to guide a subsequent intimate relationship.

It is a great paradox of intimate relationships that they can be both the safest and most secure islands on which any of us might hope to alight, while at the same time they may be as fragile as fine crystal, subject to break without a moment's notice. As a culture, Americans are no better equipped to end an intimate relationship than they are to form one. Am I suggesting that we should prepare people to **end** relationships? Not exactly. What I am saying is that if we help young people understand what is necessary for satisfying intimate relationships, if we assist them in developing the skills needed to negotiate and craft the kind of relationships they can cherish, then these skills and knowledge will also facilitate the ending of a long-term relationship.

It is quite likely that prior to reading this book, you experienced the ending of a love relationship. I offer you no guarantee that if you apply everything you learned from these pages you will never have to face such a loss again. My hope is that you will feel encouraged by what you have read here, that you will be less harsh with yourself in assessing faults and weaknesses, and that you will risk claiming what you are fully entitled to: a love relationship that satisfies and endures.

Appendix

A RELATIONSHIP INVENTORY FOR PARTNERS

There are two parts to this activity: the first calls for each partner to interview the other about what they learned while growing up about intimacy and the value of intimate relationships; the second consists of questions for partners to discuss together. Plan to spend two to four hours discussing these questions, and feel free to explore any tangential issues you discover.

Part I. An Interview for Partners

In this part of the inventory each partner takes a turn interviewing the other, assuming responsibility for guiding the questioning. The interviewer should not jump in with his or her own history or thoughts about a question—save this kind of dialogue for later. It is the interviewer's job to ask the questions, probe for details, and **listen!** The term "probe" simply means that you can expand the question by considering related matters.

1. Could you tell me a little about your family of origin in terms of intimacy—like what role you feel intimacy played in your parents' relationship? Could you describe the overall intimacy climate in your family, among and between various family members?

_ Included in this question are matters such as the expression of affection between and among family members including parents, explicit ideas conveyed by parents about intimacy and its conditions, reactions of parents to children's intimate relationships, and differences in intimacy according to the gender of each family member.

2. If you could sum up what you consider to be the most positive things you learned from your parents about intimacy, what would those things be?

✿ In this question, you should also explore any specific negative learnings about intimacy that your partner picked up from their parents. It is likely that they received more positive learnings from one parent than another, which you can explore with them in depth.

3. As best as you comprehend it, what is your parents' understanding of what love is, and what role or purpose love plays in human life?

✿ Here you can probe for the ways in which your partner's parents' religious or moral values might have influenced their attitudes toward love and its meanings. You might ask them to indicate what their parents' conversation might sound like if they were to discuss the topic of love with one another.

4. Can you summarize briefly what role you feel sex plays in your parents' relationship, and also say something about what their general attitudes are toward sexual expression in intimate relationships?

✿ Here you are not interested in knowing the details of your partner's parents' sexual activities, but rather are trying to get a sense of their general attitudes about sexual expression and intimate relationships.

5. Could you talk a little bit about how you feel your present views of love and intimacy compare and contrast with those held by your parents, and perhaps by your siblings?

✿ Here you are attempting to get a clearer idea of just what love and intimacy mean to your partner. As the discussion progresses, ask for clarification as needed.

6. I'd like to talk with you about your intimate relationship with me. Could you start by describing your initial impressions of me?

7. Can you remember what your state of mind concerning love and intimacy was just before we met and began our relationship? Were you aware of being in an active search for a partner—was this something that you had developed a plan for or had been giving careful attention to, or did it just happen?

✿ If you keep this question open, you can learn a great deal about your partner's "fix" on intimacy and intimate relationships.

8. Think now about that time period from when we first met and began our relationship up to the point where you realized that indeed we were in an intimate relationship. During this time either one of us could have decided to escalate the relationship toward more permanency, or made a decision as to whether or not it would continue to develop. Could you talk a bit about how that process occurred for you, and what your thoughts about it were?

✿ Here you can explore issues such as developing commitment, the differing ways in which you and your partner perceived what was happening, periods of doubt or separation that might have been a part of the decision-making process, the amount of time involved, and so on. You should be concerned with learning what factors your partner considered to be most important in deciding to increase their investment in the relationship.

9. Most people in intimate relationships report that there is a period of adjustment during the beginning months or years, which for some couples is pretty smooth but for others can be filled with turmoil. Could you talk for a while about this period in our relationship and give me some ideas about where our relationship seemed to work best and where you feel we may have had special difficulties during this settling-in period?

✿ This is an opportunity to explore mutual interests of your partner, their negotiating skills, problems they associate with integrating their work and relationship schedules, common values, relationship roles, and so on.

10. How would you asses the amount of power you have in our relationship in terms of being able to influence me, or to get me to do things you want me to do?

✿ You can include here questions about how your partner feels they attempt to get their way in your relationship, as well as their perception of how **you** go about getting your way. Explore ways in which your partner feels they may attempt to control you.

11. How has your life changed since you and I have been in an intimate relationship? Could you talk about this idea, thinking about how our relationship has affected your friends and your family?

✿ Look for your partner's support networks, and the impact your relationship has had on relationships with friends, fellow students, family, etc.

12. All couples have disagreements and arguments, and I assume you feel that we are like other couples in this respect, at least to some degree. Can you tell me a little bit about what kinds of things you tend to disagree with me about, and also how you feel we go about resolving these difficulties?

13. Could you summarize what you feel are the most important reasons for your being in this intimate relationship, and maybe forecast a bit about how our relationship is likely to develop and change over the next few months or years? You could also talk about any aspect of intimacy or our relationship that you think is important but that we haven't talked about?

Part II. A Structured Dialogue for Partners

With a sense of how each partner views the role that intimacy and love plays in your individual lives, you are now ready to discuss together some questions that are central to the way your relationship functions over time. Read and discuss the questions one at a time, and make notes about issues that may be raised that you would like to come back to and open up in more detail at another time. Feel free to digress into areas of your relationship that may not be included in these focus questions.

1. For most of us, our parents were the closest models we had to learn about intimacy and how to live in a love relationship. Talk together for a while about how your relationship is similar to and different from those of your parents, and to what degree you consciously work to emulate or be different from their relationships.

2. In their day-to-day lives, couples are constantly making decisions together that affect them individually and as a partnership. Some decisions are easy to make and may follow a simple script that the couple has gotten very good at, while others are extremely difficult and may involve a rather protracted process. Talk together about what you consider to be the simpler kinds of decisions you make as a couple as well as the more difficult kinds, and also describe what you see to be the processes involved in each kind of decision. You might want to give some hypothetical or real examples of each category of decision as you talk about this idea.

3. We hear a lot about the changing roles of men and women in American society today, and of course we know that the changes are more dramatic for some individuals than others. Talk together for a while about how these larger societal changes may affect your relationship, and how your sex role learnings get played out within your relationship.

4. There is a lot of folk lore and myth about why people happen to choose the partners they do— things like opposites attract and individuals pick partners who complement their own personalities. Discuss the way this kind of folk lore applies to your relationship, and why it is that you find yourselves together as a couple.

5. We often hear that love makes the world go around. Discuss what each of you feels love is and describe the various ways love serves your relationship.

6. One notion we all hear a good bit about today is that people are not as committed in their love relationships as they were in the past. Many older people say that young folks today don't understand commitment. Begin this dialogue by talking together for a bit about this idea, and at some point discuss what role you feel commitment plays in your relationship.

7. It can be pretty difficult at times for couples to gain a balance between the needs they have to develop their own lives as individuals with the needs of their relationship. Talk together about how you deal with this issue as individuals and as a couple.

8. It probably goes without saying that relationships change and develop over time, and in the individual interviews each partner talked about some of the ways they each see the relationship as changing. Talk together now about the specific things you do as a couple to develop and enrich your relationship. What is there about the nature of these activities that goes beyond the mere maintenance of the relationship?

9. Here is a hypothetical situation. Two young people who have been in an intimate sexual relationship for two years are facing the possibility of separation because one has accepted a job many miles from where they currently live together. Suppose that you were this couple. Talk together about how you would go about resolving this issue, and what factors you would consider to be the most important as well as most difficult.